It's Not the School I Hate;
It's the Principal of The Thing

The Eighty-second

COMMENCEMENT

of

HOLLAND ████ ████ CHOOL

JUNE TENTH
Nineteen Hundred Sixty-five

HOLLAND CIVIC CENTER

Volume III of My Life

Fred S. "Fritz" Bertsch

1954-1978
Publisher:
Trafford, Victoria, BC,

www.trafford.com

North America & international
toll-free: 1 888 232 4444 (USA & Canada)
phone: 250 383 6864 ♦ fax: 812 355 4082

DEDICATION

This little volume is dedicated to those members of the teaching staff of Holland High School who, during my tenure as principal, performed with skill and dedication, while suffering under the unfair observation of G.B. Shaw that *Those who can, do; those who can't, teach.* In general, our teachers not only performed well as teachers, but in addition had to perform well at something else in order to make a living. For some, it was painting houses, for others, writing, packing pickles in the local Heinz factory, photography, farming or waiting on tables.

Critics of U.S. education are mostly long on negatives, but short on entering the classroom and coping with the vast range of motivation and individual differences to be found there. My son tells me, *Let everyone proceed at his own pace.* To which I reply, *What then do you do with all those folks who remain in grades eight through ten? Do we keep them there for a lifetime?*

This book is about those of us who struggled with the situations in which we found ourselves, leaving the debates about most issues to the educationists in their ivory towers.

Previous autobiographical books by the author published by Trafford:

My Paradise; Dad's Hell

Every Day Is Navy Day

PREFACE

The genesis for this writing came after I had had a few years of striving in one of the most demanding and frustrating jobs on the face of the earth, that of the high school principal. Inspiration came in the form of a short summary, attributed to no one, but concluding with the words *It's not the school at fault; it's the principal of the thing.* Much of this volume is intended to shed some light on the impossibility of fulfilling the job description of a high school principal. The summary referred to follows:

"The high school principal should expect to please no one. He is often caught on the horns of a dilemma regardless of any action he takes, or fails to take;

"If he comes to school early, he must have insomnia, or be guilty of something; if he leaves school late, he's a slow worker;

"If he attends sports events, he is overemphasizing athletics; if he misses an event he has no school spirit;

"If he gives a teacher a poor evaluation, he's always picking on someone; if he overlooks some teacher weaknesses, he's a weak administrator;

"If he calls a teacher's meeting, he has no regard for teachers' time; if he doesn't call meetings he doesn't believe in democratic input;

"If he makes early decisions, he's an autocrat; if he's slow in making a decision, he is indecisive;

"If he makes regular classroom visits, he's being nosey; if he doesn't, he doesn't care what goes on there;

"If he buys a new car, he must be overpaid; if he doesn't have a new car, he must be a miser;

"If he supports the new program, he's radical; if he's cautious about change he's living in the past;

""If he disciplines a student, he doesn't understand young people; if he doesn't, he's a weakling;

"If he attends community affairs, he's politicking; If he doesn't he has a poor relationship with the public;

"If he attends educational conferences, he's goofing off; if he doesn't he's unprofessional;

"If he confers with the superintendent on a matter, he hasn't a mind of his own; if he seldom confers, he's assuming too much authority;

"If he lunches from the vending machines or cafeteria, he's not watching his weight; if he doesn't, the vending machine or cafeteria lunch is not good enough for him;

"If he gives the radio station the decision that there is no school on a snowy morning, why did he wait so long?; if he doesn't call off school, he must be driving a snow plow;

"If he's young or new in the job, he's got a lot to learn; If he's old or long in the job, he just doesn't have it any more.

"It's not the school at fault; it's the principal of the thing."

I attacked the job with vigor, and whatever the frustrations, I did my best to help in the education of the boys and girls of Holland.

CHAPTER ONE
A Rude Awakening

The phone at the head of the bed jolted me out of a sleep so profound that I was briefly confused. Was it evening or morning? There was natural light on the window and I decided as I picked up the phone that it was still evening. We had been sailing all day in a small boat regatta that Sunday in August, a couple of weeks before the scheduled beginning of the school year when I would resume my role as a teacher of mathematics in the Holland High School. We were dead tired from our exertions in attempting to be competitive among the locally recognized superior sailors and had dropped into bed almost immediately after returning home.

On the second ring of phone I wondered, who in hell would be calling us at a time like this? My wife, Lory, and I rarely received Sunday evening calls, so it was in a continuing state of puzzlement that I picked up the phone and uttered my standard opening, "Bertsch speaking," a response initiated by my father many years before.

The voice on the phone said, *Fritz, this is Harvey Buter. We're having an informal meeting of the school board down here in the conference room of the*

Peoples Bank, and we wondered if you could come down and join us for a little while. I had known Harvey for many years, starting from the time when he was a star player on the Holland Christian High School basketball team and I, a student at Hope College, was a string reporter for the Grand Rapids Herald covering, among everything else, the home games of Harvey's high school. We had had many opportunities, both personal and business, to become close acquaintances. I stayed in the navy after World War II, while Harvey returned to Holland after his time in the army and took a position with Holland Motor Express, a large trucking firm.

Harvey J. Buter

Harvey's influence in my life came in many forms. We were always friends, but on occasion, opponents. He always wanted to be helpful, but on some occasions his efforts were anything but helpful. He defended equality for all, but when it came to his own family he demanded special treatment. Harvey was impetuous, promised things he could not deliver, but was always a supporter of public education. Particularly in the first half of this story he was an adjunct protagonist. My sleep-dazed mind was clearing, and I wondered, "Why is the Holland Board of Education meeting on a Sunday evening?" Holland at that time was largely inhabited by people of Dutch descent, deeply and defensively religious in a tradition that prohibited both business and pleasure on the Lord's Day. My response to Harvey was a rather blunt, *Harv, I've been in bed for an hour, I'm dead tired, and I'm not about to come downtown at this hour on a Sunday night.* I had no idea what reason the school board might have to consult me, a classroom teacher, on such brief notice but I agreed to meet him in the bank's conference room at nine o'clock the next morning.....

• •

During the period when Lory and I were agonizing over whether or not I should resign my regular U.S. Navy commission and continue my naval career as a reservist, we found that we were often asking ourselves, whether spoken or not, *If I should resign, how would we make a living, and also what effect would such an action have on our growing family?*

Shortly after my return from the combat tour during the Korean War, representatives of the Martin company, manufacturers of both the PBM and P5M aircraft I had flown contacted me as a potential Martin employee after I ended my naval service, always being careful to couch their veiled offers as future possibilities so as to avoid any charges that they were actively encouraging a naval officer to resign his commission. In any case, I was not enthralled with the idea of living in either the Baltimore or Atlanta areas, sites of Martin's primary activities.

My first real shore duty was a tour as the assistant professor of naval science at the University of Minnesota, during which I was ordered back to sea for temporary duty as the officer in charge of fifteen hundred naval reserve midshipmen on a training cruise, a part of the Naval Reserve Officers Training Program curriculum, and which essentially occupied the short Minnesota summer. Upon my return, I found a marine officer sitting in the office of the associate professor, appointed to a position I had been assured by my officer detailer in the Bureau of Naval Personnel would be mine during my third year at the university, assuming I would be selected for promotion to the rank of commander, which I was. Further, I was informed that my anticipated three year tour of duty at the University of Minnesota had been shortened by a year and I was ordered back to sea as the executive officer of a patrol squadron home ported at the Naval air Station, Alameda, California.

The squadron, VP 47, would be flying the new Martin P5M seaplanes. It was at this point that I started to think seriously about where my naval career was taking me. It was to be my third consecutive tour at sea, my second as an executive officer, each of which involved year-long deployments to the Far East or lengthy periods to the far reaches of the Pacific during atom bomb tests. My next tour would be as commanding officer of a patrol squadron that would be deploying for a year following a training period. We had three children, and their well being was constantly on our minds. My absences had a definite negative affect on our daughter, Martje, who took years to accept me into the family after a long deployment during the Korean War. If I should resign, there was always the alternative of moving back to our cozy and even beloved house in Coronado and living the good life there. Our realtor friend, Lee Mather, several times in the past had indicated I could join his firm at any time I wished. He assured me that such a move would be lucrative, and we were sorely tempted. At that time we owned two houses and a five unit apartment building in Coronado. As things turned out, assuming we would keep the properties we already owned in Coronado, within a very few years, as a result of the boom in California real estate, we would have been multi-millionaires. For example, a few years later, our modest home was sold for a million, five hundred thousand dollars, quite an increase over the four thousand, two hundred and fifty dollars we had paid for it in nineteen forty-eight.

While all these agonizing mental activities were going on, I was daily searching the employment advertising in the *Wall Street Journal* for possible leads that might affect our decision. Reflecting my interest in real estate, on Fridays I would review the extensive section on properties for sale all over the world, and on one occasion there was an ad that read, in part, "Three acre lots for sale on the Big Island of Hawaii...heavily wooded...part of the old Parker ranch....$500.00 each..." The price of the land on the lower slopes of Mauna Loa and overlooking Black Sands Beach at a distance was less per acre than farm land in Western Michigan at the time, a natural comparison for us. With very little hesitation or caution beyond determining that the parcels were being offered by a well-known Hilo real estate agent, we decided to buy two of the properties "sight unseen" as "our anchor to windward" in the event we were not successful in making the move to civilian life should we decide to make that change. For the first and only time in our lives we bought a piece of property without actually setting foot on it. Perhaps it was fantasy, but we envisioned that if all else failed, we could somehow make our way to Hawaii and live in a hut on our six acres, subsisting on pineapples, coconuts, mangos and whatever else we could grow on our little "ranch." This investment turned out to be one of the best we ever made.

Previously, while serving on the staff of Commander, Fleet Air Wing FOURTEEN, my attention had been forced onto the knowledge that congress had legislated certain discrepancies in the treatment of reserve and regular personnel, favoring families of reservists recalled during the Korean War over those already serving in the regular forces. An example that lingered in my mind was the difference in treatment of the dependents of the crew members who were killed when a PBM crashed into the Pacific Ocean off San Diego. I was keenly aware that dependents of reservists killed in that crash received far greater benefits than the dependents of the regulars killed in the same crash. These differentials were later corrected, but at the time of which I write, they existed. I was an officer in the regular navy with three children; my co-pilot was a reservist with one child. Should it happen that we were both killed in the same crash, his family, under the laws that existed at the time, would receive far greater benefits than mine.

Because we had many reservists in VP-47, I necessarily referred frequently to Section H of the Bureau of Naval Personnel Manual, the personnel "bible" of the navy, usually referred to as the "BuPers Manual." On a number of occasions I took this blue book home and studied the entire section dealing with the administration of the naval reserve.

Several other things caught my eye during my perusal of this volume, and they had a considerable influence on my thinking. I learned that reservists could earn "points" toward retirement without ever leaving their homes, and that weekend drills would be credited the same for retirement as a day of flying a patrol over the Formosa Strait. I failed to take sufficient note that there were restrictions on the number of such points that could be credited for retirement. Further, one extremely important legal element escaped my attention, i.e., for an officer to retire from the naval reserve, it was required that "....the final eight years of qualifying service be in the naval reserve...."

Some time after the first of the year in 1955 our friend. Bill Van Oss flew down on navy business from Naval Air Station Whidbey Island, Washington where he was serving in a P2V patrol squadron. Bill, then a lieutenant commander, had been a friend of ours, both at Hope College, and later in the navy.

We persuaded him to stay a couple of nights with us rather than in the bachelor officers' quarters , and he and I stayed up most of the night talking about the things that had been going through my mind; deployments, promotions, family strains, unequal treatment, and the various gripes and problems that can irritate, whether one is in the navy or any other occupation or profession, but, finally I shared my thoughts on possibly resigning my regular navy commission and accepting a commission in the naval reserve. It was another agonizing discussion, but it seemed to push me closer to decision time.

The new commanding officer of the squadron was a commander named Jack Lawyer, a gregarious and likable person, and excellent aviator, who had spent virtually all of his career in aviation training commands, and thus had no operational experience in either World War II or the Korean War. In the process of getting to know him, and to know something about him, I found that his original date of commissioning was only a month or two before mine.

I flew with Jack on a number of occasions, and realized that he was a well-qualified naval aviator, but what I also discovered was that he was crude and lascivious. I developed a degree of distrust, and felt uncomfortable with some of his actions and attitudes, and thus felt uneasy serving as his primary assistant.

As the training months went by, I developed a feeling of resentment at having to leave my family once again for a tour in the Far East. Many elements entered into all of this. We thought Martje was again feeling insecure in anticipation of my departure. Lory was unhappy in Alameda. We all were wishing we were in Coronado. I was uneasy serving as Jack Lawyer's executive officer.

The culmination of all of this was a decision for me to resign my commission. We would take our chances in civilian life relocating in, or at least near, my home town of Holland, Michigan. The decision to return there was heavily influenced by the experience of my mother, following my father's death some years before. At that time, as the owner of the property on which she lived, she found it to be financially expedient to sell the majority of it to developers, one of whom was a man named Jim Klomparens. He and his partner subsequently subdivided the property and built speculation houses on the new lots for a profit. I had met Jim, and discerned him to be an honest, straightforward man. Partly because of my mother's experience I had talked to him a bit about the idea that some time in the future I might want to subdivide the fairly extensive property on Lake Macatawa's Pine Creek Bay I had acquired while on a brief leave during World War II. I wrote to him requesting information on how I might proceed if I decided to develop our property and he responded at some length and in considerable helpful detail on how to go forward with such a project.

After many long discussions, numerous sleepless nights and endless agonizing. I wrote my letter of resignation from the regular navy and requested I be commissioned in the naval reserve. Perhaps I was thinking that someone would say, *Fritz, you don't want to do that*, or *Commander, you've done a good job, please reconsider this matter*, but every forwarding senior simply endorsed the request, *Forwarded* without further comment, and when it arrived at its destination, it was accepted. My resignation was effective on June thirtieth nineteen fifty-five.

Based on my father's experiences, at least as I perceived them, we had given a great deal of thought to the idea that the local community in Holland, or at least some of its more vicious members, might undertake to torpedo our endeavors, or that no matter how valiantly we tried, our efforts in Holland might fail. In that case our Hawaiian property would become our refuge. As events developed, over time we sold all of our Coronado real estate and deposited the money in our brokerage account in anticipation of some unforeseen attack on our financial resources during the development of our property.

And so it was back across the mountains, deserts and plains in the underpowered and balky Ford Country Squire station wagon. One thing about the trip stands out particularly in my memory. The first day we made it to Elko, Nevada, than which, at least at that time, there were few more desolate places in this world. "Two Stiffs Selling Gas in Elko," was the name of a commercial conglomeration there consisting of a gas station, a poorly stocked store and a straggled group of run-down tourist cabins. "Bleak" is a word that comes to mind when I think of the setting and the accommodations.

Our underpowered 1952 Ford Station Wagon which served us well for fifteen years was similar to this later model. It was for years our family car, took us from San Diego to Minneapolis and back again; thence to Alameda and Holland before becoming a utility vehicle for both the gas station and the subdivision. The wood panels had to be refinished with marine varnish every year, but even so became discolored over time.

As we were loading the wagon for departure from Elko the next morning, Martje was sitting on the potty seat in the bathroom. We had established Buck in the back of the station wagon to keep him immobile and Susan was playing with a doll near the car. No one was in the motel room, so when Martje emerged from the bathroom, she apparently concluded we had abandoned her. She ran crying out of the room, pulling up her panties and screaming, *"Don't leave me, don't leave me.* We held her in our arms for some time trying to reassure her that we were not going to continue our cross country trip without her. I think it was as a result of that incident that I finally concluded without the previous shadows of doubt that we had not made a mistake. As much as I loved the Navy, my resignation was a necessity. Our family needed both parents to give parental presence and reassurance to our family.

CHAPTER TWO - HOLLAND
Adjustment to A New Life

During the brief period between my detachment from the squadron and the effective date of my resignation, I was stationed temporarily at the naval station on Treasure Island and relatively free to pursue my own interests. Representatives of Lear, Incorporated, with headquarters in Santa Monica, contacted me to determine if I would be interested in applying for a position with them, but I responded that we had already made the decision to return to Michigan. When they realized I would be living only about twenty-five miles from the Lear production plant in Grand Rapids, home of Lear's instrument and aviation electro-mechanical divisions, they suggested I apply for a position there, which I did almost immediately after we arrived in the Holland area.

Lear's Grand Rapids plant produced auto pilots and aircraft gyros in the instrument division, while the electro-mechanical division produced actuators for control devices of aircraft rudders, horizontal stabilizers and wing flaps. I was immediately hired and designated a sales engineer. I had not the faintest idea what a sales engineer did, but I was soon involved in selling instruments to Martin for the P6M, a proposed jet powered patrol seaplane. However, not long after this introduction to my job I was thrust into a sales team pursuing our company's largely vain attempt to sell the Lear autopilot to the airlines and to the aircraft manufacturers of the first round of commercial jet aircraft.

My mother invited us to stay with her until we could find a suitable place to live, but it was hardly appropriate for the five of us to move into the tiny two bedroom, single bath house that had originally been built to provide a place for grandpa's hired man to live. After a fire in nineteen thirty-three destroyed the five bedroom two story house left to my parents following Grandpa Daniel's death, this little dwelling had sheltered the four members of our family and frequently also housed members of our extended family.

Lory and I searched in vain for a place to live as it was the peak of the tourist season and all housing was occupied. Our Western Michigan area was one of the most sought after by those seeking beautiful beaches and nearby resort accommodations. We could find nothing other than a decrepit old one-bedroom cottage with a single bath so small that after entering, it was necessary to sit on the commode and pull one's legs aside to afford room for the door to close. We slept in the only bed while the children slept on the floor in sleeping bags. It was not easy.

One primary interest was to obtain a better place to live before winter set in. We decided, with some help from our friend, Jim Klomparens, to build a relatively inexpensive speculation house on what would eventually become a lot in the subdivision proposed for our property. A further goal was to sell this first house in due time and build our dream house on the proposed lot that included a point in the lake known locally as Boy Scout Point. Short term financing for the building period was readily available from one of the local state banks, and the friendly local banker, "Curly" Dalman, assured us that permanent financing would be available when the house was completed.

Our property was heavily wooded, primarily with huge red and black oak trees, and an understory of other varieties. The only reasonable access to our land at that time was a platted, but uncleared and undeveloped road starting almost a quarter of a mile from the southwest corner of the property. This point coincided with the southwest corner of our proposed building lot for the planned speculation house. Jim suggested that we contact Bill Brewer, a local independent bulldozer operator, who not only cleared the access promptly, but also for several years gave us prompt help in the removal of stumps, the clearing of brush and road preparation as we proceeded with preparations for platting.

With clearing of the access completed, Jim moved his building crew to the site, expedited construction, and we moved into our speculation house a day or two before Thanksgiving nineteen fifty-eight. A call to the moving company where our household goods were stored temporarily brought almost immediate delivery. We were beginning to place our furniture and unpack things, when the newly installed telephone rang for the first time. It was our long time friends, Bill and Nola Van Oss, who told us they were on a brief leave between duty stations and were visiting parents and friends living both in Holland and nearby Byron Center, a suburb of Grand Rapids, and would like to visit. We replied, as usual *Come on over,* and gave them directions to our hideaway. We drank several martinis and "swapped lies" late into the night. We insisted that they stay safely with us rather than risk the drive to Byron Center. Our daughter, Mary Jo was born nine months later.

On the recommendation of Jim Klomparens, I contacted a Grand Rapids engineering firm, Williams & Works that specialized in subdivision design and development, including a plat survey and design and survey of necessary roads or streets. Only after we approved the design and received approval from the Park Township Board, could the boundaries of the proposed roads within the subdivision be staked, and then we could proceed with the clearing of them as my time became available.

At that time, unfortunately, I did not have enough knowledge or experience about the lumber business to recognize that the large red and black oak trees, many of which did not have a single branch below thirty feet above the stump were far more valuable if sold as peeler logs rather than to a local sawmill operator. If sold to a properly equipped facility for producing the finished ply material for furniture and other fine uses the rewards to us would have been far greater that those we actually received. Instead, we sold a majority of the trees standing in the planned roadways to Slim Vander Sluis*, a sawmill operator based in the neighboring town of Zeeland for a rate based on the Doyle rule, a measure which favored the logger, no matter what size the timber. Slim's logging operation left immense piles of the tops of trees, and also the need for Bill Brewer with his bull dozer to uproot the stumps and push them out of the new roadway. This, of course, left us with the challenge of clearing the brush from the roads and eventually ridding ourselves of the immense stumps from the lots onto which they pushed by Bill and his dozer.

I decided to cut the usable firewood from the tops of the trees which cluttered the roadways with my newly acquired chain saw and burn the rest on the site, which we aimed to do. It was a simple matter at that time to get a burn permit from the township fire chief. I soon learned getting this debris to burn would be difficult and far from simple. All of it was green as were the stumps pushed out of the roadway and onto the adjacent lots of our proposed subdivision. We planned for the stumps to remain there until they were dry enough to burn. Another relatively minor problem was that I had no apparent use for the firewood, even after drying, as our new house did not include a fireplace.

As I stood by the mess of brush and that first little pile of cordwood I had cut with my new saw, contemplating what future steps to take, a strange phenomenon approached. It combined the rear end of an old Dodge pickup truck with the front end of an ancient Ford automobile. It had immense rear wheels taken from some unidentified third vehicle. These wheels with oversize tires mounted on them raised the stern of this big go-cart well above its front, giving it a distinct slope forward, making the whole look like it was forever going downhill. The driver, a rather disheveled looking individual in bib overalls and a battered felt hat, climbed out of the driver's seat with a bottle of Pabst Blue Ribbon beer in his left hand and announced as he approached me, *I'm Ted Rhudy, an' I just come by to see what yer doin' out here. Whatcha gonna do with all this brush?"*

I really don't know, but if you have any ideas, I wouldn't mind hearing them, I replied, sparring for some time to consider what might come next.

Well, I'd be willing to saw up the tops and haul away the cordwood. I burn wood all winter long...that's how I heat my house. Burn it in the parlor stove; all winter long. Haul it away, an en you'll be red of it.

Well, that leaves me with the brush, I countered, hoping for a more adequate solution for my dilemma.

I'll help you burn it. I burn a lot of brush. I'll show you how. For several weeks, Ted cut his cordwood and hauled it off to his house, two miles away, but he waited for me to be present before there was any burning. I was dressed for the woods and finishing breakfast one Saturday morning when there was a tap on the door. It was Ted, bottle of Blue Ribbon in hand. His chug-a-ma-bubble vehicle with its engine idling smoothly and emitting a rather soothing purr stood in front of the house on the dirt path which soon, we hoped, would become a county road. I tossed my chain saw and ax toward the back of this bizarre contraption onto the top of a pile of old tires and climbed into the bucket seat on Ted's right. He hoisted his beer for one last gulp, threw the bottle to the rear, glanced over at me and yelled *Hold on!* He floored the accelerator, and the purr became a roar that would have awakened the neighbors, had there been any. There was no muffler.

It was only a couple of hundred feet to the first immense pile of tightly packed green brush my new-found friend had produced over the previous weeks. The pile was about ten feet tall, its height being limited only by how high he could toss the final contribution to it. *Gimmee a hand with a couple a them tires,* he ordered. Ted was not great for the niceties of life. I grabbed two of the tires, and pulled them out of the back of the vehicle. One of them sloshed dirty water all over my legs. *Been out in the rain fer weeks,* Ted commented as he took one of the tires and threw it up as far as he could on the pile. His next move, after crumpling a wad of old newspaper and sticking it as far as he could into the base of the pile of trimmings was to pull a five gallon can out of the back of the truck. *Used oil from the gas stations, I get it free,* he commented as he poured a generous quantity on the pile. He then poured a small amount of gasoline onto this explosive mix and touched a match to it.

"Whoosh," went the gasoline, singeing Ted, and forcing me to turn away for a moment. The gasoline ignited the drain oil, and the heat from the oil fire lighted the tires. When the tires caught fire, they burned with such intensity that the brush burned with them. The burning tires poured out immense quantities of oily black smoke that rose rapidly above the tops of the surrounding trees. *Anything will burn if you give it enough heat,"* Ted observed. *This is just to give the pile enough heat. When the fire dies down and cools off in a coupla days, you'll hafta get red of the wire from them tires, or we'll have it wound all over somethin', like a rear wheel or axle.* He had further instructions. *You hafta feed that fire all the time. It'll burn out the center, so you hafta push that outside brush onto the hot spot in the middle.*

I was both pleased and horrified by what I was seeing, wondering what the overall effect would be of the burning tires and petroleum products, but the process did get rid of the brush. No one objected, at least until we were burning the very last of the brush from the roads. Environmentalists today would be horrified, and, in fact, such activities would be illegal, but I had a legitimate permit to burn the brush, and there were no restrictions on the method used. We burned a tremendous amount of brush each weekend for months.

On a Saturday afternoon toward the end of October, about a year after we started all this activity, we were burning the last huge pile of brush in the road at the far northeast corner of the plat. The only house anywhere near our proposed subdivision was owned by a Mrs. Sulkers, widow of a dentist who had been killed in an automobile accident many years before. Ir was at least five hundred feet from where we were finishing the burning for the day. As the sun was going down, and Ted and I were pushing the last bits of brush from the perimeter of the fire site onto the dying coals, by prearrangement, Lory appeared on the scene carrying supplies for a picnic; hot dogs, buns, relishes, potato salad, soda pop for the kids, beer for Ted and a couple of martinis for us.

We were just nicely seated on a few bunks from the ends of saw logs now long gone, enjoying the sips of our drinks, when the siren atop the township fire station began to wail and we speculated a bit on whose house might be burning, as only a few people had lighted off their furnaces for the winter ahead. We didn't have long to wait. With lights flashing and siren screaming, the pump truck from the fire hall, driven by the on-duty fireman, and followed by the cars of the volunteer fire department, came down the narrow, tree-lined quarter mile path from the gas station to the northwest corner of our land and thence onward on our sandy, unfinished proposed road to the site of the fire, where we were waiting for the coals to cool down somewhat before roasting our hot dogs and marshmallows. *Dad gummit, Fred, you gotta permit fer this fire?* The "dad gummit" was the local substitute for the forbidden "damn it' that others might use to express frustration under these circumstances, and the more formal "Fred" rather than "Fritz" reflected the fact that he knew who I was but wasn't among my close friends or associates. He knew perfectly well I had a permit, but I pulled it out of my shirt pocket, and showed it to him, holding it up in front of his eyes so he could report the legality of my fire to his fellow firemen just in case that question arose with them, or any others who might appear on the scene. The permit was signed by the township fire chief.

By this time there were twenty or more cars and trucks belonging not only to the firemen, but also a dozen or more vehicles of the curious neighbors plugging the single lane path behind the fire truck. There was no escape for the fire truck, except for the possibility of driving it over the dying coals and around the sandy path to the opening we had cleared for the building of our house, and thence back to the fire house on the county road hazarding the possibility of getting stuck at the muddy lower end of the subdivision. Should that occur, the township's one pump truck would be out of action much longer and be unavailable should there be a threatening fire in the community during that time. Each vehicle behind the fire truck had to back out, in turn, until getting to the opening onto the main road a quarter of a mile away. The fire chief was furious, the driver was angry, the rest of the firemen were upset, and all because poor old Mrs. Sulkers, whose vision and hearing were both impaired, saw the glow of the dying fire through the twilight at the end of a long day of brush burning.

At this point Clarence Owen, a colorful bandy legged man who generally had a chew of tobacco in his cheek and a mangled cigar in his mouth came into our life. Clarence possessed an impressive assortment of practical skills and entered our lives when he came at our invitation to negotiate for the logs from the trees that would have to be removed from the centers of the lots of the subdivision. He remained in contact with us for many years in a variety of roles. Clarence owned a steam powered saw mill on some low land on the edge of the swamp off the Black River just up stream from the River Avenue Bridge. He fueled the firebox of the ancient threshing machine boiler with the slab wood resulting from his sawing operations and the six foot blade of his mill was powered by a belt driven by the flywheel of that behemoth.

In addition to cash payment for our logs, we negotiated for his cutting to our specifications enough clear oak for the floors of our planned new house, enough cherry to panel the walls of the living room, the dining area and breakfast nook all a half level above the entry plus the recreation room occupying the space beneath the living room together with enough pine to panel the two car garage. A part of this set of trade offs was that the sawing of our portion of the deal would be done on a Saturday so I could "tail" the saw, passing the green lumber to the man who operated a relatively small saw on which the rough lumber was cut longitudinally to give the individual boards straight parallel edges so the material could be used in building. The edgings were then taken by another operator who made "little ones out of big ones" cutting them to lengths appropriate for firing the boiler, or, if there was more than enough for that use, into two-foot lengths for sale as cordwood.

When our share of the lumber had been cut, Ted and I loaded it all on a borrowed truck and moved it to Baywoodlands, where I piled it on a lot adjacent to our first house. I built this stack of green boards in our back yard with tiers of lumber separated with sticks of edgings to permit a free flow of air between the layers to facilitate drying in the outside air for a period of almost a year, when it would be transported once again to be finished by planer to the proper thickness, and then edged with tongue and groove for installation in our new house to built on the point in the lake. The loading and unloading of each board during these processes was done by me, so by the time the new house was completed I had handled each board ten times and had made a considerable investment of time in transporting the lumber from place to place and finally to the building site. In addition I played a small but vital part in the actual construction by installing the tongue and groove oak plank flooring secured with several gross of three-inch screws, all driven with my hand driven "Yankee" screwdriver. Beyond that my invaluable, as it turned out, supervision of the building process prevented one major misinterpretation of the construction plans from being built into our new home.

When the time came not much later, to build a dock for the mooring of our various boats, it was a natural for us to call in Clarence, who was one of three local men equipped and qualified to engage in marine construction. When we called he arrived on schedule, chew in his cheek and frayed cigar between his teeth. His greeting was *Where do you want them spiles for the new dock?* Fancying myself a purist of English usage, I winced at the word "spile". We walked down toward the point in the lake where I thought the dock should be built projecting northward on the deep water side of the point. *How many spiles you want?* I told him I thought eight for the dock and two about eight feet away from the dock on either side to be used for handling the mooring lines of the boats. He agreed. *You can cut them spiles right here on the place, but they gotta be at least thirty feet long so they'll stick at least twenty feet in the sand. Maybe the four near shore in the shallow water can be a little shorter, but all of 'em gotta be at least eight inches at the little end. They go in the bottom with the big end down, you know.* Well, I didn't know, but I was learning fast. *I'll come over an' pull 'em down here with my truck.* With that remark he solved one of my logistic problems. How would I otherwise be able to haul those immense logs down to the waterfront on our point?

Gotta bark them spiles before we drive 'em, was his final instruction, *Use yer drawknife an' git that done before you git me over here with my spile driver.* He assumed I knew not only what a drawknife was, but also that I owned one and knew how to use it. He was correct in those matters, as I had used my drawknife extensively as a boy while building my first wooden boat.

I cut the trees for the pilings and when called, Clarence arrived and pulled the logs down to the point, where I shaved off the bark, no small task in itself. When

I had finished barking the logs, I called Clarence and a day or so later he arrived by water with his red pile driving barge towed by a beat up old sheet metal rowboat powered with an equally ancient twenty-five horsepower outboard engine.

At one end of the barge was a ten or twelve foot strongly built tower at the top of which were double sheaves; one to accommodate a two inch line with the bitter end outboard to be tied to a piling and the standing part leading through a block on deck and thence to a gasoline powered winch. A similar arrangement was permanently attached to a length of three inch fire hose equipped with an old fashioned suicide nozzle. Another gasoline engine powered a pump drawing lake water to feed the hose. The barge was temporarily fixed in place by angle irons run through iron straps at each corner of the vessel. The irons would be lifted as it became necessary to move the barge as the different pilings were driven.

When all was ready, the two-inch line was secured to the middle of the first piling, such that the weight distribution made the large end somewhat heavier. The man on the winch then began hauling, and as the piling was lifted toward the top of the tower, its large end was down, it was vertical and approximately at the desired permanent position. At this point in the operation, the fire hose was temporarily strapped to the piling with the nozzle aimed straight down. When the pump was started sand bubbled upward and the log and its accompanying nozzle were lowered progressively until it reached the desired level. The pumping then stopped and the hose and nozzle were removed from the piling. Sand washed back in around it. With this rig all twelve piles were set in place in just over two hours. There was no real driving involved; the piles were jetted in place in the sand. It was then up to me to build the dock itself.

I was somewhat chagrined to find after consulting my dictionary that Clarence was right; *spile* is a perfectly legitimate word as he used it.

CHAPTER THREE - LEAR, INC. 1956-58
More Flying

In my new job, I was in the air, flying in tourist class on long flights to the West coast quarters of Boeing, Lockheed or Consolidated, the competing aircraft manufacturers hoping to obtain contracts for the construction of the proposed new jet airliners or eastward to the to the headquarters of several airlines, American, Eastern, United and Delta, four airlines then planning to purchase jets. Alternately we flew westward to Denver to convince Bob Six and his management team to buy our product. Although not as a pilot, I was in the air more consistently and for more hours per week than I did while flying in the navy. Our schedule for virtually every week called for our departure early on Monday and our return on Friday. The only airline then flying into Grand Rapids was Michigan Central, with a schedule that often left us stranded for the night in either Chicago or Detroit.

Sometimes, if we got into Chicago early enough, and the Michigan Central schedule was not a reasonable option for our return to Western Michigan, an alternative was to catch the return trip of a Pere Marquette train known informally as "The Rattler." This was a day train ridden primarily by folks planning either to shop in Chicago for a few hours or to accomplish some business during the day. The Rattler left Western Michigan in the morning boarding passengers during stops at every depot along the way, including Gary, Indiana as a final stop before terminating at Chicago. The train returned following a late afternoon departure. At other times we would be stranded in Chicago overnight and get back home sometime Saturday afternoon, leaving a scant fraction of the weekend for me to pursue our efforts in the proposed subdivision, where we were only making slow progress.

When we finally moved into our new house, it was also time to convert the construction loan to the more permanent financing that Curley Dalman had assured us would be available as soon as the house was completed. We were dumfounded when we went to the bank to complete the transaction, and the banker said, more formally now than when we signed the construction loan, *Sorry, Mr. and Mrs. Bertsch, but we can't give you permanent financing; the bank examiners are due to arrive within a few days."*

But you assured us that permanent financing would be available to replace the construction loan. Construction is finished and the building inspector has signed off on it, I countered, but Curley was adamant. No loan. We walked across the front of the bank to the president's office, entered without knocking, and accosted Clarence Klaasen, reminding him of the good faith promise he and Curly had made on behalf of the bank. His response was a well-rehearsed version of what Curley had said, in effect, *That was then; this is now.*

This then, we jointly concluded, was the long-anticipated test of our financial strength. Lory said to Clarence, almost defiantly, *You'll have your money within a week.* I added to myself, and under my breath, *You bastards.* As I had predicted during long discussions pro and con prior to our decision to leave the navy, there would be a local challenge to determine the extent of our finances. That time had come, and sooner than we anticipated. We verified our conclusion by crossing the street and asking my college friend and fraternity brother, Don Thomas, by now a vice president of the First State Bank, if we should apply for a loan there, and his circuitous negative reply verified our conclusion that a bankers' cabal was forcing our hands.

The following Monday, I called the Grand Rapids office of Merrill Lynch, Pierce, Fenner and Bean, to which we had transferred our previous West Coast account, and which contained the proceeds of the Coronado real estate we had liquidated in anticipation of the financial demands required to pursue our development program. I directed our brokerage man at Merrill Lynch to sell off the majority of our still rather modest portfolio of stocks, but just enough to cover our obligation at the bank.

At that time it took four days to complete street securities transactions, and thus it was the next Friday that I was actually able to pick up a certified check drawn on a Grand Rapids bank for the net proceeds. I called the bank to verify that they could not only cash the check, but also to determine that they could pay the round amount in thousand dollar bills, which they agreed to do. Neither Lory nor I had ever seen a thousand dollar bill, but now we had a bunch of them. Saturday morning we were in the bank early, and requested that President Clarence and Vice President Curley meet us in their conference room, where it greatly pleased me to peel off a dozen or more thousand dollar bills to pay off our building loan. We hoped we didn't reveal by our actions that all this put a severe strain on our resources. As we concluded our meeting, I picked up the cancelled note and said, *This is the last time I'll ever set foot in this bank.*

Over time, my determination weakened, and I frequently found myself either in the bank lobby, or passing through it, for two reasons. The first was perhaps most pressing. My mother had long had a small account at the Peoples Bank, and, during the dire days of the Great Depression, she had several times borrowed money there as short-term loans to meet some financial need, most often to buy another of the hopelessly battered old cars that served us during those desperate years. In most cases it had been either Curley or Clarence who approved the loans, and her loyalty to the bank made any change beyond her imagination.

The second reason why I passed through the lobby was that the city had procured and demolished the ancient buildings behind the bank and devoted the land to parking in an effort to save the downtown business community under the threat of competition from businesses locating outside of the city limits. For customer access to the bank, a bit of remodeling had been accomplished to provide an easily accessible path to their counters and offices. It also provided a path from the parking lots to the downtown business area and I used it often.

As important as it was to pursue our development game plan during the limited hours we had to devote to it, performance in my job at Lear was necessarily the top priority, since our financial survival now depended on it. In my role as a Lear sales engineer, and in connection with the attempt to sell Lear products to the companies involved with the new round of commercial jetliners, I was assigned to a team composed of a variety of men contributing a wealth of experience to the sales effort. There was Bob Hahn, vice president for sales, Chet Owen, a top flight gyroscopic engineer, Ralph Braverman, a persuasive and funny fellow sales engineer, and finally, me. I struggled to determine, or at least obtain, a definition of, my role in this whole thing.

I started in to learn, and I learned a great deal. Lear's organization, at least at my level, was not what a mathematician would call well-defined. I knew that the head of sales was Vice President Bob Hahn, and that Bill Bolger who occupied a glass-enclosed cubicle the end of the sixth floor of this former furniture manufacturing plant had some authority in connection with sales, while the rest of us in the sales department were assigned to desks, doubled up and facing each other in the vast open space of the sixth floor that years before had been the furniture finishing room. Facing me was an attractive young man, "Call me Andy," Anderson, who frequently left the building during his lunch period to run home for what he referred to as a "quickie."

It was some time before I realized newly wed Andy was not referring to a quickly prepared sandwich. Soon after my employment and continuing thereafter he offered his best counsel on how to survive and prosper at Lear. One of his more humorous bits of advice was, *When I first started working at Lear and complained to a fellow worker about some minor inconvenience,* he said to me, *Stick around, Fritz, things could be worse. So I stuck around, and sure enough, he was right. Things have gotten worse.*

Ralph Braverman sat at the desk behind me, so I could hear much of what went on there. One of his assignments was to convince the Martin Aircraft people that a Lear instrument system should be installed in the first jet seaplane, the Martin XP6M, presumed successor to the P5M I had flown in VP47 and PBM I had flown during the Korean War in VP42. As a former navy seaplane pilot, I was a natural for this assignment, and it soon became mine, but meanwhile I was monitoring Ralph's conversations with the Martin procurement people to learn the ropes, and become acquainted with the Martin folks Ralph had been talking to, as well as to improve my knowledge of Martin specifications and other technical details.

Ralph's reactions to unexpected telephone events, his poise and overall good humor were a revelation to me; he never was at a loss for the appropriate response and the bon mot to go with it. On one occasion, memorable to me, after a long telephonic conversation with Martin procurement people, there was a long pause. No one spoke. Eventually, Ralph ended the silence by pleading, *Say something, even it's good bye!*

The challenging efforts to sell flight systems for the planned passenger jets were soon interrupted by a strike of the Lear, Inc., hourly rated employees, largely women, who performed rather intricate jobs in the manufacture of aircraft instruments. Bill Lear prided himself in providing the best hours, wages and working conditions for his employees, so the strike was not about any of these, but rather, by what I thought was a rather superficial demand to unionize Lear's hourly rated work force, induced by an outside group attempting to unionize the plant.

Bill's reaction was to resist and he directed all salaried employees to take up the tasks vacated by the hourly rated employees for the duration of the strike. This put all salaried employees in the position of choosing either to work or quit the job. I became a strikebreaker on the spot, getting up at five in the morning to be on the assembly line, thirty miles away at seven, trying to learn how to wind electrical coils that were parts of the Lear gyrocompasses. Learning to wind those coils was not easy; despite the patience of my female instructor, a former hourly rated employee, now salaried. I didn't appear at first to have the necessary mind, eye and finger coordination to perform the job, keeping a constant even tension of the wires as they passed through my fingers and onto the coil being wound on a spinning reel that would become a part of the gyro. I broke more wires than I produced acceptable product, at least for a few days, before I became a competent coil winder.

As a result of all this, Lear dropped far behind in its contractual time lines for manufacture of its products for the armed forces, and that induced Bill Lear to direct that we all work a full day on Saturday, and could volunteer to work a full shift on Sunday if we wished. I opted not to work on Sunday, but very little was done in the woods for the duration of the strike. At the end of the week I was too tired to do much of anything in the woods.

One positive benefit of the strike was that Bill Lear decided to fly in from Santa Monica to lead us through this tense period, giving me the opportunity to meet him, and also to observe him over a period of days. Bill was one of the most intriguing people I have ever met, and although his character, personality, leadership and genius are recorded elsewhere, I must chronicle some of my limited experience with this talented man, who, although he never went to college, was the first to take off, fly a course, and come back and land an aircraft while fully "under the hood", flying completely blind using only instruments of his own design and manufacture. This feat alone made him worthy of recognition in the history of aviation, but there is much more. He established Lear, Inc. to produce both aircraft instruments and electro-mechanical devices, and as he insisted, *Lear has more product flying in more aircraft than the products of all its competitors combined.* This was true, but he never mentioned that those aircraft were almost entirely military aircraft. Selling instrumentation for passenger aircraft was quite a different challenge. Those aircraft manufacturers, pressed by the airlines, preferred to buy their aircraft instrumentation from firms with stronger financial resources and would warehouse instruments and spare parts at no cost to the consumer.

On his arrival in the morning as long as the strike lasted Bill would stop outside the building, and chat briefly with some of the striking employees he knew from the "old days," when his company was just getting underway. He knew all of his employees from that earlier time, and could call them by name. However, he adamantly refused to give in to the strikers. No union for Lear. While he was in

Grand Rapids for those few days, he gave us daily pep talks that exhibited his personality and enthusiasm. Eventually the strike wound down and ended. I was back at my desk trying to complete the negotiation with the Martin Company, and became increasingly involved in the effort to sell the airlines and manufacturers on Lear autopilots and instrumentation for the first round of commercial jet aircraft.

In order to sell anything to be installed in a new commercial plane involved selling the product both to the airlines and to the manufacturers. The airlines were Eastern, headquartered in New York, Continental based in Denver, American in Fort Worth, Texas, Delta in Atlanta, United in Chicago, Pan American in Miami and Air France in Paris. The competing manufacturers were Boeing in Seattle, Lockheed in Burbank, California, Douglas in Long Beach, California and Sud Aviation in Paris. Except for Paris, this effort meant that we traveled to every one of these destinations. Paradoxically, the headquarters for Sud Aviation, the only airline and manufacturer to which we did finally sell Lear's instrumentation system, was Paris. It was during this time that I spent about a third of my time in the air as a passenger, getting home to Holland for short weekends.

In retrospect, I perceive that period as one of failure to sell Lear's products. However, as far as I was concerned, it was also a period during which I met a large number of the pioneers of commercial aviation in the United States, including Eddie Rickenbacker of Eastern, Bob Six of Continental, C. R. Smith of American Airlines, Bob Patterson of United Airlines and Juan Trippe of Pan American.

All of these men knew and respected Bill's record of achievements. Most of them knew and liked him personally; all were willing to listen to our presentations, entertain us and take us to dinner, but none of them was willing to buy Lear products. Without going into details, one of the principal reasons our efforts failed was that the airlines all insisted that spare parts and spare systems be stocked on their maintenance sites at the manufacturer's expense. Our directions for the negotiations prohibited any such agreement; Lear either could not afford, or was unwilling to accept such contractual provisions. By the time I left Lear, the effort had failed and Lear continued to devote its output primarily to military aircraft.

Lear's chief pilot was Art Peters, an OX5 survivor, a middle aged man who was a long time friend of Bill Lear's. OX5 referred to the V8 World War I engine that powered or underpowered some of the planes flying at that time including the World War I training plane called the Jenny. Those who had flown such planes were proud to have survived this experience and had their own tontine that met in many chapters around the country. This OX5 was a water cooled V-8 in contrast with the in-line engines that powered the automobiles of the time.

Among the qualifications that brought me to Lear was my experience as a navy pilot, although I was not expected to fly in that capacity for Lear. There arose an occasion when Art, who was required to have a co-pilot because of his age and the fact he was quite deaf, was scheduled to fly to the Lubrizol plant in Wycliffe, Ohio. The other Grand Rapids Lear pilot was not available for some reason, so Art called me, asking that I fly in the right seat and I agreed, an acceptance I would soon regret.

Although the weather was deteriorating and a front lay across our path to the east, Art filed a visual flight plan for the Lubrizol air field with Cleveland International as his alternate, despite my efforts to dissuade him. In response to my efforts he offered the comment, *I hate to fly on instruments.* We took off from Grand Rapids and climbed to five thousand feet. Then, as the weather report had predicted, the ceiling kept lowering as we proceeded eastward. I kept suggesting to Art that we call air traffic control for an instrument clearance. He simply shook his head on each occasion until the cloud cover had finally forced us down to about five hundred feet and it seemed we would soon be grazing the tree tops and turning to avoid church steeples. At this point it was either reverse course and return to Grand Rapids, or request an instrument clearance from air traffic control.

Art simply nodded when I picked up the hand held radio microphone and said *I'm calling air traffic control.* Within seconds, ATC directed us to climb immediately to six thousand feet and report on reaching that altitude, which we did shortly after flying through the cone over Detroit International. A few minutes later ATC directed us to descend <u>immediately</u> to four thousand. I pulled off the throttles only to find that Art had placed his hand on top of mine and pushed them right back to where they had been for level flight, with the question, *Whadiddy say, whadiddy say?* I tried to tell him with my mike, some hand waving and considerable shouting.

All of this took some time, and just as Art finally acquiesced, a Douglas DC4 flew past us in the same direction so close that our wingtips were practically touching. This was the traffic ATC had tried to help us avoid. Then we were advised that the Lubrizol airport was closed and we must terminate our flight at Cleveland, our alternate. This seemed like a good idea to me. The De Haviland Dove we were flying had no de-icing equipment whatsoever, except for a windshield deicer. At this point we ran into freezing rain and ice began to form on the wings, and the propeller was throwing off ice, some of which rattled off our befogged windshield with a distracting rattle.

We called Cleveland control for an instrument approach to runway one-eight, and indicated we were icing up. They approved and cleared us to descend to five hundred feet in the approach. At five hundred feet we were still on instruments, the icing continued, and I was taking bites out of my seat with my glutimous maximus.

Finally we could see the runway lights ahead of us less than a quarter mile away. Art made a slightly rough landing and ice flew in every direction. Although I kept it to myself, I swore I would never fly with him again. In the turn of events, I never again piloted a plane on instruments; my flying days were over except to a few VFR hops in a flying club plane, but they hardly count.

Toward the end of my Lear tenure, a young man, Jim Van Putten, living with his parents in a cute little house they had built for their retirement on a piece of ground in the woods near our property, became a regular on my Grand Rapids commute. The reestablishment of regular working hours following the cessation of the intensive coast to coast traveling involved in trying to sell the commercial instrument system made this possible. Jim was completing his requirements for a doctorate in chemistry, and would later become a distinguished member of the Hope College faculty. At the end of his day in Grand Rapids, he would walk over to the Lear Building and wait for me to join him. We would then walk together to the Lear parking lot. Jim had expressed an interest in my career as a navy pilot and a particular interest in instrument flying. The result was that for several evenings on the return to Holland I simulated for him a flight on instruments from the Lear parking lot to the Park township airport, a little grass field on forty acres just to the north of the Waukazoo Woods, where we both lived.

Fritz two-oh-three, ready for takeoff. Request taxi instructions and instrument clearance, Lear to Holland, over. We would assume a response from Grand Rapids control, and a requirement to report all en route check points, they being, in order, Grandville, Hudsonville and Zeeland, before receiving let down and landing instructions from the simulated Park Township which in real life had no instrumentation whatsoever beyond a wind sock. It was fun, and, I hoped, interest - ing and instructional for my passenger. I don't know whether Jim ever actually flew a plane, but he made good company on those commutes.

As a result of the bank calling our building loan, there remained the problem of accumulating enough money to continue the development of Baywoodlands. Some thousands of dollars beyond what we had available were required to complete final surveys, install drainage tile at the lower end of the property and grade and gravel the road, bringing it up to the requirements of the township.

Late one wintry Sunday afternoon, Lory was bustling about caring for our children and preparing dinner, when the door bell rang. It was the first time the bell had rung since we moved in a year earlier, when we tested it before taking occupancy, just to make sure it worked. Who in the world would be ringing our doorbell on a Sunday night, when the nearest house was close to a half mile away through the woods? I went to the door wondering who or what might be there.

Hello, I'm Ed Borchers, and I'm wondering if you might own this land. I nodded in the affirmative. The man was wearing heavy duty winter clothing and peering out from within one of the wool-lined caps with ear flaps often worn by outdoorsmen and outside workers during severe winter weather. He was covered with snow from the knees down, and it was obvious he had trudged through the deep snow for some distance to get to our little house as his destination. *Do you own the lake frontage at the east end of the property?* Again I nodded, wondering what he was getting at, and a little concerned that he might be threatening some additional problem for us to solve, but to my credit, I didn't say something like, *So what?* or *What business is it of yours?* I invited him to come in out of the cold, and he stomped his feet several times outside the door in an attempt to shake off his cargo of snow, and then several more times on the indoor mat. *I was ice fishin' on Pine Creek Bay and noticed some activity on this property,* he stated. I invited him to come in and take a seat at our kitchen table. He then commented, *Looks like you're subdividing the property.*

At this point, I tentatively drew the conclusion that this rough looking man might have something more of interest to say, so I responded, *Yes, would you like to see the proposed plan of the subdivision? It has the tentative approval of the township board, subject to their final approval of the finished drainage structures, and completed roads.* Mr. Borchers answered in the affirmative, and I pulled out the rolls of the detailed plans prepared by the engineering firm of Williams and Works and spread them out on the cleared top of the kitchen table, the only place in the house where this was possible, other than on the floor.. He scrutinized the basic plan for some minutes, while I sat in silence.

Whatcha want fer this lot rightcheer? He pointed to the lot next to the one on which we hoped to build some day.

I was somewhat hesitant to reply since I didn't know whether this man was a person of substance, or some oddball hoping to steal a property legally. *Well*, I said, *we are planning to offer that lot for one hundred dollars a front foot, and the lot is a hundred and fifty feet on the water."*

I'll take it, said Mr. Borchers.

I said, *But we'll have to have several thousand dollars to hold the lot for you until the subdivision is completed and approved,* sparring for time while not wanting to scotch a deal that might alleviate at least some of our financial pain. To myself I was thinking, "Would he balk at this proposal?"

Almost immediately, the fellow sitting at our kitchen table continued, *Developing property takes money. I know, because I've done some of it myself, so I'll write you a check for the full asking price of the lot if you will just give me a receipt for the money and a written statement of what the payment is for.* I could have kissed him, but I kept a stiff upper lip. We exchanged documents, he left, and we didn't hear from him again until spring. I deposited the check the next day, and it was good for the full amount. Our financial problems were largely solved, and we could continue the process of developing Baywoodlands.

CHAPTER FOUR - MASTER'S DEGREE
"There are three reasons for teaching"

Some time after the cost problems of our projected development were alleviated to a degree by Mr. Borchers, Lory began teaching at Waukazoo School for a ridiculously low salary, an amount, I observed, that was less than two thirds the sum being paid at that time to over-the-road truck drivers, who were not required to have any education beyond high school, if that much. Although Lory had received her "permanent" teaching certificate upon graduation from college, Michigan State law required her to take a specified number of credit hours of education or get a master's degree in a subject area in order to revalidate her qualifications to teach.

Meanwhile, she could be employed under a provision of the law that allowed her to teach for a limited time while fulfilling the requirement that she successfully complete additional semester hours. This provision was probably initiated by the state to combat the loss of teachers because of the niggardly salary scales imposed by the various boards of education to "hold down costs." It did the latter, all right, but over time the effect was to build a pressure that would drive up the salaries of teachers immensely. Almost inadvertently, Lory and I became a part of that effort.

For the years Lory taught at Waukazoo School, Yvonne Rhudy cared for Mary Jo, the baby, and provided a place for the other children to come after school until Lory could pick them up. `Yvonne was pretty much the opposite of her husband Ted in that she was always well-dressed and well-groomed. She came from a respected family, and Lory and I often wondered how she fell in with the slovenly Ted. Their house was a conglomeration of materials reminiscent of the doodle bug Ted had put together from various vehicles he had procured at little or no cost. The exterior walls were a composite of used brick, concrete blocks, rough siding and tin cans filled with concrete.

The interior, although of materials different from those used on the outside of the house, was equally chaotic. On the walls there was a variety of wallpapers, evidently from samples; old newspapers and pages from mail order catalogs, together with randomly cut pieces of assorted plywood panels. Although there was a field stone fireplace, it was rarely used and the place was heated by an ancient cook stove that served both for heating and cooking. The fuel, as we had noted from our initial contacts with Ted, was primarily wood, although in colder weather Ted allowed Yvonne to use a little of the precious supply of coal he had salvaged from somewhere. We worried initially about leaving the baby with Yvonne in that atmosphere, but ultimately concluded that it was the best we could do. Yvonne herself was clean, well dressed and reliable. She gave Mary Jo excellent care in this exotic setting.

Somehow, using mostly car pooling with other teachers for transportation, Lory managed to fulfill the requirement for additional hours of college level education by taking courses offered in the Holland area during the evening or on

Saturdays by Grand Rapids Junior College, Western Michigan State Teachers College (later to become Western Michigan University) and Hope College. She also was determined to qualify for the small additional pittance paid to teachers with master's degrees.

Despite the salary situation, I was lured toward teaching by several circumstances. I had done quite a bit of teaching during my naval career, at first in informal settings, as when on board ship I had helped sailors qualify for a promotion, or when I helped my fellow officers at the Naval General Line School while they suffered through the required course in electricity, and still later, in a more formal setting, as the Assistant Professor of Naval Science in the Naval Reserve Officers Training Corps at the University of Minnesota, teaching Naval History, Naval Engineering and Navigation to college level students. I particularly enjoyed the classroom atmosphere in contact with motivated students

While I was attending Hope College as an undergraduate, the goal of most of the women on campus was to obtain a teaching degree and the associated teaching certificate with a further view of becoming a teacher, a missionary or a minister's wife. The men for the most part were enrolled in pre-medical, pre-seminary or teaching programs. I was enrolled in none of these, but obtained a degree with majors in mathematics and history, expressing disdain for those who were taking education courses.

My outstanding elementary teachers at Lakeview School gave me a strong foundation for further education although in retrospect they worked under serf-like conditions and received their paltry salaries without complaint. By and large, my high school teachers at Holland High School had been of the same ilk. For that time and place, I received an excellent secondary education, followed by my experiences at Hope College.

Despite my respect for those who had taught me, I mostly had a view similar to that of George Bernard Shaw who had written, "Those who are able, do. Those who can't, teach." Obviously, my mind set was unfair to those who taught me.

Whatever my mind set at that time, with Lory's concurrence, I came to the conclusion that education would be my next field of endeavor. From my retrospective perspective as I write, I find it hard to explain even to myself why I chose this course of action. The plan was for me to quit my job at Lear, and carry a full load of classes at Western Michigan College in order to qualify for a master's degree and my teaching certificate within two years. The regular master's program required that I enroll in classes meeting three times per week. In addition, I enrolled for Saturday and evening classes to some extent to insure that all of this could be accomplished within the planned period. Lory joined in the effort by enrolling in evening and Saturday courses in order to qualify for her master's degree. As she was enrolled in a different program, her classes did not all coincide with mine, but we managed schedules that were reasonably compatible in time.

The commutes to Western's campus were entirely over two-lane Michigan State roads that were dangerous under the best of conditions, but particularly treacherous during the winter months when the roads were often snow covered, icy and slippery. The aging Ford station wagon held together for one more campaign without giving us undo trouble.

One of our required classes was Educational Psychology, taught by a friendly gray-haired insightful older gentleman names Ellis. The college required us to obtain a tome about four inches thick bearing the same name as the course. It weighed about five pounds. After the preliminaries, when the class met for the first time Dr. Ellis cleared his throat and said, *You can read that text if you want to, it won't hurt you, but there will be no assignments from it, and no quiz or test questions from it. I will present you with the elements of this subject, but they can be summarized in just six words, 'Motivation and treatment of individual differences.' If you can gain an understanding of the meaning of those words, and all the ramifications thereof, you will be a successful educator.*

He was right, of course, and in my educational career I tried always to keep those words in mind, gaining insight into their meaning as I went through the years of my career in the profession. It is often said, and my experiences have verified it, that education in the United States is cyclical in nature, placing undo emphasis at various times to limited areas of the educational spectrum. One of the tenets of U.S. education is, *Educate all of the children of all of the people equally.* This means to educate each child to the limits of his ability to learn; it does not mean, *Make atomic scientists of everyone,*" an obvious impossibility in view of the wide spread variations of talent and intelligence across wide variations among the population. It is a parallel to the wording of the United States Constitution which states that all men, i.e. citizens, are created equal, meaning all are to be treated equally under the law. Despite all this, we have failed miserably on both counts, i.e., we have failed repeatedly to give our students equal access to education, and, perhaps even worse, we have failed to give all citizens equality under law.

One of my Saturday classes, titled "A History of Education," a course required in the master's program, was taught by a vibrant, handsome man in his mid forties named Adams. He was an excellent teacher and knew his subject well. He never used notes as he strode back and forth in the ample space in front of an ancient classroom, probably one of the oldest on the campus. He occasionally walked to the back of the room for better eye contact with the class, which was composed almost entirely of middle aged teachers who chose to sit in the back of the room. We were all there seeking to renew our credentials or complete one of the required courses for a master's degree. By choice, I sat in the very front of the room from which perch I could most closely observe his striding and hand waving teaching.

The course occupied the time between nine and noon and included a bathroom break about midway through that time. On one occasion Professor Adams returned from the break, called the class to attention and resumed his lecturing and striding. There was no interference with my view of the professor, who passed regularly in front of me. On this occasion, on the first pass, I noted that the fly of his trousers was not closed, and on the second pass I addressed him in a low voice with my hand partially covering my face and said, *Professor, your fly is open*, expecting he would turn his back, or exit the room briefly to correct the situation.

Instead, he interrupted his lecture, stepped back a couple of paces, faced his audience and announced in a loud voice, *Ladies and gentlemen, my attention has just been invited to the fact that the fly of my trousers is open*. With that he leaned backward slightly, grasped the tab of his zipper and closed it. He concluded the episode by remarking, *I missed an opportunity once by not being ready*. There was then a collective inhaling gasp from the gathering of middle aged women in the rear of the room.

When that academic year drew to a close I had completed all of the requirements for a master's degree in the teaching of mathematics except for the required thesis and one mathematics course titled, "Rings and Ideals." I planned to complete both during the ensuing summer. As Dr. Ellis was one my advisors, I wisely chose the subject, "The Role of Motivation in Secondary Education," completed the research for this dissertation, submitted it and received the expected A grade.

Not so with "Rings and Ideals." I knew the meaning of these words in everyday life, but had no concept of their meaning in the mathematical world, in which these turned out to be mathematical concepts and systems for which I had none of the prerequisites. I opened the text book and read laudatory comments about the author. I then discovered I couldn't understand a thing beyond that point.

To complicate the situation further, the course was taught by a Pakistani wearing a turban who spoke in heavily accented broken English as he faced the chalk board and wrote endless mathematical expressions that were meaningless to me, turning occasionally to face the class and inquire, *Enny Keevestyuns?* before turning back immediately thereafter to the board with the apparent impression that everyone understood the whole string of spaghetti he had inscribed on the board.

After two such wasted sessions, I went to see my mathematics adviser, who was also the chairman of the mathematics department of the university. He quizzed me a bit about my experience in the class, reviewed my college transcript and agreed I did not have the prerequisites for enrollment in *Rings and Ideals* and thus my situation in that class was hopeless. He assigned me a more elementary text and agreed that either he or his assistant would meet with me for private tutoring several days per week in mathematical concepts that were to lead to the computer age shortly thereafter, and equipped me to pass some of that knowledge on to the students who would be assigned to me for the next several years.

When this relatively heavy dose of education was finally completed, and I qualified for my master's degree, I didn't bother to attend the commencement ceremonies, but requested my diploma be sent by mail.

In March that year I was invited to address the Century Club of Holland, a group that I had once described sarcastically as deriving its name from the requirement that its members be at least a hundred years old. Actually, it was a group of distinguished local citizens who gathered for educational, artistic and social purposes on a monthly schedule. Lory and I were honored by an invitation to join a few years later, an invitation we were pleased to accept. .

The subject for my talk was *The Navy's Role in the Atomic Age,* and my remarks were well received. I was amused to note that a musical selection performed after my presentation was Handel's *Art Thou Troubled?* I had given the group sufficient information to cause the members to be troubled about the potential in the atomic age to obliterate civilization, a popular topic during the Cold War.

Even before I was fully qualified for my teaching certificate, I received a call from Ray Lokers, the superintendent schools in Zeeland, a town just six miles from Holland, who announced that he was calling at the suggestion of Randall Decker, a Zeeland attorney and director of the Zeeland State Bank soon to become under his guidance The First Michigan Bank and Trust Company. Randy was also a member of the Zeeland Board of Education. I had come to know him through my subdivision efforts at a time when I preferred not to do business with the Holland banks.

Ray had graduated from Hope College a year before me and I considered him to be a friend from those days when we were fellow students in an institution with an enrollment of fewer than five hundred, and where everyone knew everyone else. He indicated that the Zeeland schools had a vacancy teaching English at the junior level of high school, and asked if I would be interested. Seeking now, once again, to alleviate our increasingly stressed financial situation, I immediately said, *Yes,* and the contractual agreement was prepared and executed.

Although English was a minor on my record, I had almost enough hours of it to qualify as a third major. My public school teaching career would begin that fall at the handsome salary of four thousand two hundred and fifty dollars for the year. It was less than a third of my pay as a naval aviator just a few years previously.

Somewhere during the series of events leading up to this point a middle aged veteran of classroom teaching counseled me, *There are three principal reasons for teaching in Michigan, and they are June, July and August.* I had hopes that this would be true, but it never became that for me.

Teachers Sign Contracts At Zeeland Schools

Fred Bertsch Jr. is a Hope College graduate who has had teaching experience at the University of Minnesota and at the U. S. Navy Damage Control School. He held the rank of Commander in the Navy from 1941 through 1955 and still holds his commission in the Navy Reserve. He resides at 135 Oakwood Ave, Holland. Mr. Bertsch will teach ninth grade English and American Literature.

Vivian Tardiff Cook, who formerly taught at Zeeland High, is returning to teach Literature.

D. anna Deas Vaughan is a native of Staten Island, N.Y. She is a graduate of Hope College and will teach ninth grade English and a class in French. Mrs. Vaughan will reside with her husband in Holland.

Superintendent J. F. Schipper announced that there is still one position open on the 1958-59 teaching staff. The job open is that of kindergarten teacher in the elementary department.

Carol DeVries Hoffman

Fred Bertsch, Jr.

Vivian Tardiff Cook

Robert Darrow

The Holland Sentinel

We were among old friends and classmates in Holland, but we also met a variety of other people ranging from the loggers, bulldozer operators, carp netters, teachers and college professors to the surveyors, township officials and others whom we met because of our subdivision activity. One set of people who became our regular potluck group came into existence as a complete surprise to us when Charlene Sessions, the wife of the general manager of the new General Electric plant phoned and invited us to join in a gathering for a spaghetti dinner, exchange of ideas and sophisticated discussion. She told us the names of those who were invited, Ace and Margaret Candee, Jerry and Lynn Counihan, Bob and Carolyn Snyder, a group of ten people, none of whom we had met previously; all of whom were newcomers to Holland and none of whom had a Dutch name. I was the only one who could be considered a Holland native, and I had been gone for the previous fifteen years, making me an outsider and new arrival as far as many locals were concerned. The gathering was a memorable event. On arrival Charlene served each person a tall well iced glass of pink lemonade and began the introductions. The Candees and Counihans knew each other well as Ace and Jerry were senior managers at Holland Color and Chemical. The same was true of our hosts and the Snyders through their association at the local General Electric installation. We had known none of the folks present prior to this time. A lively conversation ensured. Charlene announced that dinner would begin in about twenty minutes, Ace announced that he was going outside for a smoke. The remainder of the male guests followed lemonade glasses in hand, and gathered near the open garage door. Ace, as he lighted his cigarette said, *Jees, I'd sure like a real drink before dinner* and proceeded to rummage around in the various cabinets in the garage until he found our hosts' cache of liquor. He then spliced up everyone's drink with gin. Our group rejoined the ladies for dinner feeling much more inclined to converse brilliantly.

CHAPTER FIVE - TEACHING 1958-1963
"This Genteel but Threadbare Profession"

I soon realized that Zeeland at that time was even more provincial than my home town of Holland. While there were exceptions, my students in general were ill prepared to cope with the curriculum outline provided for the teaching of third year English. The outline called for the teacher to devote approximately equal time to doses of grammar and American Literature; the former emphasized the diagramming of sentences and English composition and the latter exposed the student to the writings of American authors. Within the first day I learned that my students, by and large, didn't know a subject from a predicate, a noun from a verb or anything about the influence of an adjective or adverb in the structure of a sentence.

American Literature was supported by a well edited anthology covering selected writings over several hundred years. The contents appeared not in chronological order but in an order designed to attract student interest. I quickly accepted the de facto hopelessness of the grammar situation, and gave an assignment to read and be prepared to discuss Jack London's short story *To Build a Fire".*

The following day during the first of my five class assignments I asked a boy to outline briefly the plot of the story assigned for overnight reading. *I ain't read it* was his answer. When I asked why he had not read the assignment, he said, *I hadda milk the cows and didn't have time."* I tried to get an answer from each of the students in turn, and each, with a very few exceptions, had an excuse, varying from the girl who said she had to baby sit with the younger children while her mother went off to a church meeting, to a young man who said, *My old man told me to can that stuff and read him the newspaper.* I was devastated, but persevered through four more classes, getting similar answers to what I thought were motivating questions.

I gave no homework assignment for that night. I wanted to devote a bit of time to considering my dilemma. The following day, in each class, I asked one of the more alert students, mostly girls, to read aloud to the class O'Henry's short story, "The Gifts of the Magi". The first few paragraphs included the words, "imputation", "parsimony" and "mendicancy". I stopped the reader, believing, correctly, that no one would know the meaning of those words. On inquiry as to meanings, one person offered that he had been called impudent once by his Sunday School teacher. A second volunteered that "parsimony" probably had to do with church because his minister was often called parson. A third indicated that mendicancy probably had something to do with sewing. One by one, I looked up the words in the shabby classroom dictionary and read them to the class. I was encouraged by the appearance that this exercise was not totally lost on the class. The student reader proceeded with the remainder of the short story.

When the young lady came to the end of the story and closed her book, I asked the general question, What *did you think of that story?*

The boy who had read the local newspaper to his father the previous night said, *It's dumb,* and then in response to my query of why he thought it dumb, he said, *Because the woman shudda kept her hair, an' the guy shuddena sold off his grandpa's watch.* The discussion went onward, but not necessarily upward from that point.

I became increasingly adapted to my position, trying to support the few students eager to learn, while attempting somehow to motivate the others through a variety of devices, demonstrations, play-acting and humor. On one occasion I wore the Daniel Boone type raccoon cap we had given to our son Buck during the period when the frontier was featured in movies and songs such as "King of the Wild Frontier." I split it down the back to make it fit my balding head. Another time I wore my uniform cap to illustrate Mark Twain's *Life on the Mississippi."* In connection with an assigned excerpt from Moby Dick I wore my entire uniform, and the students paid attention, responding to the glamour of all the gold stripes. I concluded I was making progress.

The small game hunting season opened on October fifteenth, just six weeks after the beginning of the school year. In those years, when the pheasant population in Western Michigan soared to rival that of South Dakota, schools and many businesses in Zeeland closed for the opening day of the small game season, and virtually all able-bodied men and boys went hunting, along with a sprinkling of women. I contacted several of my male colleagues and persuaded them to include me in their group to insure that I hunted with Zeelanders, a move deliberately intended to demonstrate to the student body that I wasn't "different". I shot my quota of pheasants, plus a rabbit that ran before our party, an unwilling participant in the event. After cleaning and refrigerating our game, most of us went downtown for a sandwich and cup of coffee, while others illegally took to the fields to try to "fill up" again.

It was then back the next day to the difficult task to which I was assigned, but unbeknownst to me, relief of a sort was on its way, and my destiny was about to be modified through a chain of coincidences. Behind the scenes, a series of events about which I knew nothing at the time was occurring. My mathematics teacher at Holland High School during my student days was Miss Hannah Parkyn, and she was now about to retire, having taught in the same classroom for upwards of forty years. She was a small, wizened, homely woman who peered from behind thick glasses and spoke with a rattling voice as she purveyed her favorite subject. That much I knew. Beyond all that I hoped, I would become her replacement after I had completed my contractual obligation to Zeeland.

My friend, Harvey Buter, whose high school athletic career I had covered while I was a youthful reporter stringing for the Grand Rapids *Herald* and other media many years before, was now employed by Holland Motor Express, and he for some reason unbeknownst to me maintained communication with Randall Dekker, my mentor in Zeeland, who was employed by the Zeeland State Bank, soon to be renamed The First Michigan Bank & Trust Company, an institution that some years later would play a significant role in my life. These two evidently conversed regularly, including discussions of community interest. At the same time, Ray Lokers, Zeeland superintendent of schools, and Dr. Walter Scott, occupying the corresponding position in the Holland public school system, were in occasional conversations.

Whatever the collusion among these four, the result was for me to receive an invitation to visit Holland's Superintendent Scott for an interview, an invitation I quickly accepted. The meeting went well, and I became Hannah Parkyn's designated replacement, effective the following fall. In the meantime, my Zeeland contract would be rescinded, and I would be on the Holland payroll at a salary that, while still small, was larger than that at Zeeland by virtue of my being given credit on the salary schedule for teaching two years as an instructor as I had been an assistant professor of naval science in the Naval Reserve Officers Training Corp at the University of Minnesota. To sweeten the pot even further, Lory was offered a job to teach in the Holland district at the elementary level beginning at the start of the ensuing school year for a salary somewhat better that projected at Waukazoo School. She accepted.

SAFETY PATROLLER — Bill Wolters holds back pedestrian traffic at Lincoln School in his role as Safety Patrol Captain for the school. Bill was chosen to represent the city and will be a guest of the Automobile Club of Michigan at the AAA National Safety Patrol rally to be held in Washington, D.C., May 6 to 9. With Bill front row (left to right) are Steve Serrano, Mary Swain and Shirley Senters. In back are Don Schulz, principal at Lincoln School, and Mrs. Fred Bertsch who is in charge of the Safety Patrol at the school.
(Sentinel photo)

The letter transmitting my contract said, in part, "Herewith enclosed is a teacher's contract for you effective January 26, 1959, written in the amount of $2,475.00 for the second semester. This salary is predicated on the basis of four years of experience outside of Holland, and one year's credit for military service. Accordingly, you are starting in Holland as in your sixth year of teaching which on our bachelor's degree schedule calls for $4,950.00 per year...." I winced as I signed for this paltry sum.

The physical conditions under which I taught for that semester were not good. Holland High School, built in 1912, was seriously overcrowded, resulting in the need to use every space available in accommodating classes. All classrooms were occupied every hour of the day, with displaced teachers seated in the back of the assembly room for their vacant periods. Students without a class assignment for that period were also seated there. Classes were meeting in temporary Quonset huts and the junior high. One small class was assigned to the boiler room. I had no classroom for that semester, but was assigned to five classes, each of which met in a different room. I ran back and forth among classrooms in both the high school and the junior high as well as one in one of the Quonset huts. I was out of breath at the beginning of each class period.

There was no food service and no appropriate place for teachers to eat the bag or lunch bucket meals they carried from home. Some teachers with rooms munched a sandwich or piece of fruit while seated at their desks during the five minutes between classes. In many cases, such as mine, the only place with any privacy was a small space formerly used as a coal bin adjacent to the boiler room. This space contained two rough wooden benches and a smallish table on which one could place his lunch, although there was no seating at the table. The only entrance to this area was a low opening through which the coal, formerly used as fuel, could be shoveled into the huge furnace, now modified to burn natural gas.

Several of my former teachers still on the staff of the high school gave me excellent advice reinforcing what I had already learned from my past experiences teaching in the navy, and as an assistant professor of naval science at the University of Minnesota. These exposures together with the observations of Dr. Ellis, who emphasized the need to get students' attention before one could teach them anything at all helped me to become an effective high school teacher.

A useful defensive weapon for teachers came from "Prof" Hanson in whose economics class as a student I had observed one of his techniques for coping with an administrator's visit to the classroom. One day, just as the class was starting, E. E. Fell, the superintendent, stepped into the classroom, possibly for an evaluation of prof's teaching. Prof greeted Dr. Fell cordially, and then, without hesitation, announced to the class, *"Dr. Fell is more qualified than I to teach the material for today's session, so I yield the floor to him".* I don't know if the old man realized he was being conned, but he took over the class and Prof retired to the back of the room. The superintendent held forth for the entire class period, and Prof thanked him profusely for his insights.

One further bit of advice Prof gave was extremely valuable. *When grading homework assignments, if you ever give them, keep in mind that you are looking at the very best work the parents can do.* He later added that parents vote, and that our meager salaries were provided by the millage voted by the public. During the Great Depression, he told me, his salary for performing, "in this genteel but honored profession," had been reduced from $1500.00 per year to $1,200.00, and the latter amount was then paid in promises to pay, in the form of "script", pending the receipt of property taxes. These pieces of paper were frequently discounted further by the local merchants when teachers attempted to use them to buy goods or services.

During my navy days I had seen one of these tax anticipation certificates in the amount of three dollars framed and displayed behind the bar which claimed to be the deck house of the schooner in which Jack London had traveled to Alaska during the gold rush. Within the frame over such a Holland, Michigan certificate was the inscription, *You think there's no such thing as a three dollar bill? Well here is one!"*

Although a full discussion of the matter would fill at least one volume, it is important that the reader have some understanding of the political situation at that time in the portion of Western Michigan lying inland of Lake Michigan and extending from the Allegan Public School district to the south and the Grand Haven district to the north. The Zeeland school district was the eastern boundary of that area, and all of the elementary districts within those boundaries sent their secondary students to Holland High School on a tuition basis. As a result of this situation, Holland High School was seriously overcrowded.

No immediate solution was available, but Walter Scott's plan for a solution was to consolidate all of the districts sending tuition students to Holland into a single district, build an additional high school, and, as they became necessary, elementary schools. Eventually when needed an additional junior high school would be built. This was a plan or vision for the long range future, but not all of the citizens of the districts involved, including those in the city of Holland agreed, leading to a decade-long internecine battle over the many issues involved. Adding fuel to the continuing discussions and debates, Mr. Scott joined with the Holland city manager in proposing that the city limits of Holland be made to coincide with the boundaries of the proposed consolidated school districts. This would make the district one of the largest in the state. Several small school districts, including the Van Raalte district with a single small school, were so consolidated with the Holland Public Schools, but the majority resisted.

To further complicate the situation, there existed the Holland Christian Schools with an extensive constituency that was frequently less than enthusiastic about paying taxes to support public education in any form.

As far as our family was concerned, we found ourselves with attachments to at least two of the conflicting elements. We lived in the Waukazoo elementary school district to the north of Holland and our children, Susan, Martje, Buck and Mary Jo were all enrolled there. If nothing changed as a result of the forthcoming consolidation elections, Susan would shortly be attending the severely overcrowded Holland High School. The conflicting element was that Lory and I were both teaching in the Holland district. While this set of conflicts simmered along for several years, Lory and I pursued our teaching, land development and, in my case, my continuing career as a naval reserve officer in order to preserve my retirement rights, if possible.

Lory was assigned to Washington elementary school, and I came into the use of Hannah Parkyn's former room for the teaching of my five classroom assignments, four classes of advanced algebra and one of senior mathematics, which consisted of one semester of solid geometry and one semester of trigonometry, My students were all highly motivated and I was involved only with treatment of individual differences as they existed among superior students with IQs of a hundred or more. The ever-present differences of sex, family background, ethnicity, etc. were present in my classes as they were in all classes.

The second floor room inherited from Miss Parkyn faced west with the natural light on the students' left, as in my old grade school classrooms of the two room Lakeview School. The limited woodwork was all stained dark brown and covered with multiple coats of varnish applied over the years. The front of the room was entirely black chalk board, as was the wall opposite the windows, except for the door. Despite its limitations it was a pleasure to teach highly motivated students in this atmosphere.

As the school year ended, I was advised in writing, as the de facto chairman of the mathematics department, of our budget for the following school year: *The budget has been established for the 1960-61 school year. The math department requested $5.40 for special instructional supplies. This amount has been granted....I would like to emphasize at this time that because of the austerity policy established for our budget that you should not exceed this $5.40. Jay W. Formsma, Principal.* I couldn't avoid a sense of depression with regard to the austerity of it all. I would hear the word austerity many times every year for the next seventeen years. My former teachers were now my colleagues, Ed Damson, Lillian Van Dyke, Lucille (Lindsley) Donovan, Natalie Bosman, Harriet Mulder, Joe Moran and "Prof" Hanson, to name a few.

There were, of course, educational challenges. It didn't take long for me to realize the impossibility of my correcting all of the work of all of the approximately one hundred and fifty students in my classes. At the suggestion of colleagues, I developed ways of evaluating the degree of learning, including board presentations of problem solutions during which students corrected exchanged papers, frequent "pop" quizzes and other evaluations including my review of selected assignments.

One of the students in senior math was a pretty girl whose mother, it was soon revealed to me, was the president of the elementary school board for the Lakeview district, my old elementary school. I had written a problem from the previous day's lesson on the chalk board at the front of the room and covered it with the drop-down display mounted above the board. With the students settled at their desks, I announced the quiz, indicated they had five minutes to write a solution. With only one exception, the students bent to their work.

The exception was the daughter of the Lugers School board president. The young lady dissolved into tears and submitted a paper that was blank except for her name. I awarded it a failing grade. When the school day ended I was confronted in my classroom by the mother, who apparently had received a phone call from her daughter between classes. She accused me of cruelty and other high and heinous crimes even after I displayed the blank quiz paper to her. I felt the young lady received the grade she deserved and vigorously defended the grade awarded. Her mother never quite understood that doing nothing was a failure, and I never quite understood the mother. The daughter really was an above average student and at the end of the semester she received a "B" grade in what was for her a difficult course.

Peter Attalai was a former officer in the Hungarian army, a graduate of the Hungarian national military academy who had fought alongside Hitler's German army on the Eastern Front in World War II. His adventures in escaping the post war communist regime with his wife and two children and traveling eventually to Holland after a nine-year sojourn in Argentina could make a fascinating book-length story. Peter, although he spoke with a German accent, spoke grammatically perfect English.

There appear to be cycles in education which place emphasis alternately on education for the on *education for the gifted* and then in another part of this cycle *education for the learning disabled*. The emphasis at the time Peter joined the staff was on the gifted, and Walter Scott was a vocal supporter of the effort, speaking to various organizations on the merits of various parts and perceptions of such emphasis. Mr. Scott set up a meeting of the teaching staff, kindergarten through twelfth grade, to insure that all staff were sensitive to the importance of catering to the educational needs of the gifted. He held forth at some length on the subject, and concluded with a perfunctory, *I will be happy to respond or answer any questions you may have.*

At this point Peter arose and said in his heavily accented speech, *Mr. Scott, you talk about geniuses, and I guess it's true that the United States can afford kevite a few of them, but let me tell you, geniuses are very expensive to have around. In Hungary, veire I come from, vee could afford only vun at a time.* The assembled teachers responded with laughter, but for me, charged with managing the financial affairs of my brother, who tested as a genius but was incompetent to handle his own responsibilities, Peter's statement struck home.

Because of the constant threat of financial constraints, teacher salaries were always in mind, and with some teachers, the subject was close to the surface at all times. There were often occasions when the teachers, as a group, were challenged to work within the financial limits, as deficit spending was never considered by the Holland Board of Education to be an option. Jay Formsma, the principal, was in the midst of one such exhortation when Art Hielkema, a teacher, rose and interrupted him. *Mr. Formsma,* he said, *It seems to me that performing as a teacher is similar to sexual intercourse in that some of us do it for sheer love and some of us do it for money. Is it your point that those of us who expect to be paid a living wage are therefore prostitutes?* The staff greeted this with laughter, but the point was made.

During another school year among another group of students, I discovered to my dismay that a senior male student in my class could not read, and therefore could not read or solve any of the mathematical propositions that comprised the course. Somehow he had completed more than eleven years of education without learning to read more than a few words. I worked with him daily to try to develop some reading ability, and also referred him to a remedial reading teacher. He graduated the following June, somehow passed the enlistment requirements and became a Naval Air Cadet. After qualifying as a naval aviator, he requested he be commissioned as a marine. When I last heard about him, he was a captain in the United States Marine Corps flying high performance jets.

A few years into my teaching career at Holland High School, Walter Scott invited me one spring Thursday to attend a meeting of the Holland Rotary Club, an organization I had heard about, perhaps mostly from the negative inferences I had absorbed from a reading *Babbitt* by Sinclair Lewis. Beyond that bit of misinformation, I knew none of the details. I probably thought I was being asked to join a group of aging men for a weekly luncheon, and little or nothing more.

On the appointed meeting date, Dr. Scott picked me up shortly before noon and we drove to the Warm Friend Tavern, the local hotel, a former subsidiary corporation of the Holland Furnace Company, a manufacturer which some years before had been considered a mainstay of the local economy but was in its death throes by the time I was introduced to Rotary.

There were several of my acquaintances, members of the club, at the meeting including my old nemesis, Curly Dalman, and I was introduced together with other visitors prior to the introduction of the speaker for the day. I was also exposed briefly to some of the local and international programs of Rotary to which the local club contributed. On the way back to the school Walter asked me if I would be interested in joining the Holland Rotary Club. I responded, *Yes, I would like to be a member of such a group, but it would be impossible, given my teaching schedule.*

I will see to it that your teaching schedule for next year is such that you will have a couple of hours on Thursdays to accommodate your Rotary attendance obligation, as you must be present for virtually all meetings or make them up at another club within two weeks. He outlined additional Rotary responsibilities that would be mine once I was a member of Rotary which I easily accepted, and when the summer of nineteen sixty-four arrived I became a member of the club. It must have annoyed the principal that my teaching schedule was dictated by the superintendent and arranged to allow my Rotary   attendance, but he never indicated it in my presence.

I drove downtown to the club meeting each Thursday, and usually parked in back of the bank, but one Thursday, I parked on the street in a two-hour parking place and inserted my coins in the meter. As I turned away to walk to the hotel, I was greeted by Jack Plewes, one of the local jewelers, a Rotary member and also at that time an elected member of the Holland Board of Education.

There ensued a conversation that revealed some deep-seated attitudes with which I would have to deal during my career in education. I will never forget it. *What's wrong with these teachers that they keep insisting on more money? We board members can't give them more money and maintain the schools and carry out all our other responsibilities if we give them higher wages.* This was not only a rejection of salary increases, but also a demeaning comparison with hourly rated employees.

I did my best during the five minute walk to the hotel to explain to Jack that the staff was well educated, with considerable investments in their education and that their pay was less by far than that of other occupations. His only response was, *I just don't get it. They're lucky to have jobs.* By then we were at the hotel entrance. My time was up and I had failed to make my position clear to this member of the board of education. We sat at separate tables for the meeting. I felt nauseated.

With credit for nine years of teaching, my salary had become a munificent sixty-one hundred dollars as reflected in the salary schedule for that year. That spring in a letter dated March 29, 1963, the board of education directed a rather lengthy communication to the president of the Holland Education Association, an organization originally formed to promote education, but that was rapidly taking on the characteristics of a labor union. The second paragraph of the letter stated, in part,......*that contracts for teachers will be issued at the same salary rate as now exists for the 1962-63 school year.* In other words, there would be no salary increases for currently employed staff for the next year.

The third subparagraph of the third paragraph of this epistle contained a statement totally unacceptable to the teaching staff, *The normal turnover of teaching personnel may require replacement teachers to be hired. Adequate replacements can be hired only if the Board of Education is able to meet the salary competition of neighboring school districts.* The teachers interpreted this to mean that replacements would be hired at salaries above the scale which the board was asking present staff to accept.

The eighth and ninth subparagraphs read, in part, *On March 15, 1963, the Board sent to each full time teacher a contract offer setting forth the usual conditions and salary...To this date many teachers have not replied to this offer. ..The Board must proceed...(*and) unless the executed contract is returned to the Business office by 5:00 P.M. on Monday, April 8, 1963, the offer contained in such contract will thereupon terminate, the position will be considered vacant for the school year 1963-64 and the Board of Education will proceed to locate other eligible teachers to perform such work."* These were fighting words, particularly to teachers who had loyally served the district for many years,

As the deadline for the return of contracts was approaching, it was obvious that a majority of teachers would not return their signed contracts unless they were given assurance in writing that no new or replacement teacher would be placed at a salary greater than that of a present staff member with comparable experience. The key words became, *....in writing.* Because the teachers no longer accepted verbal assurances, a letter from the president of the Holland Education Association was addressed to the Board of Education advising it of the teachers' decision, and requested a reply.

To the best of my knowledge, that letter was never answered, and this failure only intensified the teachers' frustrations.

At this point, with the self-imposed deadline imminent, Mr. Scott called a meeting of all district professional staff, to be held in the assembly hall of the high school. With the staff assembled, the superintendent rose to address its members in rather high blown phrases, exhorting the teachers to see their duty, sign the contracts and deliver them prior to the deadline. He then asked for comments and questions from the floor, and there were many. Finally, I rose and said, *Mr. Scott, the issue here is not only that we are asked to sign contracts on the old salary schedule, but also that the Board of Education has not responded to our recent letter in which we simply asked that no new staff be paid outside the salary schedule at which we being asked to sign. To date no response has been received. Does this mean that the Holland Board of Education is incapable of answering its own mail?"* I had intended this remark to be simple sarcasm, but unintentionally, I had hit on exactly the right note to electrify the teachers, who erupted in applause and cat calls. Dr. Scott slumped into a nearby chair. The seeds were thus sown to produce a confrontation that had far reaching consequences, including the firing of the superintendent.

Above: Holland High School in a picture taken the year before I became the principal. Walter Scott is at the left, and Alvin D. Bos to the right. The principal's office window appears to the far right in this picture.
Photograph from the collection of Fred S. Bertsch, jr.

The salary schedule for the school year 1963-1964 is shown on the next page. It illustrates and highlights the apparently unsolvable confrontation in which the Holland Board of Education and the rapidly organizing teachers found themselves at that time. Several items in the salary schedule brought complaints from the teachers and ultimately triggered the first teachers' strike in Michigan. The most significant of these was the provision in Note 2, *The Board of Education reserves the right to adjust salaries within this schedule or change the schedule as financial needs may require.* The teachers interpreted this to mean that the board, at its sole discretion, could place newly hired teachers at salaries above those of the experienced teachers already on the staff. This provision was unacceptable to the teachers in any form and both the superintendent and the board were so advised, but nothing was done to alter the schedule in order to alleviate the teachers' concerns.

The financial stress created by the threatening language brought to mind, particularly among the older teachers, actions taken by the Holland Board of Education during the Great Depression of the nineteen thirties and they were not reticent about sharing their memories with the younger staff members. The board's first action as the Depression deepened was to cut all teachers' salaries by about a third. Then, because many taxpayers failed to pay their real estate taxes and industries in some cases went out of business or declared bankruptcy, the board issued what were called "Tax Anticipation Script and paid the teachers with it. Holland merchants accepted the script, but discounted it in various amounts, delivering a third blow to teachers' purchasing power. During the last tour of duty before resigning my commission in the regular navy, at the invitation of Martin

SCHOOL DISTRICT OF THE CITY OF HOLLAND
HOLLAND   MICHIGAN

The salary arrangement as indicated below sets forth the steps and amounts paid to teachers for the school year 1963-1964.

Year	Two Yrs. Training Or 60 Semester Hours	Three Yrs. Training Or 90 Semester Hours	A.B. Degree	M.A. Degree
1	$3500	$3800	$4500	$4500
2	3700	4000	4700	4700
3	3900	4200	4900	4900
4	4100	4400	5100	5100
5	4300	4600	5300	5500
6	4550	4850	5500	5800
7	4750	5000	5700	6000
8	4900	5200	5900	6200
9	5000		6100	6400
10			6300	6700
11			6500	6900
12				7100
13				7300

Maximum salary for non-degree teachers may not exceed $5200.

A teacher with a bachelor's degree and 20 years or more of teaching experience will advance from $6,500 to $6,700.

1. Credit for previous teaching experience is given on a corresponding year to year service not to exceed a maximum of eight years.

2. The Board of Education reserves the right to adjust salaries within this schedule or to change the schedule as financial needs may require.

3. All new teachers coming into the School District of the City of Holland are on probation for the first three years. Their services will be evaluated each year during these years.

4. Any teacher whose teaching experience in Holland has been interrupted by military service will be given full credit on the salary schedule for time spent in service.

5. Fifteen days of sick leave are allowed each teacher during the first year in the School District of the City of Holland, and ten days per year thereafter, cumulative to 100 days. One day may be used each year for emergency business — this will be deducted from sick leave.

company sales engineers, I visited a "watering hole" in Alameda's Jack London Square. There over the bar was a sign that read, *You think it's as phony as a three dollar bill? Well, here is one!* Below the sign was a framed three dollar Holland Michigan Tax Anticipation Certificate; one of those issued during the Great Depression by the Holland Board of Education.

From one of the teachers' publications I had plucked a little poem by one Stephan Schlitzer titled *Biography of a Superintendent,* which, in modified form summarizes what was happening in Holland:

The first two years he's eulogized
With lavish words of praise.
The second two years he's analyzed
And puts in anxious days.
The third two years he's criticized.
By now he's worn and tired.
The fourth two years he's ostracized
The ninth year he is fired.

While not exactly applicable to what caused Walter Scott's departure from the superintendency, it is pretty close. The school year came to an end and Walter Scott left the scene. With reference to the superintendent's departure, Prof Hanson offered two insightful comments. The first was, *The high points bring down the lightning,* and the second, referring to the newly constructed high school was, *No superintendent can outlive his memorial.* I read in the *Holland Evening Sentinel* that a man with deep roots in the city, Donald Ihrman, had been chosen to succeed him.

In our private lives, our subdivision development had gone well, and we had sold enough lots to allow us to get started on the construction of our dream house, the plans for which we discovered in a copy of *Sunset*, a magazine published on the west coast of the United States. The split level plan was for a largely open house with three levels for the living area, the entry and the bedroom area on the intermediate level. The bedrooms had Anderson double glazed windows placed above shoulder level giving privacy to the sleeping and bathroom areas. The floor of the copious entry was of quarried tile, the two outside walls were entirely double glazed insulated glass except for the front entrance door. Above an entry closet on the third side of the entry was the back of the breakfast nook and above that no wall. Oak stairs led upward to the living room and downward to the lower level recreation room and utility room. The ceiling of the entry was the underside of the open beamed roof twenty feet above its floor

The kitchen, breakfast nook, dining room and living room, were a half flight of stairs above the entry level; a half flight down was the large recreation room, the utilities and a commodious workshop for me. The whole of the roof was supported by a single beam eight by thirty inches in cross section and thirty feet long that had to be special ordered from Oregon and carried to Holland by railroad flat car.

The living room and recreation room were to be paneled with the cherry lumber sawed from the logs I had harvested on the property. The floors throughout the house were to be laid of the oak I had cut and air dried, while the limited amount of pine was devoted to paneling the utility/shop room and garage. A laundry room was included in the bedroom wing.

The fireplace in the living room, built of Indiana limestone was open on two sides, while an open grill with a separate flue opened onto the kitchen and breakfast nook. In the recreation room below the living room, and supporting the mass of masonry just described, was a brick-faced fireplace with a built in steel fire box equipped with a fan that could circulate the hot air from around the fire box into the room with the fireplace closed off with a tempered glass panel .

Lory and I were determined to build our dream house while the children were young enough to enjoy it, and we wanted them to live on the lake before they went off to college and accepted greater responsibilities elsewhere. We were never sorry we we did this although the building stressed our resources, and we made do for a number of years with the old furniture that had come with the purchase of the Coronado house many years before.

We moved into the house of our dreams in late fall. While not really finished, it was habitable, and we were motivated by the fact that our original speculation house was sold on the basis of a land contract with the purchasers' taking occupancy in the immediate future. We were content to use the few pieces of furniture we had left from our Coronado home.

Soon the Christmas season approached, and although our nearest neighbor, other than the Bill Haan and his wife next door was over a half mile away, we determined to light our new home with all the Christmas lights we could bring to bear, and this was a sizable amount. We hung lights from all the eves and lighted upa triangular frame to hang in the two-story entry which doubled as a display site for the greeting cards that were coming every day. We attached the cards with clothes pins to light clothes line running from side to side on this frame. It was a great Christmas with all of our children and our surviving parents on both sides of the family.

The great holiday celebration came to an end, we were all back in school and it was time to pay the piper. One of the bills that took us aback was from the Holland Board of Public Works, the supplier of our electric power. In indignation, I called the BPW and was directed to a woman named De Boer who would verify the meter reading and answer any questions I might have. By way of introduction, when she answered the phone she said, *Ain't you them folks in that big house out there in the woods?* I acknowledged that our house was new and it was in the woods. When Miss De Boer came back to the phone after having, as she said, *pulled our card*, she verified the record of the amount of power used and then said *You folks used a lot of power in December. Seems to me like you're livin' pretty high off the hog out there in the woods.* I ignored the impertinence. We paid the bill and began looking for ways to limit our use of electric power. The house proved very economical to operate after we took all the appropriate steps to winterize it.

Stuart Padnos, the younger of the two brothers, stopped me one spring day to tell me about a drive he had taken to show a visiting couple some of the highlights of the Holland area. He chose our new home as one of the highlights and, according to the description he gave us, he said on that occasion, *This is the home of one of our teachers. It gives you some idea of how well we pay our teachers.* In light of our paltry pay I didn't think at the time the comment was particularly humorous.

Yellow Dogs, I was told by Prof was *A national organization of male teachers, the primary purpose of which was to celebrate the fortitude, courage and wisdom of men in pursuing a career in education.* He didn't mention stupidity, but that quality seemed to be implied. Initiation of newly-employed professional educators was conducted in the fall, soon after the beginning of the school year during the annual meeting of "The Dogs" and thus, as I taught only the second semester in Holland, I did not become a member that first year. The fact that this organization met only once per year primarily for the purpose of initiating new members made me suspect two things: (1) The organization was local, not national; (2) It was social, not professional and (3) The initiation of new members was the most important entertainment activity at the organization's singular annual meeting.

In October I received a summons to appear at a Yellow Dogs meeting to be held at The Tara, a restaurant in the neighboring town of Saugatuck and to be prepared for welcome into the Ancient and Honorable National Society of Educational Yellow Dogs. What I remember most vividly is the steak dinner for which The Tara was famous, the several facetious and sarcastic speeches by older teachers and, of course, the initiation which was modeled more like a college fraternity meeting than that of serious educators. When the time came for the installation of new members, we were run through a series of pranks, demeaning demands and jokes devised by the initiation committee much to the boisterous amusement of the assembled male educators. Finally we novitiates were instructed to roll up the left leg of our trousers.

The final element of all this, after isolation of the candidates, was conducted by my old teacher, Ed Damson, who led me blindfolded to a place before the assembled membership, where he posed a rather lengthy series of humorous questions, several of which were *Do you promise to share your last bone with your fellow dogs,?* and *Do you promise when touring the neighborhood to faithfully lift your leg adequately when leaving your greetings on trees or fire plugs?* Each question was followed by the statement, *If you so promise you may respond in the affirmative by uttering the traditional "Woof Woof."* Ed then read a proclamation of membership which ended with, *And thus in recognition of you as a new Dog, we say "Pee on thee"* as he administered a gravy baster of warm water on my bared leg. With that I became a full-fledged Yellow Dog and participated in this social evening for the ensuing sixteen or more years. Annual invitations to join in these festivities continued for many years even though geography discouraged my attendance. They have stopped coming. Are the Yellow Dogs no longer in existence?

The potluck group to which we had been invited became an institution, and gathered regularly every month unless there was some serious conflict, as with holidays, but those would generally cause only a change of dates for our dinners. On one occasion when the Counihans were the hosts, Lory and I were scheduled to bring the dessert. We had recently been served cherries jubilee when dining at a fine restaurant during a visit to Chicago and felt it would be welcome as a finale for one of our potluck dinners. We carried with us to the gathering a bottle of hundred and fifty proof   brandy left from our navy days, and all the other ingredients for our showpiece dessert.

When the main course dishes had been cleared, and it was time for dessert, Lory and I left the table and went to the kitchen to ready our contribution to the occasion. Out came the cherry laden bowl of ice cream, the brandy, a ladle and the little Counihan's pretty little dessert bowls into which we planned to transfer our elegant preparation for serving to the expectant group. Certainly all eyes were on me as I poured that high octane brandy onto the contents of the bowl and struck a match. When I moved the lighted taper toward the bowl, rather than starting an attractive small blue flame over the cherries as intended, the fumes exploded in what appeared to the guests seated at table to be the equivalent of a small atomic bomb.

A collective gasp of astonishment and horror came from all present as a cloud of black smoke induced by the flaming mixture of cherry juice and alcohol ascended toward the ceiling and soot was deposited not only on the guests and the table with its elegant setting, but also on every dish in the open china cabinet, the walls of the room and the ceiling. We were devastated that our carefully planned *piece de resistance* had come to grief.

After we had collected our wits, apologized for the impact event had had on our gathering and served everyone a bit of the caramelized cherries jubilee, we offered to pay for any damages, arrange for the cleaning of the dishes and the china cabinet and repaint the dining room walls and ceiling. Our gracious hosts refused all such help, insisting that the cleaning lady was coming the next day and could clean the dishes and the cabinet. They also were kind enough to state they had been planning for some time to repaint the dining room and would take this opportunity to do so. The room definitely needed an update after our disastrous attack.

This group held together throughout the period covered in this volume, although there were subtractions and additions as members were transferred to other places; sickness or death occasionally occurred and thus the membership varied somewhat. On one occasion a member's life was saved by accident.

One winery day, when conditions were ideal, the Counihans decided to take their only offspring, Kevin, age 10, to the Holland Country club for some skiing and sledding. The slopes behind the club house are steep for golfers, but are rather tame for skiers with a few rolling unevenness to give novitiates a small challenge, and which give the sledders and tobogganers a few minor thrills as they slide over them. Occasionally the bumps are sharp enough to cause the aledders to be briefly airborne, and then land with a thump.

On what turned out to be the final slide of the day, the toboggan carrying all three members of the family with Jerry riding on the rear, was briefly airborne and landed with a considerable jar. When the slide ended at the bottom of the run Jerry could not get up from the toboggan, and willing onlookers pulled him to the top of the hill. An ambulance arrived to take him to the hospital where it was discovered that his back was fractured.

He was placed in a plaster cast from his neck to thigh, big block of inert material. While the whole sequence was far from funny, we all made light of the situation and signed his cast in a variety of colored inks. It was not a death threatening injury and it was generally thought that Jerry would be on his feet again within a month or two, but nature intervened.

Without the usual warning signs, his appendix suddenly burst and intervening action was necessary. The medics sawed his cast off on either side from head to toe, and a surgeon performed the appendectomy, loaded him up with penicillin and taped the cast back in place. A few weeks later he was released to go home, still in the body cast. He couldn't really sit, but he could stand, despite the weight of his burden, so he decided to try to resume his work, which was piling up by this time, using a drafting table as his desk.

When the body cast was finally removed, his doctor proclaimed, "I noted a few things during the appendectomy that should be checked immediately now that you are able to stand more surgery." Within a short time it was determined that one of his kidneys was cancerous and it was removed forthwith, followed by the usual preventative measures and as will be noted later in this sage, he lived a long and productive life, dying of natural causes when he was ninety-three or thereabouts. The bump on the toboggan had started this life saving process.

CHAPTER SIX - BUCK & DAVID (1958- PRESENT)
Tom Sawyer & Huckleberry Finn

About the time we moved into our house, another was built on a piece of metes and bounds property just a few hundred feet from the southwest corner of Baywoodlands. When it was occupied with it came a life-long friend for our son, Buck, a boy approximately his age, David Davis. These two, about five years old when they met, became the Tom Sawyer and Huck Finn of the neighborhood, providing cheers, tears, anguish, frustration and amusement for all as they moved through their boyhood years.

It was spring, and we had dredged a sizable amount of soil along the lake frontage of the northernmost Baywoodlands lots, and these small mountains of spoil, a mixture of sand and muck from the swamp were an irresistible attraction for two young boys. How they managed to avoid suffocation when they buried themselves in this pile of mud was due to the reappearance in our lives of Ed Borchers, the man who had underwritten our under financed real estate project at a critical stage a year or two earlier.

Borchers was a man of many trades and skills, ranging from carpentry and land speculation through carp fishing. He was engaged in the carp netting part of his life at the time of the boys' plight, and it was only through his intervention that they were saved from probable death by suffocation as they wiggled and writhed to try to extricate themselves sinking deeper and deeper into the goocy mess entrapping them. As it was, the carp fishermen arrived on the scene, launching their flat-bottomed work boat from the private lake access we had included in the plans for Baywoodlands.

The northern end of Pine Creek Bay was a spring rendezvous for carp preparing to spawn, and thus a natural place for the carp fishermen to launch their net, some thousand or more feet long. One end of this great net was secured to a tree at the private walk and the flat boat moved slowly over to the other side of the bay, paying out net as they went. When all of the net had been laid out in an extended loop which enclosed the northern end of the bay, the long lines at its extreme end were taken to a snatch block, or pulley and back to the private walk where a little gasoline powered winch would be used to pull the net.

It was during this part of the operation that one of the fishermen heard the yells of the boys, and carp fishing was set aside for a short time while the mud-drenched kids were pulled to freedom and told to go home and get cleaned up.

It must have been a Saturday, because I was at home. When our mud caked son came into view he started immediately to tell me that there was much activity down at the lake front and I should get down there right away. I arrived at the scene of action just as the game warden assigned to our area arrived. His function was not to prevent the drawing of the net, for which Borchers had the proper permit, but rather to insure that only carp and other undesirable fish were kept. As the net was pulled, it was obvious that on this occasion the catch was large. The warden watched carefully as Borchers and his crew, walking through the massive collection of fish enclosed by the net sorted the haul returning all game fish to the lake, throwing all undesirable species, as specified by the Fish and Game Commission on the shore and retaining the carp in the net as it was drawn closer to the shoreline.

With exquisite timing, large tanker trucks, resembling those delivering gasoline to service stations arrived. They were equipped with hatches at the top, through which the fish could be dumped into the tank, partially filled with water in order that they be kept alive during their trip either to Detroit or Chicago, where they would be kosher killed and transformed into gefilte fish.

For a few dollars that spring, we came into possession of a decrepit canoe, which I managed to repair enough to permit it to stay afloat. At the head of Pine Creek Bay, a few hundred yards from where our new house was being built lay a swampy area where Pine Creek enters the lake. This swamp began a few yards north of where the boys had been stuck in the pile of spoil, and extended northward to and well beyond Ottawa Beach Road which passed over the culvert that allowed the creek to flow into the lake.

The water in the creek and the associated swamp was nowhere over a foot or two deep, and was thus generally safe for exploration by young adventurers, although there were holes where the water was somewhat deeper, testing the boys' survival skills to some extent. The swamp was a subdivision of heaven as far as the two explorers were concerned. It was there they captured hundreds of turtles, pollywogs, frogs, snakes and other specimens, many of them carried home in the canoe for the express purpose of terrifying, demonizing or simply frustrating their mothers. David and Buck came home from the swamp on a regular basis ridden with muck and regularly taxing the capacity of their families' laundry machinery.

There were other destinations that tempted the two boys. "Hazelbank" was a generic name for the lake front area across the bay from our new home, an area of some forty acres which contained the principal residences of the families that had controlled the Holland Furnace Company from the days of the firm's preeminence in the home heating business. These families continued to live there even as the firm faced impending failure. The boat house which at one time had housed two powerful speedboats, a Chris Craft and a Gar Wood now lay vacant, with its big lake front door closed and locked, but the bottom of the pivoting garage type door was still several feet above lake level, allowing young adventurers arriving by boat or canoe access to its interior. There was little of value left in the old boat house, but it was a great rendezvous for Buck and David. They often went there in the ancient canoe to fish, because from the relative darkness of the windowless boat house, they could watch the numerous fish swimming below them. They found, however, that as long as they floated about in the semi-darkness above them the fish were spooked by their presence and seldom bit the well-baited hooks the boys dangled in front of them. In contrast they had much greater success when in the daylight outside the boat house.

The other attractive lake feature of Hazelbank was a sandy beach that extended southward across the entire lake front of the furnace company property. Immediately to the south of the boat house, forming a point into the lake, was a pile of the spoil from a dredging many years before in order to provide enough depth for the speedboats. The sandy beach extended several hundred feet to the south. We directed the boys not to use that beach, but they often cavorted there anyway pulling the canoe up next to the small hill of spoil.

As noted before, the renamed Lake Macatawa was home to large numbers of carp as well as other fish, and it was not unusual to have a dead carp float onto the beach and lie there decomposing. When a dead carp floated up on our property I would fork it up into the family garden and bury it as "Indian fertilizer," but over at Hazelbank they often just lay on the beach rotting away until there was nothing left but the skeleton of large carp bones lying on the sand or partially buried in the sand. Buck, as he often did, was enjoying the beach, running back and forth and leaping with enthusiasm when finally at the end of one of his leaps he landed on a pile of carp bones, one of which, almost the size of a pitchfork tine, penetrated his foot and stuck out both from the sole and the top of his foot. To the accompaniment of much yelling to get someone's attention, David paddled the victim back across the narrow bay.

We hustled him off to the hospital emergency room where the emergency physician carefully removed the bone, cleaned up the wounds and gave the "wounded hero" a tetanus shot. The next morning, he was in considerable pain, his wounds full of pus, and dark streaks were extending up his leg. It was then back to the emergency room, where a surgeon opened the entire wound area and had the young patient admitted to the hospital. It was neither the first nor the last of many such trips.

Buck and David weren't always without some malice. As the boys grew older they insisted, after taking the younger neighborhood children on a round of innocent Halloween activities, they be allowed their own forms of trick or treat, which actually became trick and treat. Unwanted corn shocks were deposited on porches, old tires were set afire in unexpected places and strings of fire crackers were thrown into yards or onto porches. There were no longer any out houses to tip over as there had been in my youth, and no more explosive streaks of fire across the road in front of speeding cars, so in the view of Buck and David something had to be done to satisfy the Halloween needs of a couple of ingenious young devils who would not be satisfied by a walk through the neighborhood carrying paper bags to be filled with tooth destroying candies and other sweets. Whatever else they might be, these two weren't going to be wimps.

On one notable Halloween evening Buck and David dutifully took the younger neighborhood children on a round of the neighborhood houses, soaped a few windows and rattled some with their homemade window rattling devices made from spools, hat pins, tin cans and resin, collecting the usual basket or bag full of goodies from smiling Baywoodlands residents.

Targeted by the perpetrators was a specific house, whose owner had aroused the ire of the boys in some way and for some reason now long forgotten. Days in advance of the big event, the schemers collected feces of various kinds, cat, dog, and perhaps human in a large brown paper bag and stored the collection in a tree out in the woods for safekeeping. After their tour with the little children, and darkness fell on the Halloween scene, the two plotters recovered the bag of feces from its hiding place and proceeded to the target area with the rest of the equipment required for their planned attack: a candle, matches, fire crackers and an oil can filled with kerosene.

They peered from the darkness through the front window of the targeted house to ascertain that their prey was available. The intended victim was reading the evening paper, seated in his easy chair with his feet resting on a padded stool, oblivious of the impending shenanigans. All was going as planned. The two plotters inserted the candle into the feces laden bag and lighted it with care, giving the brown shopping bag an aura of back lighting. They then placed it on the porch a couple of steps outside the front door. After a shot of kerosene from the oil can, which shortly thereafter caught fire, one of the boys rattled the front window, while the other banged loudly on the door. The boys then beat a hasty retreat into the wooded area across the street and waited the few seconds until the victim had had the opportunity to set aside his paper, lift himself up out of his easy chair and head for the door. From the security of their hiding place in the dark of the woods the boys had the satisfaction of seeing their enemy come out of the front door and stomp heavily on the blazing feces-laden bag, resulting in his shoes being covered with the contents of the bag..

It was a well-planned, carefully timed and successful operation from the point of view of Buck and David. The target immediately identified the culprits, and it was we, the parents who suffered the torrent of wrath Mr. "X" visited upon us, while the guilty pair took refuge in David's tree house built in a remote area of the adjacent well wooded property using materials scavenged from new construction in the area. In his youth David moved with his parents to the Atlanta area, but our Tom Sawyer and Huck Finn have remained in contact with each other for life.

CHAPTER SEVEN - OTHER INTERESTS
Rotary and Service Above Self

When Walter Scott introduced me to the Rotary Club of Holland, neither he nor I, I'm sure, had any real conception of the degree to which this outlet for idealism would affect my life. Initially my interest in Rotary was the fellowship with business and professional leaders of the community, the opportunity to mingle with peers and share a meal a week with a compatible group of men. Over the years I observed that these were the initial interests of virtually all new members, and some members never advanced in the idealisms of Rotary beyond that level, were content to sit with friends for lunch once a week, pay their dues and slough off the basic Rotary tenet of "Service Above Self ." For me, sharing initially the luncheon club concept, Rotary was an opportunity to get away from the classroom routine and exchange views with others. Often I found that my views of the world, even of the relatively tiny world of Holland, Michigan, were far different from those of other members of the club. My exposures to other nationalities, cultures and milieus while serving in the navy underlay many of these differences.

While all Rotarians were encouraged to help new members become familiar with the idealisms of Rotary, this was not adequate, particularly since not all members themselves were familiar with the broad spectrum of the organization's activities throughout the world, and further the back-bench "luncheon club" attendees, were not at all interested. On the other hand, Duffy Wade, a local druggist, an enthusiastic proponent of the ideal of service above self, was the chairman of a committee charged with the responsibility for informing and indoctrinating new members about the smorgasbord of Rotary service areas, divided broadly as club service, community service, youth service and international service.

Duffy directed all members new to the club, meaning those who had become members subsequent to the last series of such meetings, to attend a series of fireside gatherings at his home for the purpose of expounding on each avenue of service, discussing how the local club was involved in each area and answering any questions the new members might have. He included in the group several additional experienced, knowledgeable and dedicated Rotarians to assist in the indoctrination of the new members. My eyes were opened to the vast number and variety of the opportunities and challenges provided by the programs and activities of Rotary around the world. From that start, I determined to grow in Rotary service.

In 1967, Rotary idealism had not grown sufficiently to include women, a deficiency that was not corrected until some years later. A Rotary Ladies' Night was a token of affection, esteem and appreciation, and I, a relative newcomer, and for whatever reason, was appointed by Chairman Harvey Buter to serve as toastmaster for the event to be held at Point West, a restaurant on the former site of the Hotel Macatawa at the western end of the lake of the same name. The old hotel had recently been demolished and was replaced by a motel on a slightly different site. I was a relative newcomer to the club and felt honored to be requested to serve in this capacity. I took great pains to prepare in writing a detailed plan for my role. How this document survived is something of a mystery, as is the survival of other elements of my checkered past, but my discovery permits me to report some of the activities at this event. As the meeting got underway, I was introduced by Don Crawford, president of the club and I then proceeded in my role as toastmaster.

Thank you, President Don, and good evening ladies and gentlemen. It is always something of a surprise to me to be invited to appear before an audience on any excuse whatsoever, even if it's a dog fight, since my wife, Lory, regularly bolsters my ego by telling me my suits look like I just pulled them out from the bottom of a sea bag, and on one occasion recently confided to me that the moths of the country had voted me the man whose clothes they would most like to spend the season in. I bought this suit last week after uttering those famous last words, 'No woman is going to tell me what to wear.'

Before offering the toast to the ladies, I mentioned their addiction to four-letter functional words, like "wash", "iron", "dust" and "cook" as opposed to those of men such as "hunt", "fish", "golf" and "cars". I was quite pleased with the toast I had prepared, *You are gracious, you are glamorous; you are our source of resolution when in doubt and our source of solace when discouraged. You are the staunch builders of our families; guardians of the destinies of both our children and our dollars; patient devotees who wait the necessary twenty years or so while we men learn to be married. Here's to you, the ladies"*

In reviewing my notes after all these years, I was surprised and pleased that in the course of the evening, I found the courage to remark, "Has anyone thought seriously, or suggested, co-educational Rotary?" It would be some years before "Rotary Anns", groups of women who shared the idealisms of Rotary, would become full-fledged Rotarians and contribute notably to the success of Rotary programs designed to improve the lot of millions of people around the world.

Macatawa Bay Yacht Club and Our Twelve Foot Yacht

As soon as we could afford to do so, we joined the Macatawa Bay Yacht Club and became stockholders of that time-tested institution. The club had survived two wars and a depression, movements of its clubhouse from place to place and numerous threats of extinction. We were not affluent enough to have a boat larger or more splendid than the ancient and leaky twelve foot rowboat we had bought for two dollars from Bob Horner, the son of Walter Horner, the elderly retired engineer who inspired me years before at age fourteen to build my twenty two foot sailboat *Lorelei.*

Jesiek Brothers Shipyard was licensed to build and sell the *Nipper* class eight foot long catboats that were supposed to be easy for young children to handle as they began to sail. MBYC adopted the Nipper for their novice racing fleet. We wanted Susan and Martje to begin their sailing careers as soon as possible, so we stretched our finances enough to buy one. Thus began our summer enslavement to the MBYC racing schedule.

We christened the boat *Fireball* and emblazoned its sail with a huge red ball, making it easier for Mom and Dad to see where she was in the fleet during races. The Nipper was anything other than easy to handle, and a poor choice for a novice class boat. On several occasions I was the poster boy typifying this conclusion.

When the Nipper was introduced, it was decided that there should be several introductory races in which a parent would skipper the boat initially, with the juvenile prospective skipper as his or her crew. I smoked cigars in those days and in a little display of confidence I had lighted one just before the start of the first practice race.

With Susan as my crew, we got an excellent start and steadily opened the gap between us and the second boat as we rounded the short course laid out in full view of the club house. The deck along the front of the club was lined with members anxious to observe the new juvenile class boats under sail and see how well as their young crews would perform. Susan and I in *Fireball* completed three of the four legs of the short course established by the race committee and were looking forward to the sound of the gun marking our first place finish.

The final leg was directly down wind. When we rounded the last buoy marking the point between the third and fourth legs of the course, I said, *Ease the sheet, Sue*, and as she did we received a little additional puff of wind. Sue had eased the sheet all right; she simply dropped it and the line ran out most of the way, allowing the sail to present its maximum spread across the wind. At that juncture a sudden gust of wind hit the fully extended sail placing great leveraged pressure up forward. The bow of the little boat submerged and a small wall of water came back to fill the cockpit destroying the boat's stability. *Fireball* began to round up on the wind, but as she did, having very little stability, she capsized, laying the sail out on the water, leaving Sue to swim away from the boat, supported by her life jacket. My cigar was still lighted, so I climbed onto the edge of the hull to await the arrival of one of the observing power boats. All of this was to the great amusement of the spectators, both at the club and afloat.

Our rescue boat was a powerful Christ Craft. They fished our bow line out of the water, attached it to a cleat on the stern of their boat, and took off for the Nipper beach, a strip of sand reserved for our little boats. One good characteristic of the Nipper was that when towed at moderate speed it would right itself and slosh most of the water out of its cockpit. It was a bit hard on the standing rigging, but otherwise the most effective rescue method.

This event left me bobbing in the wake of the departing vessels supported by my life jacket and sucking on my still lighted cigar. The boats that had picked up Susan and me delivered us to the club's "Nipper dock" near which *Fireball* was gently adrift in shallow water where the rescuing boat had dropped her. I took a few puffs on my cigar, and we went to work bailing out the boat and preparing for the next race.

We won the next three practice races, but on the down wind legs we sat well aft in the boat to hold her bow up and made sure that the main sheet was paid out very gently.

Sue and Martje were very successful during their years as Nipper sailors; For a few years on Labor Day, when the sailing trophies were awarded to the crews of the most successful boat in all classes, those two sailors would collect an arm load of little trophies from the commodore, as Lory and I looked on with pride.

An adult yacht club on White Lake, about fifty miles north of Holland, decided that the Nipper was a suitable boat for their adult sailing group. We had been asked our opinion as a club whether the Nipper would be a good choice for them and we had responded that there were many other boats that would be more suitable for adults. Despite our good counsel, members of the White Lake club bought and started to race a number of Nippers. Toward the end of the summer, MBYC was asked to send a representative crew to sail in one of their races as a demonstration. As fleet champions, *Fireball* and her crew were chosen to respond to this invitation, and we trailered the little boat and her crew up to White Lake. The result of this demonstration was that Sue and Mart finished each race by the time the adult manned boats had reached the first windward mark.

Mary Jo was about five when the club selected the Butterfly as its novice class boat, replacing the Nipper. *Fireball II* was a fiberglass catboat about the same size as the Nipper, but faster and far easier to sail and maintain. With this development Buck became the skipper and MJ became the crew. The wind was strong during one of their initial races, and they were having trouble keeping their little yacht from lifting its dagger board out of the water thus endangering their control of the boat.

Just before reaching the finish line with a fairly brisk wind heeling the boat radically, in an effort to hold the boat down as best they could, Mary Jo fell overboard on the windward side, still holding the sheet of their single sail. In a considerable athletic demonstration, she pulled herself up onto the dagger board preparing to re-board the boat. One of the chase boats assigned to monitor the race for safety purposes was close at hand and closed in on the scene to effect a rescue, which they completed by catching a strap on her life jacket with their boat hook, and hoisting her aboard the power boat, amidst much screaming and yelling by Mary Jo, who wanted to finish the race as crew. While all this was going on, *Fireball II*, although essentially out of control, crossed the finish line well ahead of the rest of the fleet, but was disqualified by the race committee for finishing the race without part of her crew. Overall, these two were only moderately successful as a racing team partly because they spent about as much time criticizing and arguing as they devoted to sailing their yacht.

When Susan was sixteen we spotted an International 110 sailboat in a Waukazoo yard not far from our house with a sign indicating it was for sale. The 110 is a popular class at many clubs, and had been raced at MBYC for several years. It is a narrow deep keel boat with a hull shape somewhat similar to a cigar. Susan was ready for bigger racing challenges and the price for the neighbor's boat was right, so we bought it. Susan was delighted with this development in her life   and as we went into the next racing season we discovered the true meaning of the old old saying, *A boat is a hole in the water into which the owner pours money.* This was true of us for many years during our experiences with a considerable number and variety of boats, both sail and power. Nevertheless as we became more prosperous we invested in a very practical and seaworthy *Lyman Islander* which served us well for many years.

One costly event involving the near death of our beautiful Lyman brought an abrupt end to what had started our to be a quiet family event on a Sunday afternoon in September, a time when the weather was still pleasant and even balmy. Lory and a friend who was to join us for the day, packed picnic baskets loaded with fried chicken, sandwiches and a variety of other delightful foods, an with all in readiness we left the dock headed for a place called Halfway Creek, a small stream that wended its way through the dunes and into Lake Michigan at a point roughly half way between the Holland and Saugatuck harbor entrances. Susan and Martje elected to sail the One Ten and started an hour or so before us.

When we had motored out through the harbor channel, we noted with pleasure that the weather was ideal for our enterprise. There was a light breeze from the northwest and the Big Lake was almost calm. We could see that the girls ahead of us were well on their way to our destination.

On our arrival at Halfway Creek, I saw that there was a small drop-off in depth next to the shore, so I nosed the Lyman against the shore and one of the girls who by then had anchored the one ten off shore, carried our bow anchor well up on shore as we unload our picnic materials over the bow of the boat. I can never forgive myself for failing to heave out a stern anchor I had brought along for the very purpose of keeping the boat perpendicular to the shore.

After lunch some in the party, including me climbed the dune, an activity generally thought appropriate for younger people on such an occasion. I looked down from the dune and noted that the wind was picking up rapidly, and then I saw the Lyman broach across the wind and parallel to the shore, an event that would not have happened had I streamed the stern anchor. By the time we had reached the boat it was already filled with water from the waves that easily flowed across the waist of the boat. Despite the best efforts of all hands, we couldn't budge her.

We made our way over the dune to the road and called a friend who came and picked up the bunch of soaked picnickers. We returned the next day in a much larger boat and winched the Lyman off the shore, still filled with water and a great deal of sand. Despite our efforts to rehabilitate her, she was never the same again.

CHAPTER EIGHT - WINNERS, LOSERS & PHOTO FINISHES
Seeking An Income At The Level To Which We Would Like To Become Accustomed

While all of these assorted activities were going on it was obvious that to make a living "At the level to which we would like to become accustomed" the combination of our meager teaching salaries was not going be adequate. In our opinion, the proceeds from the sale of an occasional Baywoodlands lot or other windfall should be preserved as capital and expended only for vital family needs which we perceived as medical needs and savings toward the children's college expenses.

We learned from our colleagues how they supplemented their teachers' pay enough to keep body and soul together. A number of the men spent their summer months painting houses. Several were farmers, and although the seasons of teaching and farming overlapped somewhat, they survived in the dual role by choosing the right crops and working night and day during the overlapping periods. Many men filled temporary jobs in factories. Dirk Bloemendaal became a photographer for a heavy machinery manufacturing company and later wrote the copy for many advertisements and technical articles as well. A number of the women teachers earned a supplement as seasonal waitresses and a few worked a shift at the Heinz pickle factory during the fresh cucumber season.

Some of our early attempts to expand our income were humorous, some pathetic, some unexpected and a few profitable, are categorized and summarized here. Several of the successful efforts had lives that extended well beyond the scope of this narrative while others, particularly the unsuccessful ones, were brief.

WINNERS
"You Have to Be Right at Least Fifty One Percent of the Time"

HAWAII-1954
Our Potential Life Line

Before I submitted my resignation from the navy we laid plans for an alternative strategy to cut our losses should our efforts in Holland fail. Under those circumstances, we decided, we would cut our losses, get to Hawaii and somehow start over again. This probably would have seemed like impractical dream talk to anyone not privy to the fact that we already owned a six acre property on the Big Island of Hawaii, not far from Hilo. The opportunity to buy this property arose as We were making our plans for my navy departure and we paid a hundred dollars per acre, "sight unseen" for this undeveloped land.

As time went by, it became apparent we were not going to fail in Holland, and further, for many reasons, we would not be able to break our ties there. Over the years we received many inquiries, primarily from residents of Hawaii wanting to buy such a precious piece of the old Parker ranch. Toward the end of our time in Holland we succumbed and sold the property for many times the purchase price. On a percentage basis it was by far, the best real estate investment we ever made.

BAYWOODLANDS 1955-1980
The Mainstay

We had planned from the beginning that development of the wooded lakefront property I had purchased while on a brief leave during the war would be the mainstay of our transition from military to civilian life. It was a way to build our capital while providing us with a beautiful site for our dream house.

APARTMENTS 1976-1990
Opportunity

Our experience owning apartments in California inclined us to believe that building rental units in Holland could be good investments. We had given up our apartments in Coronado reluctantly shortly after moving to Holland as we needed the capital for our initial ventures in developing Baywoodlands. There were no real apartment buildings in Holland at that time, although there were many second or third floor house modifications, often built to accommodate aging parents and later used as rental units. The opportunity was there and we wanted to take advantage of it if possible.

ENTERPRISE DEVELOPMENT 1960-1980
Opportunity in Failure

Shortly after our arrival in Holland Lory discovered that the widow of one of her Grand Haven cousins had met and married a vibrant young attorney named Walter J. Roper who had established his practice in partnership with several others of his profession and opened offices over the former A&P store at the corner of River Avenue and Tenth Street. We found the Ropers to be a congenial couple and socialized with them regularly. Informally Walter J., as I often called him in response to his referring to me as Fred Stanley, was generally called Jerry. Jerry and Phyllis became our dear friends for the rest of our lives.

One of Jerry's earlier clients was a young man of some considerable inherited wealth named Howard Plagemaars, whose father was a well known and well connected Western Michigan road contractor. Howard, although only twenty five at the time, was named to have a significant part in the disposition of the assets of the failing Holland Furnace Company, once a powerhouse in the Holland community with a significant nationwide distribution and sales force, but now on the verge of bankruptcy. Eventually Howard became president of the failing company and presided over its dissolution.

It was within this setting that I was invited to join Howard and Jerry in forming a partnership with the intention of possibly purchasing some of the assets of the furnace company as they were offered publicly in a competitive bidding process.

Amazingly, our partnership outbid all competitors and we became the owners of the two hundred and forty acre Holland Furnace Picnic Grounds, including two lodges. One was a huge barn like structure built to be used by Boxer Rocky Marciano and his entourage, at that time sponsored by the furnace company as a headquarters and training camp in preparation for one of his matches. The other lodge, although smaller, was a beautifully built and equipped luxury party place. It was paneled with pine, and included an oak dance floor and full kitchen. Forming a closed loop above the first level was a balcony equipped with tables and chairs for the party goers.

We became real estate poor, presiding over a large piece of real estate in the probable path of Holland expansion. As in all real estate speculation, the underlying problem was time; how long would it be before housing development would reach this sizeable piece of land, and how would we pay the taxes and other costs of retaining the property until its value could be exploited.

LOSERS

THE GAS STATION 1959
Where Is the Help When We Need It?

The nearest store to our property was run by a couple named Meyer and named Meyer's Barbeque. The store stood at an opening of the Waukazoo woods lying eastward from the intersection of Ottawa Beach Road and Waukazoo Drive. The business was located in a concrete block building and catered primarily to summer residents and transients en route to or from the popular Ottawa Beach State Park a beautiful strip of the unparalleled beaches on the eastern shore of Lake Michigan. The business struggled to survive maintaining its services for the very limited population of the area year around. A supplement to the business was a two pump gas station operated from a small block building by the Meyer's adopted son as soon as he became old enough to handle the money, the pumping and elementary servicing of the customers' automobiles.

The Meyers had adopted Al Looman, when the young boy who could only be described as handicapped. He was smallish in stature, had buck teeth and wore glasses as thick as the glass on the bottoms of beer bottles. Despite his handicaps, Al was a hard and steady worker and as his adoptive parents faded from the scene, Al as a young adult took over the entire operation, which by that time had developed into a combination gas station, grocery store and food counter. The counter had a broader menu including a hard to resist hot roast beef sandwich but the emphasis remained on the barbecue. It was a favorite of many local people for a morning coffee break or a noontime lunch.

By the time we arrived on the scene to begin our subdivision Al as the proprietor of Meyer's Barbecue, was successful enough in his primary businesses, supplemented by income from the sale of tack to the horsy set that he wanted to relieve himself of responsibility for running both the gas station and the combination of eatery and country store that had been the backbones of the businesses his adoptive parents had established when they moved into the area many years before. The Meyers had struggled for years before the business became really viable, but now Al wanted to confine his activities to a combination of the store and the tack.

It was the end of the school year, Lory and I had just sold a lot and thus had some capital to invest. The gas station looked to us like a business that would grow rapidly as the Waukazoo area became more populated and the summer traffic to Ottawa Beach State Park, five miles to the west on Lake Michigan increased exponentially. We were in constant contact with the Rhudies since Yvonne was still caring for Mary Jo during the school day. Ted had recently been laid off from work and to us he seemed a natural to operate the station as he did show considerable skill in keeping his weird collection of vehicles and machinery operational. We offered him a share of the ownership in addition to his pay if he would carry the burden of pumping the gas, checking the oil and doing some minor repair work. For that summer, I was almost as involved in those gas station activities as I was in continuing the Baywoodlands development. The plan was for Ted to run the station by himself on foreshortened hours for the relatively slack winter season.

At the end of the summer, when I had to return to the classroom and Ted would be running the station by himself until the profitable months returned, he said, *To hell with it.* The station became a storage area for Al's tack inventory and Ted went home to enjoy a few beers.

A year or so later the station was reopened by a successful operator, "Chink" Roberts, who gave up his popular downtown station on the speculation that the growth of the Waukazoo and adjacent areas would provide a growing set of customers who would help him to grow his business. He was right.

THE *OBSERVER* 1960
"Thank God for Bankruptcy"

A group of businessmen operating in the newly-formed West Ottawa area, for various reasons, including a general feeling that the *Holland Evening Sentinel* treated the area unfairly, decided to start a newspaper to be named *The Observer*. I was not associated with this group initially, but looked on with some interest, reflecting my experiences as a reporter during my college days. Based on the self-interest of a printer who was an investor in the enterprise, the group had made a poor decision in buying a press that sucked up most of the capital they had raised and was too slow to produce the weekly newspaper in the quantity and quality needed. This fact alone left the corporation with monthly payments the operation could not afford.

One of the owners perceived that the operation was bound to fail if it continued to be operated as it had been, and let it be known that his interest in the corporation was for sale. Blinded by my experience many years before and without knowing or seeking to know the financial straits of the corporation, I bought the stock at par. This was among the poorest investments of my life. I wound up trying that summer to rescue the sinking venture, and was making some progress, driving the weekly paste-ups north to a printer and newspaper operator in Greenville where after a wait of a couple of hours the press run was loaded into the back of the aging station wagon for delivery in the Holland area. It would have been years before the operation could become viable.

As Labor Day approached, I called for a meeting of our group of stockholders and reviewed the situation with them. I almost compounded my error when I offered to take over the waning venture if all would assign their stock to me. All were willing, except for the now unemployed printer, who adamantly refused. With that decision, the *Observer* was assigned to the bankruptcy court, and I returned to my teaching job.

PHOTO FINISHES

OIL WELL 1962
"What's a Drill Stem Test?"

Toward the end of Jay Formsma's principalship, I received a phone call from Russ Klassen, Curly's brother, with whom I had done some real estate business in the past. Russ was in many ways Curly's opposite. Curly was short, Russ was tall. Curly was bald, Russ had a full head of graying hair. Curly, as a banker, sought financial security in conservative moves. Russ liked more speculative opportunities.

Russ was seeking investors who would be interested in buying shares in a proposed oil and gas well to the east of Holland in a field that had been there for years, producing just enough oil from above the Traverse rock below to make the established wells worthwhile. The proposal with which Russ approached potential investors was offered by a wildcatter who had leases on a forty acre drilling unit, the south-east quadrant of a quarter section in which the other three forties had wells producing large quantities of black gold from below the Traverse layer of rock. We were assured it was almost a sure thing to drill a well on the remaining forty acres on which the speculator held leases.

Well, it wasn't a sure thing. A group of us joined Russ and the wildcatter and pooled the money needed to start the process. After a few weeks of waiting, a big rotary drilling rig arrived from Oklahoma and then in our turn, it bored down to the oil bearing shale below the Traverse layer lying just above the impenetrable Niagara rock. There the drill went into water. The organizer called a meeting of investors, near the well site, and we all attended.

The geologist expertly explained that we had lost our money because the Traverse layer made an inside turn almost conforming to the inside angle of the other three forties. Tough luck. He also explained why we should sell our lease and the well and well head for salt water disposal to one of owners of adjacent wells, to recoup a fraction of our money.

Everyone agreed except one. Gary De Leeuw, a partner in a large lumber company, insisted that our drilling contract was "to drill down to the Niagara," and he wanted to complete the contract. The geologist tried to persuade Gary to give up. The rest of us groaned but Gary persisted, and we all gave in to Gary's insistence, knowing that the rest of our stake would be gone in a few hours. The geologist passed around a pint of bourbon, and anyone who cared to had a drink. We all went our way knowing we had lost our stakes, and that was it. Well, it wasn't all there was to it.

About two the next morning the phone next to the bed rang, and the voice on the other end was Russ Klaasen's secretary. Her message was simple. *Russ asked me to tell you to get right out to the well-head as soon as possible. Something big is going on.* I hustled into my clothes, including my duck hunting boots, jumped into the Jeep and drove to the well. I could hardly believe what I saw. The whole area under the flood lights of the drilling rig was covered with oil! My heart skipped a few beats.

I sucked in my breath and approached the group at the well head.

What happens now? I shouted over the sound of the machinery.

Drill stem test, the foreman shouted, *We'll have to pull the pipe and get a sample from the well for a drill stem test. It looks good so far. I'm pretty sure you've got a good well here.* We all had trouble containing our excitement, and were ready to congratulate Gary, the wildcatter, Russ Klaasen and anyone else who had contributed to what appeared to us to be a great success.

OILERS ARE SOLD — Mrs. Don Cook (seated left) Friday night signed the papers selling the Holland Oilers basketball team to a group of four Holland men including Howard O. Plaggemars, Walter J. Dunn and Fred S. Bertsch (seated right). Witnessing the transaction are (left to right) Walter Roper, Don Cook, former owner; William Dunn and Fred Bertsch. Plaggemars, Roper, Dunn and Bertsch have purchased the club and will take over next week. The signing took place Friday night before the Holland-Battle Creek game and the new owners met with the players following the game.
(Sentinel photo)

4 Holland Men Purchase Oilers

The purchase of the Holland Oilers basketball team by a group of four Holland investors including Howard O. Plaggemars, Walter J. Roper, William J. Dunn and Fred S. Bertsch was announced jointly by the group today and Mrs. Mary Ellen Cook, Oilers owner and Don Cook, coach.

Noting that the former ownership had expressed a desire for a public offering of Oiler shares, Plaggemars, representing the new ownership said "In order to provide a continuity of management policy and to assure area fans of the finest possible local representation in the Midwest Professional Basketball League, our group has purchased the Oiler franchise and assets, with intention of reorganizing the financial structure in a way which will permit a public offering."

"From the date of our acquisition the new Oilers will be operated as an investor owned corporation utilizing standard corporate procedures," Plaggemars said.

Plaggemars said that all of the present management, with the exception of coach Don Cook, is being retained.

An extensive search for an "outstanding coach of college caliber is being undertaken with several candidates already being considered," Plaggemars said.

In regard to the current player controversy, concerning Holland's forfeit to Grand Rapids and the use of ineligible players, Plaggemars stated that their attorneys would be looking into the league's constitution, articles and by-laws to ascertain what if any action would be taken.

"We intend to present to the area fans the finest possible professional basketball and a winning team. The community time his operation of the U.S. interest as expressed in the past will be rewarded in the future by a basketball team of which Holland citizens and businessmen can continue to be proud," Plaggemars said.

The new owners met with the Oilers players Friday night following the Holland-Battle Creek game in the Civic Center. Plans call for Cook to coach the Oilers tonight against the Grand Rapids Tuckers tonight in the Godwin gym.

A coach to handle the Oilers the rest of the season, starting with the Holland-Chicago game next week, Plaggemars reported.

Cook had announced two weeks ago his plans to sell the Oilers. He had proposed selling $7,500 in shares of stock. Details of the sale made by the new owners and Cook were not disclosed.

The former coach of the Oilers has reported he plans to be general manager of the Lansing team, expected to have a year. Cook also plans to continue his operation of the Trotters, an all-Negro exhibition basketball team.

Cook organized the Oilers eight years ago. The team has played in the Midwest Basketball League for the past two years.

I, of course, had to head back to school, change my boots for oxfords and teach a trigonometry class. En route I managed to catch Mr. Formsma and get permission to visit the well site during my next free period. When I got back to the site, all machinery had stopped. There was a big length of pipe lying in the pool of oil that had caused all the excitement. "What about the drill stem test? I inquired.

Ninety-nine plus percent salt water, came the reply. My first and last venture into the oil and gas world was over, but I have felt ever since that the modest loss involved was rewarded by the exhilaration of almost being an instant millionaire oil investor.

THE OILERS

How we four decided to buy The Oilers remains a mystery, but Jerry, Howard and I, plus Bill Coupe, another local attorney, using our Enterprise Development Company as the entity of ownership, decided to become tycoons of the professional basketball world. None of us had either played basketball or, for that matter had any strong interest in the sport. It was clear that Don Cook, the owner of The Oilers had financial problems and wanted to sell. It also appeared to us that the financial rewards from such an enterprise would be great given the strong interest locally in basketball. An added attraction was that some of the recruited stars who played regularly were truly outstanding like the Raffshanidad* brothers who later joined the Chicago Bulls.

There really wasn't a balance sheet or other hard information on the team's operation as Don combined all financial matters with his gas station records. There were few hard assets; just a few basketballs, a bunch of players' uniforms, jackets and jock straps. On the other hand there were few fixed liabilities. The players all came from Chicago, Benton Harbor or Kalamazoo, and were paid a negotiable couple of hundred dollars per game. The home games were played in the Holland Civic center, for which Don paid a minimal rental fee. It appeared that he profited greatly, particularly from home games.

Our purchase was announced at the half time of a game and we owners were introduced wearing huge new ten gallon hats inscribed "Holland Oilers." *The Holland Sentinel* gave the acquisition plenty of publicity as evidence by a clipping above. We continued to try unsuccessfully to get some hard financial data from Don. We also tried unsuccessfully to arrive at some conclusion as to the value of the "good will" and "intangibles" of the operation but got nowhere. Jerry, ever the cautious attorney, advised us to back off and discontinue the negotiation. We didn't lose anything but our time and effort. There was a lot of potential there, but at best in my eyes it lay somewhere between success and failure, a photo finish.

COLORFUL HOUSE 1963
"All Real Estate Will Sell....."

In the course of selling lots in our Baywoodlands subdivision, it occasionally became desirable to take another property in exchange. One such property was a two bedroom cottage in the Waukazoo area with access to Lake Macatawa. Although the exterior was painted with what I might describe as hideous colors, bright purple siding and brilliant orange trim it was my judgment that we could easily resell the cottage for enough to retrieve our money despite exterior colors that would be unacceptable to most prospective buyers, anticipating the buyer would repaint the place forthwith.

This proved not to be true and the little house lay vacant for months. We were reluctant to rent it and thus somewhat restrict our options for selling. As time went by with no sale, or even inquiries, we reassessed what we considered to be our options. In conversations with others, one friend said *Lower the price,* an alternative unattractive to us. Another said, *Repaint the house using off-white for the siding and dark gray for the trim. I've seen houses painted this way, and they're very attractive."* A third conversationalist remarked, *Raise the price. It'll get them every time. All real estate will sell, even if it's above the Arctic Circle. It's just a matter of time.*

We decided to repaint the house in the off-white and gray as suggested, a move that calmed the wild look purple and orange had given it. We also increased the price by the cost of the paint job. The cottage was sold within a week and we were cashed out. We didn't either make any money and we didn't lose any. We rated it a photo finish. None of this would be worth mentioning if it were not for the fact that about two weeks after the sale Lory and I went a bit out of our way to drive past the house and see how the new owners were doing. The cottage had been repainted. The colors? Purple with orange trim.

CHAPTER NINE - PRINCIPAL 1964
"Hats Off to the New Principal"

It had been a restless night for me following the brief conversation with Harvey Buter that Sunday evening after an exhausting day of sailing. Many of the thoughts expressed previously about the teachers' salary situation and their unfair treatment by the board of education had flown through my head as I lay sleeplessly. Harvey was the president of the Holland Board of Education, and at the time I describe, unbeknownst to me, he was serving as chairman of a search committee seeking a new high school principal. It was two weeks before Labor Day; the school year would begin on the day after the holiday. All this must have something to do with school, but what could Harvey possibly want from me? Holland at that time retained its loyalty to its religious heritage. To be meeting for a secular purpose on Sunday evening, even a limited secular meeting such as Harvey had proposed was out of the question.

Monday morning I drove the couple of miles to the bank, parked in my favorite spot in the city parking lot, made my way through the bank lobby and up to the conference room. Harvey greeted me cordially, extending his hand. It was a far different atmosphere from my experience the last time I had been in the room, greeted by Curly Dalman, the banker with his hand extended, not in greeting, but to receive our building loan repayment in thousand dollar bills.

My Monday morning host gestured toward a freshly brewed pot on the coffee maker and said, *Help yourself.* With the informal preliminaries thus completed and each with a cup of coffee, we seated ourselves, and I'm sure I had a look of expectancy on my face. Harvey went directly to the point. *Fritz you are aware, I'm sure, that Jay Formsma has resigned as principal of Holland High School, and that we are seeking a successor, preferably a teacher from the high school staff, and one who is well qualified and well-prepared to support our high school educational philosophy, including the open campus concept.* I was nonplussed that the president of the school board would be seeking my counsel on such an important question, but I started to run through in my mind which members of the staff might best fill these qualifications.

After Harvey had taken a sit from his cup he continued, *I have polled the board members informally, and your name has come up several times during these conversations. I've been asked by the board to sound you out to see if you would be interested in interviewing for the position.* At this point I was not only nonplussed, I was dumfounded. Harvey went on, *In fairness, I must tell you that several board members had questions about your qualifications, but Mr. Ihrman, the new superintendent, has assured me that any such barriers could be overcome, so I am asking you to consider accepting the job as principal of Holland High School if the board offers you the position. We will be holding a special meeting tomorrow afternoon at one o'clock, in the board room of the junior high school and we would like you to be there.* Harvey then requested that I not discuss this conversation with anyone other than Lory, a thought with which I agreed.

I left feeling more nonplussed than ever, and with many questions flowing through my mind, not the least of which was, *I've been critical of school administrators in the past, but what do I really know about school administration? Was I really qualified to hold this position?* My waking hours that day were spent considering these and other questions pertinent matters that had to be taken into consideration, both by us and the board of education.

As a result Monday passed rather quickly, and at the appointed hour on Tuesday I was seated on a chair outside the door of the board meeting room on the second floor of the junior high school. I realized conversation was taking place in the board room, but I couldn't decipher anything that was said until one board member, in a somewhat elevated voice said, *That doesn't amount to piss on a plate. We have to have a high school principal in place by two weeks from today and whoever it is has to have a little time to find his way around.* The first sentence was in language not normally heard during formal meetings in Holland.

A short time later I was invited to enter the room and take a seat. Present were Jim Lamb, the board president, Don Ihrman, the new superintendent, who I was meeting for the first time, my Hope college classmate, Harry Frissel, a member of the board, together with the other members, including the one who had spoken just before I was invited to join the group. Harvey started things off with an outline of my qualifications, including the fact that I was a Holland High and Hope College graduate, that I had served honorably as an officer in the navy, was in the process of developing a subdivision in Park Township, and that I was presently a teacher on the staff of Holland High. Jim Lamb noted that he knew me well, as we had been boyhood friends, although he was several years younger than I.

I was then offered the opportunity to speak. I indicated that I was honored to be suggested for the position of principal of the high school from which I had graduated. I added, *However, I have reservations and concerns relative to my qualifications and also relative to my other activities, both in businesses and socially.* At the utterance of the word "socially", several board members seemed to take a greater interest in what I was saying. I ended my little presentation with, *If you have any questions, I'll be pleased to try to answer them.*

The first question, not surprisingly, was, *Are you a church member?* I affirmed that I was a member of Beechwood Reformed Church and in reasonably regular attendance at services. There followed several questions about my academic preparation, which I answered in detail, supplemented with supportive comments by the new superintendent, who had reviewed my credentials and whatever else appeared in my record. One member wanted to know if I planned to pursue further education, to which I responded in the positive. Many other comments and questions followed, but each seemed to wind up with an affirmative statement relative to me. Finally the member whose voice I had heard through the door earlier, and who had said little or nothing during the questioning spoke up once again.

We've got to have a high school principal now, and whoever it is deserves at least to know where he can hang his hat, have time to look through the principal's desk drawers, find the men's room and get himself ready to run the place. All the rest of this is a bunch of crap, and not worth a fart in a windstorm. Let's hear from Mr. Bertsch; he may have a few things on his mind.

I did have things on my mind. The first of these was what I would be paid, and Mr. Ihrman replied that the schedule called for me, as a first year principal, to be paid the munificent sum of ninety-five hundred dollars. Harvey stepped in with, *And I'm sure we can arrange for you to have the use of a car from R.E. Barber Ford for your school use, and that's worth something.* (The "something" turned out to be zero, as such a car was never furnished in my fourteen years as principal.) The salary was less than half the pay I received in my former position as a commander in the navy, drawing flight pay as a naval aviator.

The next thing I presented to the board was my perception of a conflict between being the high school principal and my association with the Macatawa Bay Yacht Club, and I said so. I had longed as a boy to be a member of that organization and sail in boats less cumbersome than the old flat-bottomed row boat equipped with homemade sails made from old feed sacks and lee boards that had to be shifted from side to side. At the time of the interview I was the rear commodore of MBYC, and, in the normal course of events, scheduled to become the commodore in the third succeeding year. *Why do you see this as a conflict of interest?* asked an interrogator.

Well, first of all, the small boat racing schedule for the club during the three summer months is largely on Sunday morning, so for our children to race their boats we have to be there, both for support and for the physical effort needed in launching and rigging the small boats. This was greeted with an observation that we had the option of attending afternoon or evening church services; nothing more.

I then stated that when I became the commodore of the yacht club I would also become the proprietor of a bar and grill. It seemed to me there was a little gasp of surprise from some of the board members, at the end of which my Hope College classmate, Harry Frissel, asked, *Why would you become the proprietor, can't some one else fill that role?* The answer was that at that time MBYC held one of only two liquor licenses in the area between Grand Haven twenty miles north, and Saugatuck twelve miles south. The liquor license was a valuable and exclusive asset, and the commodore was listed as the license holder. Harry pressed onward, *Do you think you can hold both positions without slighting the principalship?* I replied somewhat evasively, as I didn't really know how demanding the principalship would be, but I indicated I felt it was possible for the two responsibilities to fit together reasonably well. Another board member noted that the most demanding school responsibilities would be during the school year and less pressing during the summer months. This statement seemed to remove any reservations about my position. To my surprise, it was Harry who said, *I don't see a problem there,* and the subject was dropped.

Mr. Buter, believing he had another enticement to offer, said, *Why don't we draw the contract for you to accept the job on a temporary basis, and then you could decide after the end of the year whether you wanted to continue.* I had had enough classroom experience with high school students by that time to be able to reply, *If I take the job, it will be as the high school principal together with whatever authority and strength that may carry. If the students would get a sense that I'm in the position temporarily it would destroy my authority and the kids would run me out of town on a rail.* This seemed to settle the matter, and I applied my signature to the contract.

Well, it didn't quite settle the matter. Mr. Ihrman pulled out a somewhat frayed document and handed it to me. He then said, *This is a list of the duties which you are obligated to carry out as the principal of Holland High School in accordance with the contract you just signed.* I glanced at the list Mr. Ihrman had handed me. It was fifteen items long, numbered in sequence; some were specific and objective; some were generalizations. I winced when I took a more careful look at the list and noted that the items typed there covered everything relating to student behavior, teacher behavior, teacher performance, parental and community relationships. It appeared to me the document demanded the principal correct all deficiencies in human knowledge and behavior "from A to Z." The document's all-inclusive and subjective nature told me I was taking on a job that was essentially impossible. The original piece of somewhat tattered paper on which these decrees were listed is shown on the following page.

The basic details of my new assignment seemed complete and my obligations defined clearly but basically in general terms. The superintendent then handed me a ring with the key to my new office and a skeleton key that would give me access to any space on the campus. His admonition as he passed the keys to me was, *Don't ever allow these out of your personal custody.*

The final statement was in recognition that security at the old high school had been broken many years before. A standard jibe among the townspeople was, *Every family that had sent a member to Holland High School had a duplicated skeleton key to the school building and access to everything in it.* That was pretty much a true statement.

DUTIES OF THE PRINCIPAL
Sec. 47, pages 24, 25 and 26
Board of Education Policy

1. He shall be in full and complete charge of the school to which he is appointed and responsible only to the Superintendent of Schools.

2. He shall practice that quality of democratic educational leadership that will inspire confidence, stimulate a healthy morale, and promote professional growth and development among all teachers.

3. He shall organize in cooperation with the teachers the instructional program which shall include the formulation of daily class schedules.

4. He shall be responsible with his teachers for the citizenship of all pupils in the school and on the school grounds.

5. He shall have the power to suspend pupils and to recommend to the Superintendent of Schools and the Board of Education dismissal or other disciplinary action needed.

6. He shall make available to all employees within his school all policies, rules, regulations, directives, or other information issued by the Board of Education or Superintendent.

7. He shall evaluate the efficiency and quality of teaching performance of all teachers in his school and upon request supply such evaluation to the Superintendent of Schools.

8. He shall supervise the work of the custodians in his school in cooperation with the Superintendent of Buildings and Grounds.

9. He shall take whatever steps are necessary and proper to protect the property of the school, immediately reporting in writing to the Superintendent of Buildings and Grounds any damages which may occur.

10. He shall keep a record of the circumstances and extent of any injury to any pupil or school employee, if such injury occurs on school premises.

11. He shall ultimately be responsible for all co-curricular activities of pupils which are sponsored in or through his school or its teachers.

12. He shall interpret the school program to parents and the community.

13. He shall assist in the preparation of the annual budget by listing needed equipment and supplies.

14. He shall serve in any other activity that may forward the instructional or citizenship building program of the school.

15. He shall be responsible for any other duties or changes that may reasonably fall within his scope of action and authority.

While all of this interaction leading up to my appointment was going on there had been no mention of an impending crisis with the teachers, or if there was, it was treated as a minor matter that would be resolved, as in past years, by Labor Day.

The announcement of my appointment published by media throughout Western Michigan and to a lesser degree elsewhere was followed by a torrent of letters, memos and hand-written notes applauding the action of the Board of Education in appointing me, and expressing great expectations of success for me. There was a long article in the *Sentinel* and a complimentary advertisement, one in a series, titled, "HATS OFF TO....." placed there by Holland Motor Express, the firm for which Harvey worked. My name was inscribed next to a cartoon representation of me in Dutch costume wearing the typical wooden shoes of a Hollander. All of this was done as a reminder that the sobriquet for the school was *The Holland High Dutch.*

Wednesday morning I set out to explore the school's office. The door was labeled "PRINCIPAL", and when I entered, although I had been in that space a number of times as a teacher, I couldn't do other than note that the entire area was open, with no space in which one could hold a private meeting or have a confidential conversation with teacher, student or parent, unless it would be the office restroom, a tiny space that two people would fill to capacity. It did have a door. A third door, probably required by fire regulations, led directly into the home economics classroom. I had a premonition that this degree of openness would have to change.
The new superintendent and my new boss, Donald Ihrman.

CHAPTER TEN - STRIKE! 1964
A Slap in the Face

Walter Scott, the previous superintendent, and Jay Formsma, the previous principal, had been convinced that openness in virtually all areas was the ideal, and thus the term "open campus" came into use. Just how open the campus should be was a continuing question throughout my time as principal. My reaction was that the principal's office was far too open for the conduct of many of the duties that I knew would be confronting me.

There were two large steel desks set at right angles to each other in that wide open area, one labeled "PRINCIPAL", the other, "SECRETARY." One entire wall overlooking the oval driveway off Van Raalte Avenue was double glazed plate glass. When I arrived that first morning, Mrs. Veeder, the principal's secretary, greeted me cordially, and almost immediately started to immerse me in the infinite number of details involved in the running of the school.

From among the various documents she placed in my "In" basket, she extracted a four page carbon copy of a letter dated August fifteenth, written from L'Anse, a town in the upper peninsula of Michigan and addressed to the now departed superintendent, Walter Scott. It was from Wilber Johnson, known to the staff as Webb, a chemistry teacher, and head of the science department. The copy, addressed to Mrs. Veeder, called for extensive changes in the schedules for chemistry classes, particularly those assigned to Webb Johnson. Hand written at the top was the penned note, *Betty: No doubt you are now doing the Principal's job, so this copy is for your decisions. I hope you can make the changes without too much trouble. Much luck, Webb"* This was typical of the torrent of documents, notes and conversations I was to have with Mr. Johnson over the next thirteen years.

My response, perhaps also typical, observed that I was new in the job and thus not prepared to make large changes in the scheduling for the forthcoming school year. The final paragraph of my letter ended with, *It is too late in the summer to do the necessary research and schedule changing that your request involves; this is something to keep in mind for the 1965-66 school year.*

On exploring my desk, I found a brief list of suggestions and tips left by my predecessor. Betty introduced me to the process of generating the student schedules for the forthcoming semester and modifying them as necessary. The more I explored, the more I found that there was much to be learned about my new job, and the feeling intensified as I returned each day to try to get ready for the big day on the Tuesday following Labor Day, two weeks hence, when I would meet with the staff and prepare for the arrival of students the next day.

Negotiators Reject Final School Offer

School May Not Open On Sept. 5

$5,900 to $9,000 Is Board's Offer; HEA Meets Tonight

The negotiating team of the Holland Education Association Tuesday night rejected an offer of the Board of Education listing a salary schedule ranging from $5,900 to $9,000 for the coming school year.

It was the board's final offer and the best offer possible under financial circumstances, Board President James O. Lamb said.

A counter offer by the teachers' negotiators calls for a range of $6,000 to $10,500, Ted Boeve, head negotiator for the teachers, said details would be explained at a meeting of the Holland Education Association tonight at 7:30 p.m. in the auditorium of Holland High School.

"In the light of how teachers felt at our last meeting, we could not accept the board's offer and we have made a counter proposal. We also are petitioning the state for a fact finding survey taking a close, hard look at all things involved, and we have been assured such service will be provided as soon as possible," Boeve said.

In explaining the board's action at a press conference this morning in the administration building, Board President Lamb reiterated the board's policy not to deficit spend.

"We have thoroughly studied all angles and made the best offer possible. On the basis of a 1967-68 school budget of $2,652,874, covering the board's latest proposal, the estimated balance June 30, 1968, will be $3,938.22," he said.

Under the board's proposal, the average teacher's salary for the coming year would be $7,827. Average salary per certificated person for 1966-67 was $7,520, based on a schedule which ranged from $5,300 to $8,420.

"Approximately 50 per cent of our teachers are at the top of the salary schedule," Lamb said. "This makes for a fine, experienced teaching staff but it poses difficulties in balancing budgets. Most other school districts in the area do not have such a high percentage of teachers at maximum salary," Lamb said.

The newest offer provides an average salary increase of $557 per certificated person or a 9.3 per cent increase. This com-

(Continued on page 2.)

Teachers Reject Board Offer, 153-7

During the final week before the planned opening of school there were indications that the opening of the school year might not be as routine as I or many others might think. Rather than the usual articles about the schools reminding parents and older students of the days and times involved in the routine beginning of the school year, *The Holland Sentinel* on Wednesday, August 30th carried the news that negotiators had failed to resolve the issues between the Holland Education Association and the Holland Board of Education. The board's "final offer" of a salary schedule ranging from $5,900 to $9,000 per year was rejected by the HEA. There were other issues to be resolved, including one regarding what salaries would be offered to newly hired experienced teachers. James Lamb, school board president reiterated the established board policy against deficit spending. Following the breakdown in negotiations, the teachers gathered in the high school auditorium for a briefing on the situation by the association's negotiator, Ted Boeve, and expressed their support by voting to reject the board's offer by a vote of 153-7.

When I returned home from the high school Friday evening looking forward to the Labor Day weekend I picked up the *Holland Evening Sentinel* at our mail box and noted a front page story headlined, *LETTERS SENT TO* 219 *TEACHERS*. The article quoted exactly the text of a letter written on behalf of the Holland Board of Education. I read this letter with considerable interest, and noted that it was sent by registered mail to each member of the teaching staff:

You have been informed by a letter from the school district on Aug. 18 of the schedule for the opening of the school year. According to that communication all teachers are expected to be on duty Tuesday, Sept. 5, by 8 a.m. in the building to which they have been assigned.

This letter will serve to emphasize that nothing has happened to relieve teachers pf their obligation to report as scheduled. Whatever develops in the course of bargaining between the Holland Education Association and the Board of Education will not change the schedule as set.

"Statements by the Education Association point to the possibility that some teachers in the district may act as a group in refusing to work as scheduled. Any such action by teachers will be regarded as a breach of the teachers' obligations to the school district and a disregard of the provisions of the State Labor Mediation Act and the Tenure Act and will be treated accordingly.

"The Board of Education is hopeful that all differences with the Education Association can be quickly and amicably resolved. In the meantime, it is the hope of the board that everyone will recognize that the welfare of the boys and girls in the system should not suffer and that nothing will be done to jeopardize the students' educational opportunities". The teachers interpreted this statement to mean *Let's compromise and do it the board's way*

The letter went on to caution the addressees against acting as a group in refusing to report for work as scheduled, an action that would violate the provisions of both Michigan's State Labor Mediation Act and the state's tenure act. The final paragraph of the letter appealed to the teachers to consider the welfare of the boys and girls in the schools.

The newspaper indicated that negotiations would continue that Friday evening with a representative of the State Board of Appeals present. Teacher protests in other Michigan districts were summarized as involving several thousand teachers.

Friday night's meeting lasted for almost five hours, but was unproductive, with both sides locked into their respective positions. Following the meeting, School Board President James Lamb stated the board was willing to instate previous offers and meet with negotiators at any time until the beginning of the school year at eight o'clock Tuesday morning, the day after Labor Day. John Vander Ark of the State Labor Mediation Board, who had presided at the Friday meeting, announced that he had ordered the case to a fact finding panel, and Ted Boeve announced that the teachers would meet on Monday, Labor Day evening, emphasizing that should schools not be in session on Tuesday it would be due to teachers "withholding their services," not a strike, his interpretation being that if the teachers were not employed at the time of the action, due to the failure of negotiations, they could not be considered to be on strike.

That Labor Day weekend, Lory and I spent most of the time at the yacht club with our family. All four of the children participated in the racing, while we followed in our newly-acquired Lyman motor boat with a group of friends, mostly parents of the young sailors. At the end of the day on Monday the winners of the various summer racing series received their trophies for the victories of the season. Susan and Martje received some recognition during the ceremonies and after a light meal at the club we headed home up the lake to Pine Creek Bay and flopped into bed for some well-earned rest.

Tuesday morning at six o'clock the radio alarm clock at the head of our bed snapped on and, after the *Star Spangled Banner,* came an announcement stating that Mrs. Earnest Penna, president of the Holland Education Association had announced that teachers would withhold their services until further notice, due to the fact that no agreement had been reached with the Holland Board of Education. Members of the association were to meet at the Enterprise Development Company picnic ground at 168th Avenue and Lakewood Boulevard north of Holland at nine a.m. Shortly thereafter was an announcement by the superintendent of schools that there would be no school that day.

Suddenly, Lory and I were on opposite sides in an interface between the teachers and the administration. This interface could be viewed as further complicated by the fact that Enterprise Development Company, owner of the lodge where the teachers were planning to meet, was a partnership in which I, our attorney and friend, Jerry Roper, and a young client of Jerry's, Howard Plaggemars, were the principal partners. Lory and I were, potentially at least, to become benefactors of the dispute, while having an interest in both sides of the matter.

That Tuesday morning I parked my little Ghia in one of the staff spaces behind the West Unit, a separate classroom building of the three and a half year old campus and then walked through the door leading to and from the staff parking lot. It had been unlocked by a custodian, and I proceeded to my new office where I sat behind my desk wondering what the day would bring, Betty Veeder, the principal's secretary arrived, and I greeted her cordially, she having been my office contact and problem solver during my previous years as a teacher. I expected that I would soon see my teacher colleagues marching back and forth outside the big window of the principal's office which overlooked the oval driveway providing access to the school offices, and limited short term parking. I wondered if my wife, Lory, would be one of the marchers and then I devoted a few seconds to considering what effect this confrontation was going to have on my home life.

Negotiations had continued all weekend without progress. There had been no *Sentinel* on Labor Day, but the Tuesday afternoon paper was full of information about the situation. The flare headline across the top of page one was, NO PUBLIC SCHOOL HERE TODAY with the sub head, "Board Seeks Legal Action In Crisis." After a review of the situation until that time was the statement: *No contract was signed up until noon today…… Meanwhile, the local teachers were spending the day at the pavilion on the grounds of the Enterprise Development Co. lodge north of Holland, formerly the Holland Furnace Co. picnic grounds.* As Lory and I were major stockholders in Enterprise Development, this action by the teachers' group created a situation which potentially could be an embarrassment both to Lory and to me.

The article continued, *Ted Boeve, the chief negotiator for the Holland Education Association, playing on the term picnic grounds said the gathering was 'not a picnic.' He said a full program of orientation, workshops and department curricular meetings was scheduled.* In another section of the lengthy article was included the statement, *Monday was truly a 'Labor Day" for negotiators….sessions were held from one p.m. to midnight….* The rest of the paper was sprinkled with numerous articles describing teacher negotiations throughout the state and many pieces on the situation in Viet Nam.

Ted Boeve, Chief negotiator for the teachers.

The paper's flare headline on Wednesday, September 6, 1967 read, *TEACHER STRIKE IN SECOND DAY,* with a sub headline, *Hearing Set Today in Court; Outcome Awaited on Injunction; Fact Finding Slated.* Accompanying this was a five-inch four column picture of ten students, including Harvey Buter's daughter, Jane, holding signs objecting to the strike. In another lengthy article in the same issue it was stated that the board was willing to increase the teacher salary offer by $100 per year, but gave no indication of a change of intention regarding the possibility of paying new teachers more than present staff. The teachers at the lodge voted 197-9 to withhold services "until a master contract is signed."

Thursday's headline was, HEA THWARTS COURT INJUNTION. The board late on Wednesday had received a temporary injunction from the

STRIKE IN SECOND DAY

llies Stop ong Attack t Tam Ky

epulse 2,500-Man vasion Force; 9 Communists Killed

WE WANT SCHOOL — Young fry of the neighborhood gathered at Thomas Jefferson School bearing posters plumping for the opening of school, delayed a second day by the "withholding services" policy of the Holland Education Association. Kneeling, (left to right) are Kelin Kapp, Karri Israck, Dave Israck, Mike Wood and Beth Kapp. Standing are Dee Dee Newell, Kathy Kapp, Jane Boley, Cindy Wood and Nancy Stewart. (Sentinel photo)

The Holland Sentinel

Hearing Set Today In Court

Outcome Awaited On Injunction, Fact-Finding Slated

Ottawa County Circuit Court ordering the teachers back to work, but quick action by a combination of the Holland Education Association, the Michigan Education Association and the National Education Association, obtained a stay of the injunction from the Michigan Court of Appeals.

Tom Carey

A battle in the courts was thus enjoined, starting with the Ottawa County Circuit Court, presided over by Judge Raymond L. Smith, father-in-law of Holland High's head of counseling services, Tom Carey.

In his ten page opinion, Judge Smith said the law spells out the meaning of the word "strike" and clearly states that public employees may not strike. This ruling set the stage for a succession of appeals all the way to the Supreme Court of Michigan. The lengthy *Sentinel* story on the subject includes this paragraph, *In his summation, Judge Smith said the case deals with a dedicated group of teachers, and it is a shame that truck drivers and other workers earn more than teachers, but I will not concern myself with the economic side of the question.*

From the teachers' point of view the economic side of the matter, having been neglected for years, was *the* issue. Until the issue was confronted, the general public in all of the state's school districts, with the exception of the teachers, was quite content with things as they were. This was particularly true in Holland. As Judge Smith had pointed out emphatically, the truck drivers and factory workers were content being paid more than teachers; the taxpayers were content with low taxes; the board of education was proud of itself and its policy of no deficit spending (even though it was neglecting its duty through this policy of striving to maintain the best staff possible), and, finally, many voters in the very large group supporting the Christian Schools would prefer to pay no taxes at all in support of public education.

Thursday's paper also gave emphasis to the situation by publishing a photograph of Lory's empty classroom at Lincoln school and made the point that the room was fully equipped with supplies for the year. The teachers continued to meet at the pavilion outside the school district, emphasizing that each day was devoted to "Development of Educational Activities." Observations were sought from many organizations having expressed positions on education, ranging from the Holland Area Chamber of Commerce to the Parent-Teacher Association.

Aggressive and contradictory statements were issued by both the participants and the general public, and Friday's paper contained lengthy articles on the processes being used in the various courts and other school districts to settle the assorted conflicts, primarily about salaries. There was also speculation on possible outcomes with Holland's situation being recognized state wide as a test case.

On Saturday, the Michigan Court of Appeals met in a large auditorium in Grand Rapids packed with interested people to consider the case of the Holland Public Schools, and twenty-seven other Michigan districts.

On Sunday, September 10, the Court of Appeals directed the teachers to report for work Monday and the teachers complied, although amidst much grumbling. The often delayed teacher orientation sessions in all buildings went smoothly. At the high school meetings I strived to welcome the teachers back, and emphasized the need for educating the students. I tried to build on my status as a colleague and most of the teachers, but not all, accepted my position.

The Sunday ruling created the opportunity for my friend Harvey Buter to run down Eighth Street on Monday morning yelling, *We Won! We Won!* to the embarrassment of many of the onlookers. The teachers were back in the classrooms but had the board really won? Even though the Michigan Supreme Court, in a 5-3 decision upheld the Appeals Court ruling, the Holland Education Association was now firmly established as a labor organization, and the administration of the schools had been made far more difficult over the short span of a couple of weeks, a fact of life I would be facing, with varying degrees of success, for the next fourteen years.

Teacher orientation sessions were held on Monday, September 11, with all the teachers present. Tuesday's paper reported, *Fact finding in Holland's stalemated teacher negotiations adjourned at 9 p.m. Monday after a five hour session.* The lead of Wednesday's issue read, *The Michigan Supreme Court ruled Tuesday night that it would hear an appeal of the Michigan Education Association in Holland's current school dispute, but refused to lift a court injunction that had ordered teachers back to work.* Students returned to school on Tuesday.

Negotiations between the board and the HEA continued without progress. On Monday September 26, the teachers voted 201-7 to reject the latest board offer, which was widely viewed by teachers as a "slap in the face." Included in the *Sentinel's* front page story were two paragraphs presenting the HEA position: *Mrs. Ernest Penna, HEA president said today that teachers do not question the board's integrity or its financial statements, but the HEA feels Holland is a prosperous community able to pay salaries comparable with communities elsewhere, and that it is the responsibility of the board to obtain the necessary funds from various sources. Holland is a fine community and takes pride in many things –cleanliness, well-kept homes, yards and parks, and we are sure Holland wants quality education too. We feel the people will be willing to pay for quality education when they know all the facts."*

A part of my job, as I saw it, was to assuage the teachers' anger and frustration and proceed with the education of Holland's youth. My efforts involved long exchanges between the teachers and me. During one of our many teachers' meetings, Art Hielkema, a teacher of English rose to offer this comment, *The rewards for teaching in the Holland school district are similar to those for sexual intercourse. Some of us do it for money, and some of us do it for love.* He added emphasis to this statement by adding, *I must be a prostitute because I need the money to care for my family.*

An almost uninterrupted challenge during the years I was involved with public education in the city of Holland was to provide enough money to support an educational program that would meet the needs of a community that was growing rapidly. This meant repeatedly presenting millage proposals to voters who were not uniformly in agreement about the need for additional funds. My obligation was to lead a staff that sought what in their minds was a "living wage" and to provide the best education possible for the young people of the community under these circumstances.

CHAPTER ELEVEN - THE FIRST YEAR
1964-1965
On the Learning Curve

Plenty of help came my way during the post-strike days, primarily in the form of useful suggestions and good counsel from Betty Veeder, the principal's secretary, who knew how to cope with the vast array of problems that came up on a daily basis. She and the capable Dean of Students, Edna Dyk, shielded me from many of the annoying little matters that were always cropping up. It was my responsibility to cope with the big ones.

At the end of the very first marking period after the strike, my sponsor, Harvey Buter, addressed a two page letter to me complaining that his son had received a grade of C plus in geometry, when, in Harvey's view, the boy deserved at least a B minus in the traditional marking scales then in use. Most of the letter was devoted to a description of the son's tendency to interrupt verbally whatever was going on whether in or out of class and in a concluding statement said, *We hoped that during his high school years teachers would be able to provide some of the motivation he needs.* I could hardly believe that such a letter would come from a school board member who had expressed strong support for me and any judgments I should make.

In my reply, supporting the teacher's position, I suggested that motivation had to come not only from school and parents, but from within. I heard no more on the subject.

I soon figured out, doing the arithmetic in bed during one of those sleepless nights early in my tenure, that the job of being a high school principal was impossible because of the demands of time to be devoted to the assorted duties of the assignment. Such a calculation required some assumptions or postulates, so I assumed a twelve hour day, to use a nice round number, even though the principal's day often exceeds that number of hours. The principal's day then equals seven hundred twenty minutes or almost one hundred thirty thousand minutes per school year of one hundred eighty days. With a total enrollment of twelve hundred students, the principal then has a little less than eleven minutes per student per school year to be divided among his many responsibilities, and not necessarily devoting any actual time to each individual enrolled student. In my reverie, I conceived the possibility of writing a book, or at least an article, to be titled, "The Arithmetic of the Principalship."

Some, but by no means all, of the principal's responsibilities include conferences with parents often taking up to an hour apiece. These are not always happy events, particularly when the son or daughter has conducted him or herself in a manner such that parents are called to participate in the discipline of the student. Further, there is hise involvement with teachers, coaches, negotiators, police and/or sheriff's officers, the school psychologist, juvenile officers, the probate judge, probation officers, social workers, interested or frustrated members of the public, and, finally, certainly not to be ignored, the superintendent and board of education, no matter how cordial and cooperative that relationship might be. The list of responsibilities the superintendent handed me directly after I had signed my initial contract fleshed out in considerable detail these and other functions assigned to the principal. The duties, both specific and general, were enumerated on the list Superintendent Ihrman handed me a few minutes after I had signed the contract to serve as high school principal.

At the entrance to our driveway of our new house on the lake stood a relatively small maple tree dwarfed by the huge oak, maple and cherry trees spread across our subdivision. That first Halloween the short maple tree in our front yard was teepeed with enough toilet paper to last the average family a year or so. This decoration remained on display until in a few days the fall rains brought most of it down to earth to be raked up and added to my compost pile. I considered the innocent and harmless prank to be a recognition of my status. I described it with a laugh for the entire student body at the next student assembly, and there were no recurrences during my tenure as principal.

One Sunday morning I was surprised when I looked out toward the end of the point in Lake Macatawa on which our house stood to see the back of a large sheet metal sign erected there. It turned out on further inspection to be a rather handsome sign, a wood frame covered with sheet metal advertising Budweiser beer. This was another student prank, harmless at least as far as I was concerned. It had to have taken some considerable late night effort on the part of the perpetrators to remove the sign from its original position and reinstall it on our point. I called the local Budweiser distributor Monday morning thinking he would know the original owner of the sign. He removed the sign and presumably returned it to its rightful owner.

Commencement activities at Holland High School were always carefully planned and highly disciplined showcase events, and I believed, since I had participated in a number of them as a teacher the graduation activities for the class of nineteen sixty-five would not be notably different from those in the past; all would be planned by the superintendent, as I knew they had been under Dr. Scott. As springtime began, and the crocus were blooming, I was startled one day when, in a conversation with Mr. Ihrman, he suddenly inserted the question, *Who are you planning to have as a commencement speaker, Fritz?* It developed that he expected me to do all the planning formerly done by the previous superintendent for both a baccalaureate service and the commencement. I was somewhat taken aback by this addition to what I perceived as my already daunting burden, but I began forthwith to start the planning.

The scheduled dates for these activities were just a little over two months in the future, so it appeared to me that the first aim of my efforts should be to get an appropriate principal speaker for each occasion, and I further concluded that the best source of speakers would be our own list of alumni. Baccalaureate was easy. I called Reverend Russell W. Vande Bunte, pastor of the Third Reformed Church, and he readily accepted the charge of delivering the sermon.

After a weekend of pondering the matter of a commencement speaker, I made an almost fatal error; I decided that the speaker should be a distinguished graduate of Holland High School. I failed to realize that all graduates who have been successful in life after high school, with very few exceptions, are, in the inner reaches of their minds, waiting for that great day when an invitation to address a graduating class would arrive. My premise was correct, but the execution on my first attempt was almost fatally flawed. As it was I wrote carefully worded letters to each of three distinguished Holland High School alumni, and therein lay the flaw. Had I written to a single potential speaker and he did not accept the invitation, I would be free to seek another.

The letters I wrote to these three old grads were simply inquiring whether, if invited, they would accept the charge of delivering the principal address at commencement on June tenth. The three I selected were all graduates of both Holland High and Hope College with doctoral degrees from famed universities. One was the son of the city engineer, Jacob Zuidema, the second, John Olert, was serving as the pastor of Knox Presbyterian church in Louisville, Kentucky, and the third, John Pruis, was a vice president of Western Michigan University.

Within days, all three wrote that they had cleared their calendars for the date of our graduation and accepted, without equivocation, my kind invitation to speak at commencement, ignoring the fact that my letter was a query, not an invitation. I had three speakers and only one vacancy. Although it didn't help the current situation, I resolved never again to invite a commencement speaker by mail, but would make a discreet inquiry by telephone until I had a firm commitment. During the subsequent thirteen years of my principalship the recipient of each call to a graduate of Holland High accepted the invitation immediately with pride and pleasure, offering in each case to come without either honorarium or reimbursement of his expenses.

After an uneasy weekend considering what to do I finally concluded that I could only "bite the bullet", choosing one honored graduate to speak and unquestionably offending the other two. On Monday morning I attended to routine school matters, and, as I often did when pondering difficult situations, I delayed the ultimate as long as possible. About ten o'clock the redoubtable Betty Veeder, my secretary, who had been busying herself opening the morning mail, appeared at my desk and announced, *Mr. Bertsch, I think you will be interested in this letter.* The letter she handed me was from John Olert, the Louisville pastor, containing the news that he had been climbing a tree in his back yard to prune a few of its branches when he lost his grip and fell to the ground, breaking an arm and a leg. He would thus be unable to participate in our graduation. I don't recall ever feeling so selfishly relieved at the news of another man's misfortune. It was then one down and one to go.

Probably because he would travel a shorter distance than the others I decided the speaker should be Dr. Pruis. Having made that decision, I called Dr. Zuidema and informed him of my quandary and decision, offering my regrets. I fully expected that he would be less than happy with this decision, and he was, but he also expressed some understanding of my predicament. His Holland parents, his sister, Florence, who was a teacher at Holland Junior high, his brother and numerous other relatives in the area were not so gracious, and so informed me both by mail and by phone. Despite my sincere apologies, I won no points with the Zuildemas for my decision, and was left with the impression the Zuidema family would have me burned at the stake had they had the power to do so.

My nephew, Charles D. Bertsch, jr. was a member of the first class to graduate during my tenure as principal. He was a dour and bitter person at the time, undoubtedly reflecting his difficult experiences. Ever since the boy was a toddler, his father, my brother, suffered from both tuberculosis and diabetes, and had also developed a dementia that resulted in his confinement to the Michigan State Hospital in Kalamazoo. An additional result of this situation was that his parents were divorced, although our parents, his grandparents, continued to maintain a

AT HHS COMMENCEMENT — Representative of persons participating in commencemnt exercises for Holland High School seniors Thursday night in Civic Center was this group. Left to right are Supt. Donald Ihrman, High School Principal Fred S. Bertsch Jr., Dr. John J. Pruis of Western Michigan University, commencement speaker; William Elenbaas, senior class president, and David Lauridsen, school mayor. (Sentinel photo)

supportive attitude toward both of the former partners and their children.

My brother was considered well enough to attend his son's graduation ceremonies, and from where I was seated on the stage before the processional for the occasion began I spotted him in the audience seated next to the center aisle beside our mother, who was then in her early seventies. She had obtained special permission from the hospital to bring him to the commencement and had driven a special round trip to Kalamazoo to get him there. When the graduating seniors marched forward, Chuck waited for his son to pass his position in the audience, at which point he rose and shouted dramatically, *My son! My son! Charles D. Bertsch, jr., my son."* No other parent performed in such a theatrical manner. It was humiliating both for my nephew and for me, although I received no comments on the subject from anyone in attendance. Our mother sat calmly in her seat throughout this incident, apparently feeling that such an outburst was a perfectly normal thing in the midst of what most of the audience considered to be a solemn event.

Overall, the graduation ceremonies went well, and I was greatly relieved when they were over. As a memento of success that first year, I have kept a letter dated June 15, 1965 from a student suspended from another school who later had enrolled in Holland High. It read, *I would like to take this opportunity to express my thanks to you and all of the teachers of Holland High School for all the help and encouragement you have given me these past two years. Without you all my tasks would have been much harder. My only regret is that more people do not take advantage of the opportunity to return as I was able to do.....Thanks again,* The letter was signed *Darlene Boersen,* and it alone made it all seem worthwhile.

CHAPTER TWELVE - ROGER & DIRK
1964-1978
Roger Was an Advocate For Every Perceived Gripe and Grievance

Roger Plagenhoef came from a family of fire fighters and policemen who served, had served or would sometime serve with either the Holland fire department or police force. Brothers, cousins, uncles and nephews were all fire fighters or policemen. Roger was different; he chose to go to college and become a teacher. He was determined to be a good teacher, and, in fact was one of our best classroom instructors, innovative, entertaining, knowledgeable and well liked by the students. He was a supporter of student extra-curricular activities. He served as a tennis coach and instructor in that sport for many years, both at Holland High School and the community in general.

He was also a strong proponent of labor unions, whether for fire fighters, teachers, plumbers or carpenters. Shortly after the perceived victory over the Board of Education, Roger became the elected president of the union, and thereafter remained its *de facto* head by holding every union office in a succession of such offices during my entire principalship. Management was the enemy and Roger was determined to make life as miserable as possible for administrators while pursuing each and every perceived gripe and grievance a teacher might have, no matter how trivial the grievance, how incompetent the teacher or how much that person might be in non-compliance with district policy or the current labor contract. All that having been said, Roger was an excellent innovative teacher and competent tennis instructor and coach; a valuable if difficult member of the high school staff.

Roger and his fellow biology teacher, Dirk Bloemendaal, were particularly innovative, I thought, when the subject of the theory of evolution inevitably arose each year. Until about the time I became the principal, if the word evolution was mentioned, whether in the classroom or the community it would usually bring a deep silence or a strong statement upholding the creationists' beliefs. With the influx of newcomers, many of whom had beliefs outside that notion, evolution became a hot topic, causing occasional disputations or arguments.

As a classroom approach to the subject, Roger and Dirk collaborated on developing a method of coping with the inevitable controversy the subject would bring to the classroom. They devoted an hour to a debate on the subject, dividing the each class into three groups, evolutionists, creationists and pragmatists, allowing each student to decide which group he wanted to join. Several days were allowed for out-of classroom preparation, and then the debate was held, with alternate points being hurled back and forth in good order among the participants with very little instructor interference.

I purposely scheduled one of my classroom visits so I would be present during such a debate, and listened to the interesting interplay among the three groups. Finally there was an exchange that went something like this:

Student #1: (evolutionist): ....*evolution does exist. Humans today are far more developed than the Neanderthal man, who, in turn was more highly developed than the Cro-Magnon man...that preceded him."*

Student # 2 (creationist): *Yah, but where did Cro-Magnon man come from?*

Student #3" (A proponent of accepting and forming an accommodation to both positions), announced in a very loud voice: *He came from AKRON, OHIO!*

After a round of laughter, the debate went on, as it does in our society, even as this is written. *Dirk Bloemendaal*

These two teacher/collaborators were at different poles as far as their relationships with the administration (usually meaning me) were concerned. Roger was constantly stirring the pot and endeavoring to create some sort of problem, while Dirk, though not necessarily an administration man basically devoted himself to his teaching and his outside activities, the combination of which was aimed at making an above average living for his family.

An illustration of this difference was the fact that Dirk and I would occasionally go fishing together at any season of the year if we thought the fish would be biting. Toward spring one year after the ice had gone out, we heard the word that the perch had been biting *out by the white light,* referring to a navigational light set on the north side of the shipping channel at the south side of a shallow area known as middle ground. For several days during the week we suffered the scene of clusters of boats out there hauling in the perch, but couldn't join in the fun because of our school commitments. We had great plans to fish on Saturday, but were almost thwarted by Old Man Winter. It froze hard that Friday night and when we got ready to launch our twelve foot boat, we discovered there was about an inch of ice on the lake. We could see no boats out at the light. Should we give up? We decided to launch and break our way with some difficulty through the ice. On arrival at the white light we found it unnecessary to anchor, as the ice around us held us in place, and we had to push it aside to get our lines in the water. We were prepared to use the two poles allowed for each fisherman, but the fish were coming in so fast, often two at a time, that we couldn't handle a second pole. Another memorable day!

With the development of the salmon and lake trout fishing in Lake Michigan, we were becoming successful in catching these beautiful fish during the milder months, but a wintertime effort on our part almost resulted in disaster. It had been a severe winter and the icebergs along the shore were far more extensive than most years. Dirk was wearing cleats over his shoes, and thus had good footing on the ice. I stupidly climbed out there on the ice wearing my heavy hunting boots, slippery on ice under any circumstances. My stupidity continued, and I climbed out to the edge of the berg to cast my line. When I did, my feet went out from under me and I landed on my backside at the edge of the ice. I looked down over the edge of the berg and realized that had I fallen or slipped over the edge, there would be no way I could recover or be recovered. Without additional equipment, neither Dirk nor anyone else would be able to rescue me and the prospect would be I that I would drown in freezing water. I withdrew, packed up my gear and retired to the car. I would never again try to fish from the ice bergs. It was more fun to fish for those species during the summer.

Through all of these adventures, and there were more, Dirk and I never got into any rancor about school or anything else, while Roger held me at arms length for fourteen years with an attitude, expressed verbally only once toward the end of my time as principal, but always apparent in during our prickly relationship. On that occasion, as he left my office dissatisfied, he turned an said, "Damn you, Fred, you win again." It was not always thus.

Evaluation was always on our minds. Dirk annually sought student evaluation of his performance as a teacher and also some input relative to the importance of biology in our lives as human beings and asked students to write briefly on the subject, *Why do we study biology?* Among his responses one year were a couple of dandies he passed on to me for my collection.

Why I would like Boiloily

To learn the physical way the body of a human and the brian works and the hart. To learn a lot more about the human body. I wood lean about the way the animals body is to. The differic kind's of animals to.

Why Study Biology

You study biology so you don't have to come back next year and sufure it again. You can learn about a lot of neet stuff like different plants and animals that you never new before. You learn a lot about plant celles, roots and leaves and how to adentafie different trees by the way the leaves look. You also study hard so you can get a good grade like an A or B, but I wouldn't mine a C. And so you git to no what his testes are about and Big words he said's when he talking.

You should study hard if you want to be a sientice, but I am just going to be a hafassed welder and make a few bucks to buy a pickup truck. (P.S. Did ya ever stuff them ducks I give ya?) (Dirk was, among his many talents, a taxidermist.)

CHAPTER THIRTEEN - CIVILIAN
NAVY; ACTIVE DUTY FOR TRAINING (1957-1974)
At the Top of the John Hancock Building

My naval career as an every day obligation was at an end as a result of the resignation of my regular commission, but there remained years of sacrifice, a few high p
oints, one almost overwhelming concern and several thrills for me as a reserve officer during the eighteen years of naval reserve participation following my regular navy career.

The great concern developed a few months after my resignation from the regular navy. My friend, Bob Donley, the former executive officer of VP 42 at the time I was flying with that squadron during the Korean War was aware I had resigned my regular commission. He called one day to caution me about a potential problem in the course of action I had chosen, and to invite my attention to it. As carefully as I had read Section H of the Bureau of Naval Personnel Manual, the section dealing with naval reserve matters, prior to my resignation, I had overlooked one sub-section of the manual that dealt with retirement, and this oversight could have cost me all retirement credit for the time I had served on active duty. The provision stated that an officer who resigned his regular U.S. Navy commission and accepted a commission in the U.S. Naval Reserve, in order to retire with pay, would be required to serve the last eight years of qualifying service in the naval reserve. As I was already a commander, this effectively meant I would have to be selected for the rank of captain, or I would be involuntarily placed on the retired list without pay.

There were other complications. I was a designated naval aviator committed to living in Holland, Michigan, while the nearest naval air stations supporting reserve units were at Naval Air Stations Glenview, Illinois, and Grosse Pointe, Michigan, each about a hundred and eighty miles from Holland. This obstacle might have been surmountable, but when I investigated the possibility of getting an assignment to a reserve aviation unit, there was another barrier I had not foreseen. There were few billets for commanders, and there were informal internal structures in place in the various units that would make it virtually impossible for a newcomer to obtain a billet. My visits to the two naval air stations also revealed, from discussions with senior reserve naval aviators at each station, that I could not realistically expect to be assigned a billet in any of the air station reserve squadrons for two reasons, the first being my seniority, a level for which there were few billets, and, secondly, the available billets were all filled by aviators with much more flying experience than I had, many of them pilots flying for the commercial air lines.

At the time of my resignation I didn't realize it, but there was no possibility that a naval aviator not actively flying would be promoted. Aviators assigned to any selection board would immediately place a non-flying naval aviator's service record on the pile before him designated "not eligible for selection."

I received orders to various billets in the Grand Rapids reserve battalion in a non-pay status, and managed to be assigned two periods of ACDUTRA, both to ships supporting naval aviation. I attended the weekly drills regularly and each year was ordered to fourteen days of active duty for training.

Although I intensified my reserve participation, I was busy in my efforts to develop BAYWOODLANDS, and was blissfully ignorant of the approaching threat to my reserve career. I finally concluded, almost too late, that I should turn in my wings and request designation as a surface warfare officer once again. I had, after all, far more experience in surface warfare than aviation. Upon reaching this conclusion I requested in a letter to the Chief of Naval Personnel that my designation as a naval aviator be revoked and I be designated a surface warfare specialist once again. This bureaucratic change took time, and by the time my name came up before a board to select officers at my level of seniority I was still designated as a naval aviator and was duly passed over for promotion. This was to be anticipated, but a severe blow to my pride nonetheless.

1962   On the third of January I received a letter from the Chief of Naval Personnel with an endorsement by the Commandant, NINTH Naval District that struck terror to my soul and threatened to end my naval reserve career two years short of my having completed the last eight years of required service in the naval reserve to qualify for retirement with pay. *A review of your record indicates that on 30 June 1962 you were credited with at least twenty years of satisfactory service and note your completion of this important requirement for retirement with pay at age sixty. Additionally, it is noted that you have not been selected for the grade of captain...*

I was aware that the selection board for captain would be meeting in January, and that it would be considering my eligibility and qualifications for promotion in competition with other surface-designated officers rather than in competition with naval aviators amidst whom I would probably not be selected. Now the letter in my hands was telling me that my record would not even be presented to the selection board for consideration! Our telephone bill which included early January 1962 recorded calls to my friends in Washington, Arlington, Falls Church, and other DC area localities, seeking advice on what to do to insure my record was at least considered by the selection board. We had never had a phone bill of that size, many times our normal amount, but in the end I was assured that my record would be among those presented to the selection board. While I wanted assurance that my record would be included with the others being considered, I was careful not to imply that I was seeking any intervention with the proceedings of the board, which would be both unethical and illegal. The board met and reported out in early February. My name was listed among those selected. Several long time navy friends wrote congratulations, as did several of those whose help I had sought to insure my record was considered by the board. I was to be promoted to the rank of Captain, with date of rank 1 July 1962, but I did not get authorization to wear the four stripes of a captain until mid 1963. This promotion, made against the raw odds of the rank structure, was needed for my planned naval reserve career to succeed. Actually, based on my record, both active duty and reserve, the odds were much better; I was aware that the field of officers eligible for consideration by the promotion board was filled with records of surface officers who couldn't reasonably compete with mine, and I had strived mightily to keep it thus.

1963: ACDUTRA orders were received to the U.S.S. PROCYON a refrigerator ship lying alongside a pier in San Francisco. I had essentially no experience with ships of the train except for the numerous fuelings and provisionings I experienced in World War II, so it was a good opportunity for me to get some exposure to ships of this broad genre. We elected to have Lory, Martje and Buck accompany me at our expense, and made a reservation for accommodations for our entire party at a family type hotel just off Market Street, a short commute by street car to where the ship was docked. A few weeks before our departure for San Francisco, I received a letter from the Secretary of the Navy:

To: *Captain Fred. S. BERTSCH, JR., USNR*
Via: *Commandant, NINTH Naval District*
Subj: *Temporary Appointment*
Ref: *(a) Title 10, United States Code, Section 5910*

1. Pursuant to the provisions of reference (a) the President of the United States temporarily appoints you a Captain in the Reserve of the United States Navy to rank from 1 July 1962.... The rest of the letter was routine boiler plate covering the necessary details involved in any navy promotion, i.e., promotion physical; oath, etc.

This document was signed by the Secretary of the Navy for the President. I was elated by the promotion, which I felt was well-earned, and I lost no time in getting my blue uniforms delivered to the tailor for the addition of the fourth stripe. A modification to my ACDUTA orders changed my rank therein from commander to captain. It was official!

Aboard the PROCYON, I found the officers and crew preparing for a materiel inspection by the Underway Training Group, San Francisco, based at Treasure Island, at that time a naval station in San Francisco Bay. Although not familiar with auxiliary ships such as the PROCYON, I was very familiar with the nature and procedures of the materiel inspections, having served as the Ship Training Officer on the staff of Commander Fleet Air Wing FOURTEEN following my combat tour during the first year of the Korean War. My fitness report for this period, signed by the commanding officer of the PROCYON acknowledged my assistance in preparation for the ship's inspection and marked the entire report OUTSTANDING.

1964 My application for ACDUTRA was denied because of insufficient funds allocated the reserve forces that year.

1965 In April I received ACDUTRA orders to attend a course in the administration of the naval reserve. This two week period included that of the annual spring vacation of the Holland schools. It was my first opportunity to meet Rear Admiral "Red" Yeager, Commandant, Ninth Naval District, an officer I had admired from a distance for a number of years. Later that year I accepted orders to an unpaid two-day period of active duty at Headquarters, NINTH Naval District over a weekend for a seminar on the duties of a Group Commander, a position for which I had been selected. I would preside over all of the reserve units based at the Naval Reserve Training Center, Grand Rapids.

1966 In April I was advised that I had been chosen to participate in a seminar for selected senior reserve officers of all the United States military to be held at Fort Leslie J. McNair, the site of the National War College in Washington, D.C. starting in late June. This was an opportunity for Martje and Buck to accompany their parents to the nation's capital and have some additional exposure to its treasures.

The seminar itself was an invaluable and unforgettable experience, an opportunity to hear talks on the international situation of the time, the military commitments and the resources of the United States in comparison to its international friends, rivals and neutrals, and other major defense issues, all presented by senior officers of the military services and their civilian counterparts in several governmental departments and agencies including the Departments of State, Treasury and Commerce. All made themselves available for questions and gave answers with the condition that their responses not be discussed or even mentioned outside the hall in which we sat.

Fort McNair had a beautiful officers' mess where we took our midday meals, and Lory and I took advantage of the beautifully served evening meal on several occasions during that time in Washington. Several of the presenters at the seminars joked that *Security is so tight at Fort McNair that even the mess attendants are required to have secret clearances.* I never ascertained whether or not it was true, but security was paramount, lending credence to the statement.

In early November I received a two page letter from the Chief of Naval Personnel which read, in part:

Subject: Reserve Selection Board Duty, Selection for (What a beautiful example of bureaucratese!)

"1. .....you have been accepted as a member of the Lieutenant Commander to Commander Reserve Line Selection Board, convening on 17 January 1967. Appropriate BuPers orders will be issued.....

4. Correspondence and personal inquiries from individual reserve officers to the Chief of Naval Personnel or any individual in the Bureau of Naval Personnel regarding duty on selection boards convened un Title 10, U.S. Code are not desired...

8. Your attention is invited to the fact that membership on an inactive reserve selection board is not to be divulged to anyone except on a need to know basis. (I felt it necessary that Don Ihrman be notified of these orders immediately and requested interim help during my absence for the already overworked dean, my sole professional assistant, Edna Dyk.)

9. You will receive a letter from the recorder of the selection board giving information on required uniforms, housing facilities, parking and other pertinent facts.

1967 : I continued in a non-pay status as commanding officer of the Naval Reserve Officers School 9-15. My six-week tour of active duty as a member of the board to select reserve lieutenant commanders for the rank of commander was truly an educational experience. When I walked into the room in which the board was to meet, the first person I saw was my old shipmate from the U.S.S. CASE, Bill Elliott, now a captain naval aviator. We renewed old ties and had several wonderful dinners together during that period of temporary active duty.   .

As to the functioning of the board, and my part in it, I found it most interesting to review the records of those officers who were in the zone for possible promotion. Captain Bedillion, the commanding officer of the CASE at the time I joined her had told me, many years before, that it was easy for members of selection boards to discard the records of those officers who had little operational experience, as well as those whose strongest recommendations were relative to musical ability, social graces, or athletic ability rather than to their qualities as a naval leader. Likewise, it was not hard to pick the "shoo-ins", those officers whose leadership qualities were outstanding, and whose operational experiences under pressure indicated that they would perform well in the next higher rank. The difficult problem was to pick potential leaders from among the remaining officers in the zone of eligibility; those who would most probably perform ably in the next higher rank.

Each member of the board was assigned a pile of records for the purpose of placing each record in one of three categories, shoo-ins, or "fully qualified and recommended for promotion", "unqualified and not recommended for promotion" and by far the largest category, "worthy of consideration". These were not the exact adjective descriptions during the board's considerations, as time has erased them from my mind, but they will do. At the end of all this sorting, each record in each category was presented by the reviewer for consideration by the entire board. On a majority vote of the board, each officer under consideration was either "Recommended for promotion" or "Not recommended for promotion." ACDUTA this year was a two week tour at the headquarters of the Military Sea Transport Service in Washington, D.C. starting in mid June for orientation to a command within this service if recalled to active duty.

Son Buck was fifteen and Mary Jo eleven, so it was a good opportunity for them to get their first exposure to the historic sites and sights of the nation's capital. Lory could escort them on tours daily while I attended my duties at MSTS. The flag officer commanding MSTS at that time was Vice Admiral Lawson Ramage, older brother of my long-time friend, Captain Don Ramage. This was my opportunity to rub elbows with another of the navy's World War II heroes. Lawson P. Ramage was a lieutenant commander when he was ordered to command of the submarine, U.S.S. PARCHE (SS 384). While on a war patrol he took his boat into the center of a convoy of Japanese merchant ships and sank several of them. For this exploit he was awarded the Congressional Medal of Honor. He was an affable and outgoing man, far different from his brother Don, my friend, who was comparatively quiet and more introspective. On returning to Holland, my mail, held for the two weeks of our absence, contained the letter from the Chief of Naval Personnel for which I had strived during those twelve years of naval reserve service after resigning from the regular navy:

Subject: Notification of Eligibility for Retired Pay at Age 60

1. This is to notify you that, having completed the required years of service, you will be eligible for retired pay upon application at age 60 in accordance with the provisions of Title 10, U,S. Code, Chapter 67....." These were the golden words I needed to assure me that my years of service, both regular and reserve, had not gone for naught. I heaved a great sigh of relief that this protection for me and my family had been achieved.

<u>1968</u>   This year I was ordered to the staff of the Commandant, Ninth Naval District, with headquarters at Great Lakes, Illinois for orientation to a new mobilization billet as ship training officer on the staff. The commandant was still Rear Admiral "Red" Yeager, who previously, as a vice admiral, had commanded the naval task force assigned to evacuate the marines from Lebanon after the terrorist bombing of the marine barracks there. I respected this fine officer, not only for his outstanding naval career, but also for the fact he had requested assignment as commandant of the Ninth Naval District in the lower rank of rear admiral in order to be with his ailing wife.

I had barely met the admiral during my several previous tours at Great Lakes, but it became apparent he was aware of my presence in his command when one morning toward the end of the second week he called me personally and asked if I would like to accompany him on a trip downtown, meaning to Chicago where he would be delivering a speech at a gathering of American Legion members. Naturally, I accepted the invitation, and enjoyed being in the company of this personable flag officer. The admiral delivered his speech, and then we motored to the Chicago Yacht Club for lunch at the invitation, I was told, *of the lift contractor on the John Hancock building, now topping out at a site on Rush Street...* We had a pleasant luncheon at the yacht club, during which the our host explained what a lift contractor does. He went into much fascinating detail, and his summarizing sentence was, *We lift all the people, and all the material needed to construct the building, up to the level where they are needed.* At the conclusion of our lunch, he said, *And now we'll show you the operation.*

At the site, we looked at the lift machinery and the gigantic coils of cable that were involved in lifting the tons of material required at the top and all the intermediate levels of that tremendous structure, then the tallest building in the world.

Following our inspection of the operation on the ground, our host invited us to join him on a trip up to the eighty-first story of this great building. We stepped into a cage-like car and our host worked the controls to hoist us past eighty open doors through which we could see workers laboring at various stages of the building's construction. We stepped out onto sheets of plywood laid over the girders that represented the eighty-first level, and the contractor explained in detail the building process to that point.

With that little tour completed, he led us to another elevator shaft and onto a car that looked like it might have been put together by some kids trying to build a tree house. There were no sides to this basket; just a rail to lean on, if one dared lean. Through the expanded metal floor, one could look straight down the elevator shaft for eighty-one floors. The basket swung loosely in the shaft, guided only by gravity, and the lift cable attached to its top. *Now I'll take you up to the ninety-fifth floor and show you the world's highest swimming pool,* our friend announced as he stepped aboard this wobbling monstrosity. I wasn't at all sure I wanted to accompany him, but there really was no alternative, so I joined him and the admiral on board that ridiculous-looking makeshift elevator car swinging loosely far above the bustling street below.

There was a bundle of varicolored wires hanging out of a box loosely nailed to one side of the contraption in which we were standing. All the wires had bare ends for several inches. The car swung lazily from side to side under our feet, and I took a quick glance downward through the expanded metal mesh of the floor. There were eighty floors beneath my feet. *Let's see, I can't always remember whether to connect the red wire to the white wire, or the red wire to the black wire to make this thing go,* said our host. I hoped he was kidding.

Eventually he selected two wires and momentarily allowed them to touch. There was a spark between the wires and the make-shift car gave an upward jerk. *I guess that's right,* he said, and held the wires together. The car moved upward with a hesitant motion, swinging loosely in the shaft as it went. *Ninety-fifth floor, everybody out,* said our guide cheerily as he stepped out of the car and onto a two-inch by twelve-inch plank lying across the I-beams representing that level. There was no floor. There were no walls, interior or exterior. We were looking out at a panorama of Chicago, standing on two-by-twelve inch boards.

Let me show you the highest swimming pool in any city in the world, exclaimed our host. We followed him along the plank, stepping with care along the narrow path until we were looking at the empty steel tank and expressed appropriate amazement that a swimming pool was being installed so high in the sky.

I felt I had had enough of this kind of sight-seeing, and was ready to reenter the swinging basket for the beginning of our descent to the civilized world, when our Our host then led us around what was soon to be a wall on the ninety-fifth floor, and said, *"I have a real surprise for you, Admiral, I want you to be the first person who is not a construction worker to be present at the topping out of a major building. Follow me."* He was walking along a plank leading toward a ladder, the top of which was resting on another I-beam ten or twelve feet above us. *Admiral, you're going to love this,* he called back over his shoulder, and started to climb up that damned ladder.

I wasn't at all sure the old man was going to love it, and I was absolutely certain I wasn't going to love it, but as the admiral started up that ladder, there was no turning back. If he went up there, I was honor bound to follow.

Resting on the I-beam representing the ninety-sixth floor was another ladder, this one extending to the ninety-seventh level from a position to the right of the top of the first ladder, so a few steps along the I-beam on which the second ladder rested was necessary to reach its foot. The admiral was already climbing the second ladder when I stepped off the first with my knees knocking together. There were no hand rails. I had to make the few steps along that I-beam to the foot of the second ladder, or face oblivion.

I made it to the second ladder, gritted my teeth and followed the admiral to the top, where there was no structure above the bare beam on which we stood, except for the beginnings of the TV tower, above which extended a gin pole for the erection of the mighty antenna that would extend from it. The United States flag fluttered from the top of the gin pole, and a welder working on the base for the antenna swung from the gin pole in a harness from which streamed a tail of welding hoses and wires. Sea gulls were gliding past us, eyeball-to-eyeball. A plane climbing out of Midway airport appeared to be at about our level. There was nothing to hang on to, and one misstep would mean a fall of at least two stories, or, possibly, ninety-seven.

Eventually my knees stopped knocking together, and I started to enjoy the scene. The flange of the beam on which I stood was at least fourteen inches wide. At ground level, I wouldn't have any trouble walking along a pavement fourteen inches wide, so why should it be difficult here? It was another experience I was happy to have had, but one I don't care to repeat. I've visited the top of the John Hancock building a number of times since, and on each occasion I have returned to the observation deck under circumstances considerably different from those during my first time there.

1969 I was notified my application for ACDUTRA was denied due to lack of funds.

1970 In order to maintain a continuing record of accepting regular ACDUTRA orders, I requested duty without pay in my mobilization billet and was given orders to the Fleet Training Center, Norfolk, Virginia. This was my opportunity to participate in the activities in preparation for the commissioning of a new ship, the U.S.S. MOUNT WHITNEY. I entered into these preparations with considerable enthusiasm. At the end of this two week tout, my fitness report in part read,

Captain Bertsch has performed all of his assigned duties in an outstanding manner. He has served with great skill and professionalism in his mobilization billet as Director, Precommissioning Training Department....Captain Bertsch left a favorable impression on all who met him.

<u>1971</u> In mid April Rear Admiral Draper L. Kauffman, then serving as Commandant, Ninth Naval District, made an official visit to Grand Rapids and inspected our facility and personnel. I had the opportunity to visit briefly and informally with the admiral during which time I expressed concern that the selection system for promotion of senior officers in the Naval Reserve was having an adverse effect on the selection of Ninth Naval District officers due to the fact that the district, although the largest in the navy, was represented on these boards by a far lower percentage of members than the smaller districts lying along the coasts. The admiral expressed considerable interest in what I was saying, and requested that I write an expanded version in memorandum form and mail it to his personal attention. The following is what I wrote in this informal letter.

Dear Admiral Kauffman,

I am concerned with what I believe the results of the fiscal year 1971 inactive USNR officer selection boards to be. Before indicating the bases for my concern I note the following with respect to the U.S. Navy selection system:

(1) While subject to human error, it is probably the best promotion system thus far devised;
(2) With respect to equity, the system is subject to the wisdom with which the board members themselves are selected;
(3) While geographical origin of membership composing regular navy selection boards is presumably not significant, geography is extremely important to the composition of naval reserve boards, since inactive USNR officers may serve virtually their entire careers under the aegis of a single naval district;
(4) The leverage of district representation on selection boards is obviously greatest on boards convened to select officers to the grades of rear admiral, captain and commander.

The observations that led to my concern are as follows:
(1) The NINTH Naval District contains roughly 23% of all USNR personnel;
(2) No line Rear Admiral was selected in FY '71 from 9ND (not in itself particularly significant for any given year);
(3) Although 176 line captains were selected, only <u>nine</u> were from the NINTH Naval District, when a pro-rata share would be approximately forty;

(4) Although to a degree incidental to point (3), above, only four of the nine officers selected to the grade of captain were surface officers, the group that carries the brunt of the selected reserve program, other than air;

From these observations, and assuming that NINTH Naval District officers are on average as well qualified for promotion as those of other districts, I draw the following inferred conclusions:

(1) Naval district representation on selection boards is _very_ important in the USNR selection process in contrast with the relative unimportance of geography to USN boards;

(2) By intuition I conclude that the NINTH Naval District was not adequately represented on the Rear Admiral and Captain boards in FY'71 .....

(3) If these perceptions are correct, or even partially correct, then morale of the officers of the district junior to the grade of captain is bound to suffer.

If these observations and conclusions appear to you to have any merit, I recommend:

(1)That the validity of these observations be examined by your staff;

(2) That the NINTH Naval District nominate the strongest possible candidates for the FY'72 boards, soliciting the participation of well-qualified officers at the earliest possible time so they can arrange their affairs as necessary to permit participation if selected by the Bureau of Naval Personnel;

(3) That any and all appropriate measures be taken to insure NINTH Naval District representation on _all_ selections boards and that this representation be as nearly pro-rata as possible;

(4) That officers selected to serve on promotion boards be carefully briefed by senior member of the staff on the selection process and the stake of 9ND in receiving some measure of equity in the selection process. In no way do I mean to suggest any compromise of the oath of a selection board member; rather I suggest that ComNINE be adequately represented on all boards by well-qualified officers.

Your consideration of these comments is solicited.
Very respectfully...."

Avid readers of my autobiography will note how carefully I adhered to protocol in my complimentary close of this communication. This was in marked contrast to that I used in a memorandum, a copy of which was addressed to the assistant chief of staff, a newly promoted rear admiral, during the Eniwetok atomic bomb tests, when I closed the memorandum with a simple "Respectfully" rather then "Very respectfully." The result in that case was an explosion from the officer addressed that far exceeded any necessary to get my attention,

In marked contrast to the frigid response I received in Eniwetok, shortly after my submittal, the admiral replied in some detail, but included the following:

Thank you very much for your letter...I have looked into the matter...your facts are quite accurate...be assured that I will do everything I can to ensure proper Ninth Naval District representation in future years....

Although my action could have been viewed as presumptuous, I felt justified in doing my best to improve the system and NINTH Naval District's part in it.

Shortly before the end of the school year, I received orders to an unpaid tour of ACDUTRA at the Naval War College, Newport, Rhode Island where I attended the instructors' course in advanced Naval Planning. At the end of the tour all blocks on my fitness report were marked "outstanding." Comments included, "Captain Bertsch has enthusiastically and effectively participated in an intensive two-week seminar on Military Planning. His presentation on the functions of staff in Military Planning benefited all attendees....Captain Bertsch is recommended for retention in the Naval Reserve and further promotion...While flattering, I could hardly put much stock in the recommendation for promotion.

I received orders to serve as director of the Naval Reserve Officers School attached to the Grand Rapids Naval Reserve Group at the Grand Rapids Naval Armory, and served in this role for the rest of my reserve career.

I received ACDUTRA orders to attend a reserve officers seminar at the Naval War College, Newport, Rhode Island the last two weeks in July, and took advantage of the opportunity to include Lory, as a vacation for her. During this period we had an opportunity to renew our association with Don and Helen Ramage as Don was serving as a War College instructor.

It also was an opportunity to review some films recovered from the Japanese, a few of which showed our makeshift task force of destroyers and ancient mine sweepers "hidden" in Makushin Bay in the Aleutians during our phase of the battle of Midway. Apparently the enemy didn't consider our little ""Kodiak Defense Force" to be worthy of attack.

1972   For this year I had requested duty on a major seagoing staff, preferably to the staff of one of the numbered fleets. I was delighted to receive my orders about the time of our commencement that year to spend two weeks on the staff of Commander, Second Fleet based in Norfolk, Virginia with the admiral's flag aboard a heavy cruiser. I was assigned as an understudy to the chief of staff, a regular navy officer of about my seniority and age. He let me know immediately, and in the most explicit terms that he had expected someone much older than I, one who was completely out of date as far as the active fleet was concerned, and of very little potential for filling a fleet billet in time of war.

In the face of this challenge, I set about immediately by my performance to correct his misapprehensions. First of all, he had not had much if any, contact with reserve officers since World War II, and was not familiar with the legislation that assigned reserve officers "running mates", gave them seniority on the same basis as those of the regular navy, and directed that the "up or out" system would apply equally, thus retiring officers who failed of promotion on the same basis as their regular navy contemporaries. By the end of the first week I had impressed my boss favorably, and any barrier that had existed, disappeared. I became involved, albeit in a minor way, in the planning for a fleet exercise to be conducted several months hence. Vice Admiral Vincent P. De Poix, a gracious and scholarly flag officer presided over the flag mess and made a point of engaging me in conversation and exploration of my naval experience.

In a reflection of the thinking of naval personnel serving in surface vessels in those days of nuclear confrontation with the Soviet Union, one response to the question, not entirely humorous, of what action SECOND Fleet would take in the event of war was, *Sortie Chesapeake Bay and turn right to course 180. Set standard speed at fifteen knots and proceed until entering the ice field of Antarctica.*

By the end of the training period, I was detached with a copy of an outstanding fitness report to be submitted to the Bureau of Naval Personnel. The remarks section of the report read, *Captain Bertsch's overall performance of duty, interest in garnering as much professional knowledge as possible, and his grasp of the immediate problems of both the regular component and the Naval Reserve have been most impressive. His ability and willingness to participate in open and frank professional subjects has been superb. Although my experience with senior reserve officers serving on active duty for training is limited, I have observed that this officer if far above average and I would welcome the opportunity to have Captain Bertsch as a full time member of my staff.*

1974 My active participation in the naval reserve came to an end on 30 June 1974. Eventually, time catches up with all of us. I had had transient dreams of sometime wearing the broad stripe of a rear admiral myself, but if that had been a possibility before I left the regular navy, circumstances did not permit me to post a record that might have qualified me for selection to that rank in the naval reserve. The navy system is one of "up or out", and the consequence for me, was retirement from the naval reserve as of 1 July, 1974. I trust it is evident from this chronology that I am proud to have served.

CHAPTER FOURTEEN
THE SECOND YEAR AND BEYOND
Better for the Most Part, 1962-'78

After struggling through the first post-strike year, my efforts to support the teaching staff and heal the wounds resulting from the strike appeared to be paying off. I received much advice from all sides, much of it from teachers whose counsel I appreciated and utilized. Of the rest, mostly from unhappy parents, I discarded ninety percent or more.

However, the second year commencement activities did not go well at all.

Despite any rulings the United States Supreme Court in the matter and supported by all of the fairly broad variety of conservative churches in Holland a baccalaureate service remained a mainstay of the sequence of events leading to commencement and under Superintendent Ihrman, planning of the service was also a responsibility of the high school principal. Thus, if things went poorly, the principal became the goat, and if they went well the service, if recalled at all, became a part of a whole series of events producing a general feeling of happiness surrounding the overall graduation process.

Since I was seeking to cope with the already limited funding that second year, I hit upon the happy notion that there were almost always senior students whose fathers were ministers, and thus in situations such that they could hardly refuse to serve as participants in the baccalaureate, all at no cost to the school district. I checked with Don and he agreed with my concept; it would save a few bucks. I carefully screened the personnel cards of the class and quickly discovered four preacher/fathers:

The Reverend Asaph Bayard* a retired missionary who was working in a local furniture factory;

The Reverend Rabid C. Millsome*, head of a small congregation that labeled itself the First Bed Rock Fundamentalist Church;

Dr, Alburtus George VandeHeuvel*, ThD., professor of Theoretical Theology at the local seminary, and

The Reverend William C. Van Veen*, the college chaplain.

I surveyed these qualifications and drew what I thought to be logical conclusions:

(1) The most learned of the group was the professor, so he should deliver the sermon at baccalaureate;

(2) The Reverend Bayard, the missionary should deliver the invocation, read the scripture passage and deliver the benediction;

(3) The Reverend Millson should deliver the principal prayers, and

(4) The college chaplain could carry off the invocation and benediction responsibilities at commencement.

All would have a part and no one slighted.

I had never met any of this group of potential participants, except perhaps briefly at parent-teacher conferences the previous fall. If I had, I might have been more cautious. In my innocence I called each of the participants on the telephone, carefully outlined his assignments and each accepted with pleasure.

In a follow up letter addressed to each person invited I stated with precision the time factors involved, and emphasized the importance of staying within the time restraints I specified in order insure that neither baccalaureate nor commencement would last longer than one hour. In summary and in the order of time allotted the plan was this:

Reverend Bayard would start the service, reading a prescribed passage of scripture;

Reverend Millsome would deliver a principal prayer not to exceed three minutes;

Dr. VandeHeuvel would deliver a sermon of not more than twenty minutes.

With only a few exceptions the two-hour rehearsal for baccalaureate went well. I briefed the students, *At the end of the processional, when all of you are lined up with a seat, the Reverend Bayard will approach the lectern and say, 'The audience will please rise for the invocation,' BOYS REMOVE YOUR CAPS. When the invocation has been completed, Reverend Millsome will say, 'The audience and the class of 1959 may be seated.' This will be the signal not only to be seated, but for boys to replace their caps; tassel on the right side.* Everyone understood, or so I thought.

All participants were directed to be present at least a half hour early, and all were prompt. I had labeled the chairs on the stage for myself, the superintendent, the board of education, the clergy and Harvey Meyer, the choir director. Chairs were in place on risers for the entry of the choir. I carefully reviewed the program with the clergy, emphasizing that the entire program would proceed based on the signals built into the wordings they would use. I re-emphasized the importance of each completing his part within the prescribed time restraints. I might as well have saved my breath, but at least no member of the stage group tripped getting onto the stage and each sat in his labeled chair. The choir entered in good order, and the processional began

Two of the first five couples in the procession of graduates were out of step. George*, one of the class jokesters, was missing. The processional ended, and all, save George appeared to be in the proper row and place. George appeared in the back of the auditorium in cap and gown, came limping down the center aisle, a processional of one. He took his time, grinning sheepishly all the way, found his proper row and pushed himself past his standing classmates to get to his assigned place. The Reverend Bayard rose, got the audience to its feet and pronounced the invocation, at the end of which he grabbed his Bible opened it, and said, *Our reading* *to day is chapter _____ of the Book of _____,* the selection chosen by the scheduled speaker, and he then started to read. I winced; our time frame was already broken and the audience of over three thousand, together with the graduating class was still standing, and becoming restless.

Eventually, the reader glanced upward, realized his error and uttered the prescribed words *The audience and the class of 1965 may be seated.* Pandemonium reigned, Chairs scraped, several members of the class dropped their caps and had to stoop to retrieve them, everyone in the audience coughed at least once and a not inconsiderable number felt constrained to cough three or four times. The senior girl in the second row aisle seat was left without a chair, apparently due to the return of George. There were a few titters from the members of the audience who could see what had happened, but the young lady initially solved the problem by sitting down on the knee of the boy who was seated in the aisle seat. The Reverend Bayard droned on and finally said, *"....and this concludes our scripture lesson for today."* I could have shot him, but no one was seriously damaged and it looked like the dignity of the service might be reestablished if all other participants carried out their roles as prescribed.

Harvey Meyer, the choir director, had joined our staff at the beginning of the school year. He was a real professional, demanding great music and great precision from his student performers. The choral anthem scheduled to follow the scripture reading was beautiful and I started to relax, at least as much as is possible during an extended baccalaureate service being conducted in an ambient temperature of a hundred and six degrees with sweat pouring into the eyeballs.

Harvey Meyer

As the anthem ended, Reverend Millsome rose. He got the audience on its feet handily, and then with a resounding, but somewhat tremulous voice, he said *Let us p-u-r-raay,* and started in to invite the Lord's attention to every conceivable detail in the world's existence. His voice shook with emotion as he really got going, and I could readily see that no one was going to stop this guy in any five minutes. He had hardly covered the missionaries in Micronesia in that much time, and hadn't even started on those in darkened Africa and Asia.

At the fifteen minute mark he started to wing his way back toward the home area with a plea for the forgiveness all the sinners in the audience and by implication the sinners on the stage, *....if it be thy will.....* At the twenty-five minute mark he glanced at his watch, realized he had set a new endurance record, and in a fast sequence of high-blown sentences, he concluded his prayer. Harvey's baton was poised for the choral conclusion, but before a note could be sung, Reverend

Millsome declared *AHHH..MEN* and quickly added *The audience and the class of 1969 may be seated.* Once again pandemonium reigned.

Several members of the choir behind us sat down. The remaining members seemed to be in doubt as to whether or not they should be singing. Harvey's baton came down and the remaining members of the choir sang a somewhat straggly *a.a.a.-men* Chairs scraped on the floor, caps dropped, everyone, it seemed, coughed and it appeared that no one heard the choir. I looked back to get a glimpse of Harvey. His eyeballs looked at me along the ridge of his nose as though he was looking over the sights of a rifle. I was happy he didn't have one. He stomped off the stage and I fully expected I would never see him again. The Reverend Millsome sat down looking very pleased with himself. I wanted to shoot him.

True to the examples already established, the college chaplain's sermon ran ten minutes beyond the time suggested. Eventually the recessional began. George marched out without a sign of a limp. I lingered a bit after the service to give anyone who wished to do so the opportunity to offer comments. When the floor was cleared, I started my exit and was greeted by two little old ladies who apparently attended the service every year, even though they had no relative graduating. They delightedly announced that this year's was the best service they had ever witnessed.

I went home and had a martini.

We reverted to my idea of selecting as our commencement speaker a "Distinguished Graduate" of Holland High, believing, correctly, that no graduate so identified would turn down the invitation. This plan worked well and all of the speakers did well in their respective roles, with only minor glitches usually identified only by parents decrying some detail in the activities. These years were dominated by the Viet Nam War, and there were considerable effects on several of our graduations.

Pronunciation of names was always a challenge, and even though I was raised in Holland many of the Dutch names were tongue twisters for me. For several weeks before graduation, I would take the class list and practice. When I didn't know the proper pronunciation, I would ask the student, just as the marine instructor had asked us on board the old U.S.S. WYOMING many years before. In 1966 Amanda Asusana Arredondo was the first name on the list of graduates in that class. I practiced it diligently, coached at first by the young lady herself until I got just the right roll to the Asusana. Amanda would be among the first, if not the first, Mexican American to graduate from Holland High School. Many more were to follow.

Preparations for the third commencement of my career as principal again proved to be a memorable period of my career when I reverted to my original idea that the speaker should be a distinguished graduate of Holland High School. When I phoned the man I selected for the honor he had graciously accepted and I considered the first task of commencement planning complete.

As with planning for the second commencement of my principalship it was not to be. Within a few days after receiving the acceptance of my chosen speaker, Mrs. Veeder entered my office with a letter in one hand and a postmarked envelope in the other. *I think you will want respond to this letter immediately.* She handed me a piece of stationary headed with the logo of the University of Michigan, a side bar reading, "Office of the President" and a brief letter which read, *"Dr. Hatcher appreciates invitations to give commencement addresses for a limited number of Michigan high schools each year. Please reply by return mail giving the date, time and place of your commencement in order that I may clear his calendar for that date if possible. Subject to these limitations, you may consider this a tentative acceptance of your kind invitation."* The letter was signed "Secretary to the President." I was stunned; I was back into the business of having multiple commencement speakers after having taken precautions to avoid the problem I had encountered earlier.

Not only that. In the next day's mail was a letter signed with the facsimile signature of Thurgood Marshall, first black member of the United States Supreme Court, stating that court business made it impossible for him to accept my invitation to be the commencement speaker. I hastened to dictate a letter to President Hatcher's secretary declining his kind offer. I wiped my brow and wondered what was going on. Was this some sort of fantasy?

One can imagine my astonishment when the following day I received a letter signed personally by Senator Barry Goldwater indicating he would be pleased indeed to be the commencement speaker for Holland High School in June, since his schedule already called for him to be in the Midwest during that period of time. It would only be necessary to change the date from Thursday to Wednesday to avoid a conflict with his already scheduled appearances. I hastily dictated a letter to the senator tactfully advising him that in no way could the commencement date be changed, as the other two local high schools had already scheduled their graduation activities for Wednesday by agreement among the three high schools. I remained very much in the dark as to how this whole mess had come to pass.

The following day I received letters declining my kind invitation to serve as commencement speaker from Paul H. Todd, member of congress from the third district of Michigan, Don Lubbers, the president of Central College in Pella, Iowa, and now the distinguished president of Grand Valley State College, Congressman Guy VanderJagt, Justice Byron White of the United States Supreme Court, Martin Luther King,Jr., George Meany, president of the American Federation of Labor/CIO, Colonel John Glenn, Senator Bob Griffin, Congressman Jerry Ford, Justice Hugo Black, together with an unequivocal acceptance from Dr. Averill, vice president of Kalamazoo College. I derailed the acceptance of Dr. Averill with a phone call and awaited the arrival of the next day's mail with something approaching terror in my heart.

When the mail came the next day, sure enough, there was what had come to be the usual shower of letters regarding our commencement exercises. There were regrets from Admiral Hyman Rickover, J. Edgar Hoover, Walter Reuther, Senator Everett Dirksen and Justices Potter Stewart, Arthur Goldberg and William O.

Douglas. At that point I had a fine start on an autograph collection containing signatures of many significant leaders of the time.

I was held in suspense for a period of time during which I lost sleep once again over a situation I had no part in creating, but finally came to believe that the blizzard of letters accepting or declining my "kind invitation" had ended. About the time I had finished reading what I hoped would be the last of this torrent of letters, and responding where this seemed appropriate, Bill Elenbaas, the president of the senior class came into the office with a bit of a flair. It was not to see me, but to inquire, *Have we received any replies to the invitations I sent out?* It developed that somehow he had gotten the idea that recruiting a commencement speaker was his responsibility and had sent out the invitations on a wholesale basis, using my name and official Holland High School stationery. Further, he had filched my facsimile signature stamp from the office safe for long enough to get the letters stamped with my signature without either me or my secretary knowing it.

My choice for commencement speaker one year was Rear Admiral Mayo "Mike" Hadden, a Hope College graduate, three or four years older than I, a genuine naval aviation hero and an ace based on his victories against both German and Japanese pilots during World War II, a rare combination and distinction shared by very few U.S. pilots. Considering the times, the graduation went fairly smoothly, although interrupted from time to time by shouts of "Peace" from the audience. Mike's address, aimed at the students was decorous and considerate, with no references to either war or peace.

We planned a small reception for Mike in an anteroom off the stage following the ceremonies, in order that local friends of Mike and his family might exchange personal greetings. I included a small general invitation in the commencement program aimed at anyone in the audience who wished to attend. Punch and cookies would be served. In contrast with our expectations, when we in the stage participants left the stage in company to join the group, we found our speaker confronted by a man shaking his fist in Mike's face yelling obscenities and accusing our speaker of being a *"F- - -ing war monger. You're no hero, you're murderer."* He then threw his cup of colorful punch at Mike, staining the front of his immaculate white uniform. Mike smiled, wiped himself off somewhat with his paper napkin and continued his conversations with family and old friends, explaining as he went, that the gold buttons, shoulder boards and decorations of a navy service dress uniform are all removable, and the uniform itself washable.

Another year our speaker was Robert Rowan, president and chairman of the board of Fruehauf Corporation, manufacturers of large trucks. His success in the world of business was enough, in my estimation, to qualify him as a distinguished graduate of Holland High, where, during his high school years was known as "Hoots" Rowan. The only problem with this choice was that Hoots, unbeknownst to me, was under indictment by the U. S. attorney's office for some alleged violations in connection with the truck manufacturing business. His indictment did not dissuade him from accepting our invitation. He delivered an inspirational speech which was applauded by the audience, and our little reception following the ceremonies was well attended by old friends from his days in Holland and comrades from his days in the local national guard unit, most of whom addressed him as Hoots. Most attendees were smiling, chatting and enjoying the occasion when a man of a differing persuasion broke into the conversation, pushed a couple of guests out of the way and delivered a strong right punch to Bob's chin, together with a few loudly expressed and vulgar epithets. I was nearing a conclusion that being a commencement speaker was a dangerous activity.

At this point in the story of my career in education, it becomes difficult to maintain a sequence of events and the narrative becomes one of sets of topics that were spread across fourteen years. I have attempted to include the year or time span within which the incident or incidents occurred.

The enrollment of Mexican-American students steadily increased each year as the population of former migrant families settling in Holland increased. Many such students, particularly boys found it difficult to succeed in the realm of education for a variety of reasons, including, but not limited to the language interface and the lack of preparation due in part to the transient history of their families.

In an effort to make the commencement ceremonies more understandable and meaningful to the Latino families in attendance, about 1974 or 1975, I invited one of our better Latino students to address the audience in both Spanish and English in addition to the customary presentations by the valedictorian and guest speaker. I was so impressed by what she said and how well her thoughts were organized that I spoke to her at the end of the ceremonies and requested a copy of what she had said. She handed me her carefully prepared hand lettered double spaced speech. I regret that I failed to inscribe the author's name on that aging document. Here is what she said:

THE NEW LIFE

Respect for education and for educators begins in the home. Like many Spanish speaking people, my parents have had less than a fifth grade education, bu they know that education is the key to their children's future.

To complete the first twelve years of schooling is not easy for a bilingual, bicultural child. He lives in two different environments. In one, he speaks Spanish, eats fryoles con chili with tortilla, and learns not to meet the eyes of an adult, a sign of respect and obedience. In his other environment, he speaks English, eats hamburgers and French fries and must meet the eyes of adults he meets to show respect and obedience. As you can see, the child must already be confused. He doesn't know which way of showing respect for an adult is the right way.

A misinterpretation of our culture's body language and our speaking Spanish in school sometimes cause problems for the Latino child. Thank goodness Holland's schools are now encouraging bilingualism and are becoming more aware of our culture instead of penalizing it. These cultural differences are not so serious that they should interfere with the Latino's secondary education. The Latino drop out rate is high because Latinos never learn how to read well. They are not encouraged to read in their homes. When they enter school they are already behind the rest of the English speaking children. Problems with the English language also hold them back. By the time the youngster gets to high school this inability to understand what he is reading smothers the learning process and confuses the student to the point he no longer wants to attend and he quits.

The Latino students present here tonight are quite fortunate to have overcome this obstacle. In fact, we are the largest Latino group graduating from Holland High School thus far. On behalf of all the graduates, I would like to deeply thank all of our teachers for being educators, and our parents for being the guides in our lives.

Now it is up to us, the Mexican Americans, Chicanos, Cubans, Puerto Ricans, Latinos asnd so forth, to share our traditions and language with more people. The Latino minority has an important place in American society because all minorities have an important place in this society. The United States is a nation composed of minorities. Each one has made important contributions to our civilizations. Each one is essential for the success of this great nation.

I am very proud to have had this opportunity to speak to you in Spanish not only because I was able to share with you my beautiful language, but also because non-English speaking people have been able to share is memorable evening with us. Good luck, fellow classmates and God bless you until we meet again.

Adios y muchos gracias.

How could anyone have addressed her responsibility more accurately and beautifully? I was proud to be the head of an institution that could produce such a graduate.

CHAPTER FIFTEEN - DEANS 1964-1979
It Will Take Two Men to Replace Her"

Edna Dyk was an English teacher who voluntarily became an assistant principal charged with attendance and the relatively minor disciplinary problems that exist in every high school. She and the reliable Betty Veeder were all but indispensable during the first four years of my principalship. Edna was an attractive, graceful and empathic person by nature but forceful enough to be most effective carrying out her responsibilities in dealing with both students and parents in a demanding job. I admired and greatly appreciated her effective assistance.

Edna's only weakness, as I perceived it, was an abiding faith in the honesty of parents. From my experience in the real world, I knew that all human beings will lie under certain circumstances. In the school situation I learned early that parents will avoid the truth by lying or distorting the truth about many things. For example, mothers who consider themselves to be honest will say a student is sick when in fact a shopping trip to Chicago or Grand Rapids is planned. Thresholds will vary and many humans do hold themselves to high standards of honesty, but in the long run, whether the individual is threatened with death, the failure of a child, the revelation of an unsavory situation within the family, or other such circumstance, all parents will lie. It just depends on the degree of pressure the parent feels to do so.

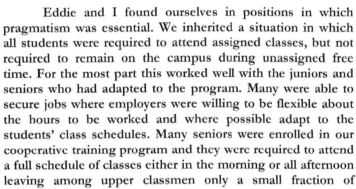

Eddie and I found ourselves in positions in which pragmatism was essential. We inherited a situation in which all students were required to attend assigned classes, but not required to remain on the campus during unassigned free time. For the most part this worked well with the juniors and seniors who had adapted to the program. Many were able to secure jobs where employers were willing to be flexible about the hours to be worked and where possible adapt to the students' class schedules. Many seniors were enrolled in our cooperative training program and they were required to attend a full schedule of classes either in the morning or all afternoon leaving among upper classmen only a small fraction of students who might not be able to use their time responsibly either on or off the campus. We could schedule them into instruction in personal discipline (IPD), which we established for the purpose of coping with this problem.

That of course left the sophomores who were in the majority of cases prohibited from employment by the child labor laws as they had not attained the magical age of seventeen. It was our observation that sixteen year olds were often unable to use their time on campus profitably, or went downtown during their free periods, skipped classes and otherwise managed, unintentionally, to convince some adult members of the community that the entire philosophy of the school was wrong. We felt it necessary to take action to stop unacceptable behaviors by assigning these young students to IPD a class in which they received counseling from a teacher who could persuade the offenders to accept a more disciplined approach to their high school careers.

On occasion Eddie would refer a disciplinary case to me, and sometimes these turned out to be joint ventures in which we tackled the problem with the student together. We were striving, one day, to persuade a student to see the error of his ways, and, it was hoped, convince him to improve his behavior. In retrospect, it's easy to understand he might see our performance as another good guy; bad guy scenario. After a fairly large dose of the Dean and me lecturing him, the student gave his response, *What is this, stereo?*

The dean, as I called her professionally, also was of the old school in many of her ways and perceptions, although she struggled successfully with the concept of freedom with responsibility. Student dress was a problem for her in that she perceived proper dress for female students to be dresses and for the males something more dressy than dungarees or blue jeans. This was fine as long as the style for women called for dresses at or below the knees, and Edna insisted, *No shorts and no culottes* for our students. Suddenly the style changed and women of all ages were wearing dresses with hemlines, it seemed to me, that were about at the hips and far more revealing than any culottes

Parents understandably perceived culottes and even shorts as being far more seemly than the short-short dresses prescribed by style authorities of Paris and New York. Somewhat to my amusement, the dean stood her ground, trying to enforce her self-imposed restriction against culottes and dungarees, until finally she recognized that styles are dictated from sources elsewhere than Holland High School. These matters were emphasized by the fact that mothers visiting the school on behalf of their children were often wearing culottes, accompanied in many cases by husbands wearing bell-bottomed blue jeans or cut-offs. The rules changed.

By the end of my first two years as principal I had concluded that the load we were carrying in administering the growing program of this comprehensive high school was greater than two people could handle effectively. This led me to recommend to Superintendent Ihrman the hiring of an assistant principal to be designated for supervision of the day-to-day functions of the school under my direction. Given the ever-present financial condition of the district, my recommendation went no further than occasional mention of the need by members of the board of education.

Two years after my recommendation, Mrs. Dyk, worn out in the job, threw up her hands and resigned from the staff, both teaching and administration. My efforts to persuade her to change her mind were to no avail. With that development, the board of education authorized the hiring of two assistant principals, the board having concluded that two men were now needed to fill the position Mrs. Dyk had been carrying on her own for four years.

The staff was scanned for candidates to fill the open positions, but those with the personality and experience to qualify declined to apply. Their decisions, I'm sure, were based on observations of how demanding the jobs could be. I then sought applicants among attendees at the annual meeting of the North Central Association of Colleges and Secondary Schools, meeting in Chicago. Two of the young men who came forward, and applied for the jobs, Richard Giordano and Dennis Shufelt impressed me favorably enough that I recommended them for the positions. The two were interviewed separately for the jobs, Shufelt for operations and Giordano for the position of dean.

I was half right in my perception of these two young men. Dick Giordano, although inexperienced, fit readily into the fabric of Holland High School and its philosophy of education, growing in his position in a generally professional manner. Dennis Shufelt, on the other hand, was less amenable to cooperation, and went his own way on many occasions, often in conflict with my wishes and intentions and those of the superintendent and board of education. This led to a situation that could be resolved only by his departure or mine, the resolution of which came at my insistence.

Dick became increasingly adept at handling the routine of his office, many dealing with attendance and some involving more serious disciplinary problems. There were two incidents involving student discipline that remain in my memory. In the first, Dick had asked the mother of one of our recalcitrant male students to join him in his office for a discussion of the latest offense. Joe De Feyter* lived up to his mnemonic name as a fighter and offended in many other asocial ways. His mother was a single parent doing her economic best to raise the rebellious son while holding down two modest jobs. Mrs. De Feyter sat in the dean's office while Dick reviewed the behavioral problems of her son.

Finally the son, waiting outside of Dick's office, was asked to enter the office and have a seat. The scene reminded me of the one in Jock Riemersma's office many years before when I was on the hot seat of the student. Dick began the little sermon he had rehearsed in his mind so carefully before confronting the young man with it, *Joe, it's not my purpose here today to harass.....*

Not allowing another word to come out of the Dean's mouth, Joe interrupted with, *Look Gio,* (purposely omitting the customary "Mr.) *It ain't gonna be her ass an' it ain't gonna be my ass. It's gonna to be your ass if you don't stop this discipline shit."*

In the second incident, Dick, having exhausted himself in entreaties for better behavior, brought the young offender to my office, where upon entering, the student asked, *What is this, team teaching, or is it the good guy/bad guy act like we see on TV?*

As Dick continued to develop maturity and experience his reputation in educational circles increased commensurately, and he began to receive feelers from other school districts needing administrative talent. In mid-year, January 1977, he was offered a position as principal of a small high school in Hartford, a district in the southern part of Michigan where the principal had left hurriedly, for reasons I don't recall.

In September, after serving as principal of his new high school for one semester, he wrote me a gracious letter of appreciation that included the following:

I can say I am enjoying the experience of being the principal thus far. The students here are not quite as sophisticated as Holland students are, but they are not much different in other respects; kids are kids!

I have had excellent training as an assistant principal under your guidance at Holland High School, and have come to realize this more and more every day. Many of the issues that are unresolved problems here were confronted and resolved under your supervision during my experiences in Holland. This gives me a distinct "edge" and people here have come to believe that I have all the answers. In fact, it's just that I have been through these situations in the past.

When you open school on Tuesday, I would appreciate it if this letter could be read to the H.H.S. staff as from me to express my regards and thanks to them and to you. I was pleased to do so.

Dick and I exchanged occasional notes, but I knew of his activities mostly through teachers who remained in more regular communication with him. After a few years he accepted a position as principal of Durango High School in Colorado and I heard nothing from him for several years. Three years after I retired, I received the following: *Dear Fred,*

As you might expect, my current position carries with it (responsibility for) the level one response to all grievances. I expect that you well recall your bouts with the omnipresent Mr. Roger Plagenhoef. You will be unsurprised to know that there are 'Plagenhoefs' in all parts of the country. Their names may vary and their faces are certainly different, but their purpose remains constant, i.e. to file ridiculous grievances.

I have enclosed a copy of such material with the thought that you might like to rejoin the battle, if only from your arm chair overlooking the lake. My main purpose in enclosing the grievance material is to again let you know that I remain indebted to you for the training you provided which allows me to perform my job today in Durango, Colorado. While I am sure that my writing talents will still be subject to your critical eye, I want you to know that your criticisms have been invaluable to me. I continue to appreciate your prominence in my career on a daily basis." The remainder of the letter consists of observations about the Durango area not related to education.

Teacher absences were not usually a large problem in the Holland schools as there existed in the community a number of retired or otherwise well qualified teachers who were willing to substitute and who could, with proper notice fill in for those who became ill overnight. To provide for this contingency the high school staff was directed to call me before six-thirty a.m. if they were going to be absent, in order that I might call Mrs. Gould, the superintendent's secretary, who would arrange for substitutes if possible. This made it advisable that the clock radio at the head of the bed be set for six o'clock, the time when WHTC, the local radio station began its daily broadcasts with the national anthem followed by an advertisement for R. E. Barber, the local Ford franchise.

The ad followed a fairly standard format in which two of the company's salesmen,
Joe Den Tassel* and Pete Van Dam* would alternate in giving portions of the daily sales pitch winding up with an invitation to visit the agency's showroom.

One morning following the *Star Spangled Banner,* the two presented the following ad reproduced here to the best of my memory:
This is Joe Den Tassel down here at R.E. Barber Ford with the best auto deal of the day;
And this is Pete Van Dam. Today we have a beautiful Ford Victoria, six passenger with a powerful V-8 engine and power steering;
Joe came in and said, *And yes, it does have white wall tires and FM radio;*
Pete followed with, *Grab your title and come on down to R. E. Barber Ford. Bring your wife with you and we'll dicker.*

That was the first and only time that recording was aired, but enough people heard it that it was a conversation piece in the community for days after the broadcast as those who had heard the ad related the story to their friends and neighbors.

I had never met the two errant broadcasters previously, but fifteen years later I met them in a social setting and we were introduced by a third party. I would not have been able to recognize them unless they were introduced or identified by name, but somehow their names remained in my memory. When the first of these car salesmen was introduced there was instant name recognition on my part and I blurted out *Are you kidding me?* and then *Are you one of the guys who uttered those great lines for R. E. Barber Ford?*

And he said *Oh dammit! Not again! Can't we ever live that down?*

CHAPTER SIXTEEN MACATAWA BAY YACHT CLUB II
COMMODORE (1963-'65

One of the considerations involved in my appointment as principal of the high school was the fact that I was the vice commodore of the Macatawa Bay Yacht Club, and scheduled, by succession, to become the commodore in 1965. I felt honored to be in this position and was anxious to undertake the responsibility.

In previous years the clubhouse had been enlarged, and a beautiful new stone fireplace added to the bar area. In 1963, when I was the rear commodore and Leonard "Bud" Verdier was the commodore, we had just celebrated the opening of a swimming pool on the club property. Bonds were sold to cover the cost of the pool, and members who bought bonds were shortly thereafter encouraged to contribute the bonds to the club rather than receive the funds at maturity. Most of us followed this request.

A celebration of these developments and in celebration of the Fourth of July an extensive fireworks display was planned to be launched from a barge moored at the lakeside of the club. As darkness fell following a beautiful dinner in the clubhouse, four past commodores who had cheerfully volunteered to fire the display, manned the barge. All were veterans of several end of season rendezvous celebrations of the past, when heavy duty fireworks, mostly block busters, were fired on the narrow streets between cottages in the hills of Macatawa Park until in due course sheriff's deputies arrived at the request of fellow cottagers. The fireworks display deployed from the barge was far more colorful than those in the hills, and spectators declared them *the most beautiful seen in these parts for years.*

I recall standing at the bar afterward and exclaiming about the magnificent event and its significance in the history of the Macatawa Bay Yacht Club. Unbeknownst to me, apparently impressed by the potential danger to the club from a demonstration such as had just been completed, and cognizant of the fact that the club, with its recent renovations, was grossly uninsured, two members collaborated and despite the hour called a local insurance provider from the bar and arranged a binder to increase the club's fire insurance by fifty thousand dollars.

We all went home after that eventful day of racing, eating, partying and enjoying the fireworks. The club was secured for the night by the staff sometime after midnight. For Past Commodore Beach Gill, one of those who sponsored me as a candidate for rear commodore, summer home was his motor yacht *Wanderer*, in the first slip west of the club house. Beach was profoundly deaf in one ear, and when he retired to *Wanderer* that night he lay down on his good ear. Our house was about five miles from the club in a direct line, and I vaguely sensed the howl of sirens, but I knew nothing about the compete destruction of the club by fire until the next morning, when a member called to insure I knew the news. Lory and I jumped into the Lyman and raced to the scene, a smoldering pile of ashes. As we arrived, Beach Gill was just climbing out of *Wanderer* and seeing the devastation for the first time. He had slept on his good ear and heard nothing of the noise and clamor of four fire departments wetting down the ruins. There was no significant damage to the yachts and motor boats in slips attached to the club. The only significant remaining part of the clubhouse was the recently built brick fireplace. It was toppled shortly hereafter in preparation for rebuilding.

This event left the new swimming pool and its relatively small dressing rooms as the only significant structure on the site. However, the social committee, of which Lory was a part, began immediately to plan social events centered around the pool, while several of the traditional parties such as the commodore's ball were held in one

of the huge winter boat storage sheds, kindly contributed temporarily for this use by the Eldean brothers, who had purchased the former Jesiek Brothers Shipyard.

As a result of the foresight of two of our members in binding additional insurance, construction funds were immediately available to produce a structure far more spacious and practical than the former railroad depot that had served so well. Design and construction proceeded forthwith and the new clubhouse was completed in just eleven months.

Holland Sentinel Photo

In June, 1964 the new facility was commissioned in an impressive ceremony in which I, as the vice commodore played a significant part. A few feet toward the lake from the clubhouse stood a grand flag pole, a gift from Past Commodore Beach Gill in honor of his late wife. In addition to the staff for the national colors, and the club's burgee at the head of the pole, there was a yard arm accommodating six halyards. Although not exactly in accordance with flag etiquette, on this occasion the halyards flew the personal flags of the club's flag officers and those of several past commodores.

Following he completion of the new clubhouse, the commodores' ball that year was a particularly festive affair, with membership generally congratulating itself for a successful recovery. Naturally, there was much continuing speculation regarding the origin of the fire. Was it started from the fireworks display? Had the help overlooked a smoldering cigar or cigarette? Was the club subject to the ire of some disgruntled neighbor? Rumors seemed to flow from every mouth, but in the end the fire marshal determined that the cause of the fire was a short in some of the ancient wiring in the old part of the building that had outlived its earlier existence as the interurban terminal and subsequently moved to the Macatawa Bay site where it served for many years until its destruction.

The club had its share of off-beat characters, several of whom were past commodores. Most notable of these was Bill Lowry, a prominent Holland and Grand Rapids furniture manufacturer, whose exploits could fill several volumes. In one case, returning to Macatawa Bay in his high powered Chris Craft speedboat from an evening of celebrating in Saugatuck, the next harbor to the south, whether from haze of weather or alcohol, he misjudged his position and drove the boat at high speed onto the outer breakwater where the boat, although damaged, rested on an even keel. The outer breakwater was long known in club circles as Lowry's Reef.

Lowry detested pompous airs and sometimes attributed this characteristic to people unfairly. One such case came about when an eminent World War II admiral, Jerry Bogan was invited to join the crew of a Macatawa Bay yacht entered in the Chicago-Mackinac race. The admiral joined the crew for lunch at the Chicago Yacht Club, and was introduced to each crew member in turn as Admiral Bogan, with repeated emphasis on the word Admiral. Lowry attributed this emphasis to pompousness.

After the start of the race Lowry uncharacteristically volunteered to aid in serving lunch to the rest of the crew and catered particularly to the admiral. Addressing the admiral from the hatchway, he said *Admiral we're having hot dogs for lunch. How would you like yours?* The admiral replied *Yes, with mustard, a bit of relish and a beer.*

Shortly thereafter Lowry reappeared in the hatch and handed the admiral his lunch, accepted a few words of appreciation, and then waited for the senior officer's reaction, which came emphatically when the admiral took his first bite. Lowry had substituted a rubber hot dog for the real thing.

CHAPTER SEVENTEEN - LANDLORD
"Beneath All Lies the Land"

Although immersed in our educational commitments, our overall investment objective remained constant. We wanted to convert the capital represented by Baywoodlands, and other pieces of real estate that had come our way through exchanges into more stable income producing properties. Our informal analysis told us that Holland needed some multi-family housing, as there was nothing of that nature in the city. The city's building code had scattered the zoning for multi-family housing to limited areas, with some attempt to recognize that the closest thing to apartments that existed were large houses remodeled to include one or two apartments on the second story, often with access often via stairs built on the outside of the house.

None of the houses we had taken in exchanges were located in areas zoned for multi-family use, so if we wanted to proceed, it appeared we had to purchase properties suitably zoned. I consulted on many occasions with the city's building inspector, who also served as the zoning administrator, seeking a way in which properties we already owned could be used for multi-family buildings. Although friendly, he repeatedly advised me that only the city council could make such a change, and they were not likely to make such a change to a zoning ordnance only recently adopted.

I talked to several serving members of the city council, and they advised me that in their view zoning changes were not necessary because the zoning ordinance already designated adequate areas for multi family housing, and we could meet our objective only by buying property already zoned for apartments.

With the assurance that rezoning would not be approved, we bought a piece of property on west Twentieth Street already zoned for multi-family use on which there was a tumbled down windowless building, filled with well rotted cow manure, that for many years had been used as a mushroom farm. Adjoining this property to the east, was a narrow brick building on a thirty-seven foot lot. When a "For Sale" sign appeared on it, we bought it on a land contract basis, seeking to preserve our capital for the major project. Another incentive for buying this building was that it was zoned for commercial use because of its status at the time of the passage of the new zoning ordinance. Its commercial status was preserved by its previous continuous commercial use and thus could be of value in the pursuit of our plans.

Returning to Holland from an educational meeting in Detroit, during a stop for gas, I spotted a group of buildings that appeared to be similar to what we had in mind for our apartments. They were two-story buildings, each containing eleven two bedroom apartments and one single bedroom unit on the lower level, with the remaining space there committed to utilities and coin laundry equipment for tenant use.

We made arrangements to procure the building plans and started the pre-construction process. For construction financing, we turned once again to Bob Den Herder and the friendly folks at the Zeeland Bank, which had now become the First Michigan National Bank. The bank would require a land survey and plot plan, an executed construction agreement as well as assurance that permanent take-out financing was available upon successful completion of the buildings. Also required was a city building permit, which was issued after some quibbling on the details of the plan. The required guarantee that permanent financing would succeed the construction financing was provided by the New York Life Assurance Company, from which organization I held a sizable amount of insurance still in force from my military flying days.

For the construction of the buildings themselves, we turned to reliable Russ Lamar, who had built our house some years before, and based on his estimates, we negotiated a fixed price contract with only limited adjustments for changing economic conditions and modifications to the original plans.

Satisfying these myriad details and more occupied many of our evenings and weekends for months. To some degree we concerned ourselves with seeking a person or persons who would live at the site and manage the apartments once they were built although we recognized that for us to be the on-site managers would be unfeasible.

We continued to get assurance from responsible city personnel that no rezoning of any properties not already zoned for apartments would be allowed. Accordingly, with this assurance we became increasingly committed financially. Almost immediately after we started actual construction, an apartment builder/speculator from out of town, appeared on the scene with a consort of assistants, a fancy slide projector and a set of plans for buildings not dissimilar to ours, together with a vague but convincing statement that over time he would be building fifty or sixty of the apartment buildings. This entourage somehow arranged to meet with the city council at a special meeting seeking rezoning of several properties to accommodate his plans. All this took us completely by surprise and naturally, given the history of our project, our long series of the negotiations with the city, the city's steadfast statements that they would not rezone properties for multi-family as long as there was property available that was already so zoned, we felt strongly we were being treated unfairly.

We attended the special meeting of the city council and aired our objections. They were noted, but in the end, the council approved the rezoning of several properties, all of which were under tentative purchase agreements held by the newcomer from out of town and subject to the necessary readings required by the zoning ordnance.

This "railroad job" continued and the properties selected by the man from out of town were rezoned. Our conclusion was that a fast talker from somewhere else was preferred over a local resident who had complied with all the red tape and requirements of the zoning ordinance.

*********   *********   *********

Action on the academic front continued unabated. I tried throughout my time as principal, to inject some humor into what could otherwise become tedious. An example is a memorandum I wrote and addressed to all staff:

Past experience has shown that much of the confusion experienced at the high school between teachers and administrators has emanated from poor communication between and among the respective parties. In an attempt to initiate and maintain clear communications at an optimum level, the administration here presents some of its more commonly used terminology. It is hoped that all staff members will devote careful study to this offering so that understanding will prevail in future conversations. The following phrases are among those to be used, together with their meaning in each case:

IT IS IN PROCESS ---- It's so wrapped up in red tape that the situation is almost hopeless.

WE WILL LOOK INTO IT ---- By the time the wheel makes a full turn we assume we both will have forgotten about it .

CONSULTANT ---- Any ordinary former school teacher with a briefcase who is more than fifty miles from home.

UNDER CONSIDERATION ---- We never heard of it.

UNDER ACTIVE CONSIDERATION ---- We're looking in the files for it.

REORIENTATION ---- Getting used to working again.

WE ARE MAKING A SURVEY ---- We need more time to think of an answer.

WE WILL ADVISE YOU IN DUE COURSE ---- If we figure it out, we'll let you know.

FORWARDED FOR YOUR CONSIDERATION ---- You hold the bag for awhile.

SEE ME ON THIS ONE ---- Come into the office; I'm lonesome, and I need someone to help me get my head back on straight.

LET'S DISCUSS ---- I don't understand this.

LET'S GET TOGETHER ON THIS ---- I assume you're as confused as I am."

CHAPTER EIGHTEEN-ROTARY I (1960 –
A Major Influence On My Life

After some years in the principal's chair, I was invited to speak to Rotary about my experiences as a high school principal. By this time I felt much more comfortable in my position than had been the case a few years earlier. In keeping with my general view that humor and comic relief are important to one choosing to lead a balanced life, I chose to address the humorous aspects of operating a high school for the most part omitting the more dreary and threatening parts of the job. Once again, my friend, Harvey Buter introduced me with a few flattering, if undeserved comments about my performance as principal.

My succinct introductory remarks identified my intention to speak of the amusing rather then the depressing aspects of the job. *It is a strong temptation to say, as others have relative to other situations, 'The events related here are true; only the names have been changed to protect the innocent.' However, my experiences as a principal have made me skeptical, indeed, as to whether there are any innocents; to me it appears there are only degrees of innocence, or lack thereof. All of what I say here this noon is true, but the names of the participants have been changed in most cases.*

I went on to retell the story of the co-operative training student who was fired from his cooperative training job for his adventures in driving a police cruiser on a post-maintenance test drive; the tale of the all "A" student carrying seven subjects who, with several other students aboard his vehicle, drove several times through the center approaches to a neighboring high school; I reviewed in detail the frustrating problems in organizing my first commencements. All of these subjects have been included in other chapters of this book, but one event, minor but important in my memory, occurred at the end of one of those first years. At that time, Holland Christian High School and we at Holland High used the civic center on consecutive nights for our commencements with theirs on Wednesday; ours on Thursday. The programs for both high schools were in a similar format, including the presentation of the colors and the playing of the national anthem by the band at the beginning of the ceremonies,

Our new band director decided that since Christian High had left the heavy bases used to place the colors when they were advanced at the beginning of the ceremonies, he would use them the next night rather than take the trouble to replace them with Holland's bases. Although we had always had the color guard walk through the ceremony during the commencement rehearsal, in this case we did not bother to have the color guard actually place the standards in their bases. When the colors were advanced that evening the staff on our national colors was too large for the Christian High base. As a result, the color guard had to hold the staff with his left hand, and salute with his right hand throughout the recitation of the pledge of allegiance and through the singing of the national anthem. Fortunately, at the conclusion of the national anthem he had sufficient presence of mind to remove the flag from the stage and remove himself from the premises, as the bearer of the state flag did likewise.

Excerpts from my speech: *In the first year of my principalship, I found that we have a copious supply of people in this town who have vocabularies that would make a boatswain's mate blush, and also that the high school principal is one of the people upon whom these four letter functional terms are lavished on occasion by frustrated parents.*

On one such occasion early in my career a mother called and rained upon me a shower of such epithets, winding up her tirade with the statement, 'You don't know half of what goes on up there at that high school. By this time I had learned to keep my cool while under this kind of fire and after taking a deep breath I responded by saying, "Lady, if I knew one tenth of what goes on up here at this high school, I'd consider myself to be remarkably well informed, and now, if you will tell me what your problem is, I will attempt to take care of it.' She even laughed a little at my response. Her problem turned out to be trivial, and I did take care of it.

Teaching staff often provide amusing sidelights to the day's activities. A veteran, highly structured lady teacher used Time magazine as a text for her course in current events. She collected the subscription money from the students at the beginning of the semester and then submitted a group educational subscription at a price heavily discounted by the publisher. When the magazines arrived for the first time, her name was spelled L-A-M-P-O-N, rather thean the correct L-A-M-P-E-N. I thought it a wonder they didn't spell it L-A-M-P-O-O-N! She immediately and indignantly fired off a letter to the magazine to correct what in her view was this serious misspelling. The only problem then was that in her letter the word MISSPELLED was spelled M-I-S-P-E-L-E-D." In my talk to Rotary I added the parenthetical comment, *You have to be able to spell to understand that one."*

Lory, a long time elementary teacher says *On the first day of school, send a note home to all parents saying, "If you promise not to believe everything your child says happens in school, I'll promise not to believe everything he says happens at home"*

I concluded my talk with, *All in all, I would like to end with the observation that by and large, the high school principalship consists, in part at least, of conducting oneself in institutional administration in such a way that when the inevitable disaster occurs, one can find himself in a posture which gives the impression he is leading a parade rather than being run our of town.*

"And now a word to the representatives of the media: If you are going to publish anything about my remarks, I would plead with you to couch your account of these proceedings in the most general terms

Thank you very much" The applause was both gratifying and reassuring.

CHAPTER NINETEEN--
CONFRONTATION
"Laying Down the Gauntlet"

In contrast with Dick Giordano's increasingly competent and cooperative performance, growing with the task, my young assistant for operations seemed at times to deliberately insert his will, even when it diverged from mine or that of other higher authority and his will was often destructive of good order. After months of deliberation on the subject, I determined in my mind that Dennis was more destructive than constructive of our school program, and would have to go, or in any event, one of us would have to go.

I wrote a letter to the superintendent in early March recommending that "for cause" the employment of Dennis Shufelt as an assistant principal be terminated. Mr. Ihrman requested that I amplify my reasons for this action, and I replied in a letter dated March 12, 1973, essentially outlining the reasons for my loss of confidence in the assistant principal and my recommendation that his employment in that position be terminated. My letter is quoted below in its entirety:

Dear Mr. Ihrman:

You have asked that I expand on my letter of March 6, 1973, outlining more specifically the reasons why I recommend that Mr. Dennis Shufelt not be continued as an assistant principal of Holland High School beyond the expiration of his present contract.

Among these reasons are the following:

(1) Lack of Loyalty. Over the period that Mr. Shufelt has been employed in this district he has repeatedly and openly criticized me, the superintendent, other colleagues, the Holland School System and the Board of Education in circumstances that I consider to be inappropriate. Examples:

> *(a) He has openly suggested that I seek Mr. Ihrman's removal in order that I might fill the position; likewise he has been highly critical of Mr. Ihrman in the presence of subordinates (teachers);*

> *(b) He has repeatedly criticized the organization of the Board of Education;*

> *(c) He has discussed my shortcomings as he envisions and interprets*

> *(d) On the occasion of a North Central Association visit to a Grand Rapids area high school last year, by the account of the visiting team chairman, Brian Callaghan, Principal of Grandville High School, he was so "acid tongued concerning the nature and function of the North Central visit, the ineffectiveness and*

indolence of his principal, the lack of quality of performance of the Holland Public Schools in general, that the chairman called the state chairman of the NCA (Dr, G. Sutherland Hayden) to request that Mr. Shufelt not be assigned to a North Central Evaluation Team again. He also advised me of this action. Mr. Shufelt has denied that his comments over the period of the three-day visit were of the acidulous nature alleged, but others who were present have affirmed to me without prompting that they considered them to be inappropriate and disloyal.

(2) _Indiscretion._ Closely related to (1) above is the fact that I have found that Mr. Shufelt lacks understanding of what are appropriate topics of discussion and what are appropriate actions in many circumstances. Example:

(a) At a recent teacher meeting, after I had indicated to the staff why, in my opinion, I could not take a certain action under the membership rules of the State Board of Education, he asserted loudly that he believed he could devise a way to take the action without being detected by the State Board of Education;

(b) He frequently voices opinions in public or with staff that, in my opinion, are harmful to the orderly educational process;

(c) A frequent, and to me particularly obnoxious indiscretion, is for him to express disdain for the desires of the electorate, stating that their opinions are of little account to him, since he is "nothing but a paid mercenary" in education;

(d) He not infrequently makes comments to or about female members of our staff, which, in my opinion, are inappropriate or repugnant.

(3) _Disobedience._ In an example of direct disobedience this year, I assigned Mr. Shufelt a project to complete. Since the project included a policy matter, and since I had been having difficulty in getting him to do things in accordance with my direction, I was explicit in respect to how the job was to be approached _and_

(a) That I wanted to review his completed work in the rough;

(b) That when the work was prepared for submittal to the superintendent, I would sign it as principal;

(c) I established a deadline for the completion of the work

"As the time for completion approached, I reviewed with him several times the three points outlined above. Later, he requested an extension of time, which I granted, and reminded him of my requirements (a) and (b). On the morning of the extended due date I reminded him again of the matter and laid particular emphasis on points (a) and (b).

He acknowledged what I was saying on each occasion. When that afternoon he presented the completed project, it had:
> *(a) Been typed in the smooth and*

> *(b) Been signed by him.*

> *(c) Indirectly, he disobeys (or is purposely ineffective) by the simple expedient of failing to do the job; failing to do it in the way in which I would expect it to be done; or neglecting to do it at all.*

(4) <u>Deviousness</u>. Mr. Shufelt has used a considerable amount of school time in attempting to woo a group of staff loyal to him as a person and his concepts of how things should be. This activity has contributed to divisiveness rather than unity of staff.

As a recent (to me) validation of this characteristic, Mr. Shufelt has spent a very considerable amount of time since receiving a copy of my letter of March 6, in contacting staff members to sound them out on their positions on a matter which, although it affects all staff, is beyond their jurisdiction. His activities are imprudent and insubordinate.

(5) <u>Lack of Tact.</u> If tact is "a nice discernment of what is appropriate to do or say in dealing with others," and particularly that "ability to deal with others without giving offense", Mr. Shufelt falls far short of that ideal. While we have consulted frequently over the past three and one-half years on this subject, and he has made some improvement, he continues to be brusque with students and staff.

Lest the above be interpreted as outright defamation of Mr. Shufelt, I wish to add the following: He is an intelligent young man;

> *(1)He has many good thoughts on education;*
> *(2) He is aggressive (sometimes too much so);*
> *(3) He has great desire to do well for boys and girls.*

It is possible that he would do well in another school situation elsewhere, and he has indicated during each of the last three years by the end of the first semester that he was planning to leave either to:

> *(1)Accept a job as principal;*
> *(2)Complete work on his PhD., or*
> *(3) Enter theological seminary.*

This approach has tended to minimize his effectiveness during the second semester of each year until such time as it becomes clear that he is not leaving.

In summary, analysis of the matters discussed above has eroded my confidence in Mr. Shufelt to the degree that I recommend he not be placed under contract for the school year 1973-74.

> "Very truly yours,
> Fred S. Bertsch, Jr.
> Principal"

This letter quite clearly laid down the gauntlet. One of us was going to have to leave the employ of the school district.

I recognized that others were involved in the matter, particularly several staff members assigned to the west academic unit. I also realized that Dick Giordano might be affected by virtue of his position in the administration and some of his relationships with west unit teachers. I invited Dick into my office for a discussion of the overall scene, and I then advised him to confine his activities strictly to his assigned functions until the matter was settled, to stay away from the teachers lounge of the west unit and remove himself, insofar as possible, from contact with Dennis. I'm sure I said something in summary like, "Dick, stay out of the line of fire."

A special meeting of the school board was called to consider the matter, and Dennis and I found ourselves seated next to each other outside the board room waiting to be called in for whatever was required of us. We greeted each other cordially, and made a bit of small talk before Dennis was summoned. His period with the board was brief, perhaps five minutes. When I was called in the board asked me to verify what I had written and asked for additional details in connection with several of the issues I had with Dennis. My recommendation was accepted.

I effectively limited Dennis to his office for the remainder of the semester, asking him only to perform a few perfunctory duties, primarily in connection with the year's commencement activities. On the day his contract expired he departed abruptly, and I thought I would never see him again.

I was wrong. Three years later he reappeared in my office, ebullient as ever, and introduced himself as "The Reverend Mr. Shufelt," having received his ThD degree from a Baptist seminary in the south. We displayed no rancor. He requested permission to visit the West Unit, where his plotting and acid tongue had initiated so many problems. I thought it best to accompany him on his visit, at the end of which he departed, never to be seen again in the Holland area as far as I know.

The vacancy left by the Shufelt departure was once again put forward within the school district to attract any talent that might be appropriate for the challenging position of assistant principal for operations The only staff member to apply for the job was David Lightfoot, a teacher of English and husband of our teacher of Home Economics and Restaurant Management, Janet Lightfoot. Following an initial interview with me, he was interviewed by the superintendent and a special committee of the board of education. All deemed him well qualified, and he was appointed to the position.

David was intelligent, competent, energetic, cooperative and ambitious. He appeared to be everything I could wish for in an assistant principal, except for, perhaps, a desire to remain in that position. He had originally been hired as a teacher with the understanding that his wife, Janet, would fill an existing vacancy in the Home Economics/Restaurant Management position. It seemed at the time to be a perfect and stabilizing fit that would ensure that both would remain on the staff.

Dave entered his new job with enthusiasm and adapted readily to his new surroundings and responsibilities. I was pleased with how readily he fit into our management team and how well he exerted his influence in a professional way in marked contrast with the brusque "know it all" manner of his predecessor. He presented a calming atmosphere to the entire staff

In an effort to assist in healing any continuing hurts left over from "L'affaire Schufelt", just before Christmas vacation in 1974, I wrote another staff missile to be signed by me and both assistant principals:

> *"As you leave for a well-deserved holiday period, we want to thank you for all for the things you are doing to help young men and women, our students; your high order of professionalism and your willingness to do the "extra" things without which educational programs cannot be successful. Through the cooperative efforts of all, we are having a good school year at Holland High School, and we want you all tom know that the fine things you do are sincerely appreciated.*

> *"It is also appropriate at the Christmas season for us all to enter into a bit of personal reexamination and evaluation. Is each of us the person he or she wishes to be? Are our professional attitudes and performances what they should be? Are we working effectively with each other in a joint effort to produce the best possible program that we can for the students of Holland High? We can all benefit by devoting some of our Christmas thinking and and perhaps some of our New Year resolutions to such appraisal.*

> *"Whatever your activities over the next two weeks, have a good vacation and come back refreshed and ready to cope with the "long pull" until spring vacation. Merry Christmas and a Happy New Year!!*

> > *"The Triumvirate,*
> > *Fritz,*
> > > *Dick &*
> > > > *Dave"*

David was doing a good job in his first year and was effective with both students and parents. Where he perceived serious problems in communications with a student's home, he occasionally would take the time to make a call on the parents, even though this was not an efficient use of time in most cases. In the spring of his first year on the job, after consulting with the student's special education teacher, he decided it was desirable to make a visit to the home Jerry Box*. Jerry and his family had moved to Holland from their previous surroundings in the hills of Kentucky.

David was confronted shortly after he knocked on the door by a bearded and toothless senior citizen who invited the new arrival to join him in a disheveled living room, where the old man began immediately to expound on the value of schooling. After an extended build up regarding his educational experiences, which terminated after four consecutive years in the fifth grade, he described with some pride his final experience in school.

The highlight of this final year of education, David learned, was Mr. Box's participation in as spelling contest, which he described as a spelldown. *I was supposed to be the ninth in line at that spelldown, an' I wuz sposed to spell a particallar word that I had practiced time after time getting' ready fer the spelldown. But win the whole thing come off, a feller afore me missed a word, an' I got a differnt word and was spelled down.*

David was intrigued by the story and asked the old man to identify the word. Finally the old geezer commented, *My hearing never was much good. The word was ship, but I thought it was something closer to home than that , havin' to do with a outhouse an' when I spelt it, they threw me out of the spelldown. That was about the last of my schoolin.'*

The school year 1973-74 had taken a great deal out of me, but I evidently carried things off to the satisfaction of most of the staff. A note card from Natalie Bosman, teacher of French and English, written at the end of the school year was uplifting:

Dear Fritz,

I daily marvel at the way you hold things together. It is always more apparent at the end of the school year When fatigue and temper are our constant companions!

This has been a difficult year for some people who have voiced numerous dissatisfactions, but I commend you on looking at the humorous side of things and rolling with it.

In my opinion yyou do an outstanding job of knowing "what's what" at the right time, and I enjoy working for and with you. Sincerely, Nat.

Expressions of this kind made it possible for me to stay the course.

Some time in the fall of 1974, after all of the events of the past year, I was looking forward to a more tranquil school year. Class assignments for students had been completed, although as usual not to everyone's satisfaction, whether teacher or student. Class sizes had been leveled to the best of our abilities. I was seated at my desk pursuing routine administrative matters when in an unprecedented event a woman whom I identified as a teacher suddenly pushed open the door between my office and the home economics room with a violence that was completely out of character for this person who, at least in my perception, was a quiet, mild mannered teacher. I was seated at my desk at the time she entered, and when I rose to greet her she burst into tears, sobbing and falling into my arms with a declaration between *kill him.* I did my best to console her without a great deal of success.

Toward the end of the school year in 1976, my friend and colleague, John Noe, who had served as principal of E.E. Fell Junior High School for many years resigned his position and requested reassignment to the senior high school as a teacher. This provided David with an opportunity to advance a level in his educational career; all considered the exchange to be appropriate and he was appointed to the position.

Alice Beukema

The vacancy left by David's reassignment was posted throughout the district in a memorandum requesting interested and qualified staff to contact the director of personnel, but there were no applicants. After a talent search and numerous interviews a young man named Jerry Burg was hired and served capably as assistant principal during my final years as principal. Alice Beukema, the popular teacher of psychology served as dean for a time, and then became the principal for a year following my retirement at the end of which she elected to return to the classroom.

After two years at Fell, David was offered and accepted the position of Superintendent of Schools in Ravenna, a small town east of Muskegon. Janet refused to move, leaving her tenured position in Holland, and divorce became inevitable. With that development, David dropped off my radar screen and reappeared only as I was writing this narrative and after I had exerted some considerable effort to contact him. With Janet's help I was successful.

Baywoodlands, the subdivision we developed, was populated by a diverse group of people much as was the potluck group to which we already belonged. The potluck gatherings of the neighbors in Baywoodlands came into existence in a very different way. We, as the proprietors of the subdivision were interested in promoting the way of life that our development represented and we attempted to insure that all residents knew each other and gave support to common interests. One step that promoted common interest was to include in the subdivision design exclusive access to the waters of Lake Macatawa's Pine Creek Bay and to encourage use of this access by the residents. Another was for us as the developers to encourage good relationships and friendships among the residents.

Shortly after several families were established in their new Baywoodlands homes, we invited all of them to dinner. The few pieces of living room furniture we owned consisted of an odd grouping of aging things from our California house. We had consigned these items to the recreation room on the lower level as they would be dwarfed and entirely inadequate in our new and comparatively large living room where there was no furniture at all pending a time when our finances would permit the purchase of appropriate furnishings.

Our guests were served a home cooked dinner at which the adults were served on a table consisting of an unhinged door resting on two saw horses and were seated on folding chairs we had borrowed from our Beechwood Church. The children were served in the breakfast nook off the kitchen, where there was a built in bench at the end of the cherry table I had glued up from the scrap left over after the paneling was installed throughout the living and recreation rooms.

Either in reciprocation or simply an act of neighborliness Jim and Tommy Lou Mooi invited this group for a potluck dinner and a rotation among the residents began. In summer month some of these gatherings were held on the private lake access and swimming and boating became a part of the pre-dinner entertainment.

CHAPTER TWENTY - INCIDENTS ALONG THE WAY
El Gordo

There was another "cherries jubilee" tale in which a new teacher of public speaking allowed a student to smoke up her classroom with a demonstration speech describing the preparation of cherries jubilee, thus violating in a single incident, (1) common sense, (2) the fire regulations and (3) the school rule prohibiting alcoholic beverages on campus. As I had created a similar incident in a pot luck dinner situation a few years earlier, I was hardly in a position to be unduly severe in my reprimand of a young teacher who used poor judgment. I was also reminded that in a similar incident when as a student I had given a talk on how to field strip a sidearm, and was sent to the principal's office for having carried a gun to school.

The integration of the increasing number of Latinos into the local culture caused difficulties of understanding in both groups. A number of the male students from Spanish speaking families were named Jesus, pronounced "Haysoos." To the Latinos, this appellation was intended to honor the deity of Christ while to much of the Holland population this was a sacrilege, and many teachers insisted on calling students with that name "Jessie." This represented only one of many language oriented conflicts that in many case discouraged Latinos to a degree that they dropped out of school.

My late wife, Lory, taught at Washington elementary school, and told this story:

It seems incredible, but an overweight student arrived one year in a Washington school fifth grade classroom with the appellation, used by his fellow students, "El Gordo," or just "Gordo." The teacher recognized it as a nickname, but as she knew no Spanish, she didn't know the nickname meant "the fat one" or essentially "fatso." She continued calling the boy Gordo until he finally broke down in tears and told her he preferred his real name, Henriche.

Sometimes students were identified with several different families. On one occasion a student formerly classified as a ninth grader was sent to the high school as a sophomore, but she indicated to me she didn't know why. She was a most attractive and polite young lady. The record that accompanied her was titled, "Rosa Gonzales", but she claimed that was not the correct name. I started our interview with the routine question, *What is your name, young lady?* She replied, *Rosa Fuentes.*

How old are you?

She replied, *Sixteen, Sir.*

I asked, *Do you live in the Holland School District?*

She said, *Yes sir*, and recited her address.

I asked, *Did you go to school last year, Rosa?*

She said, *Yes, Sir.*

I asked, *Where did you go to school?*

She said, *Jefferson School on Tenth Street, across from the college.* And then, after what seemed to me to be an extended pause, she continued, *Would it help if I told you my maiden name was Gonzales?* The truth will out, but I was not very perceptive in getting there.

The principal's office is inundated with mail, much of it of no interest at all after the first class mail has been extracted, but included in the rest of the deluge are the journals of school administrators, some of which contained useful information, suggestions, descriptions of successful school programs. As one can surmise, these were not exactly humor magazines and thus not a barrel of laughs. Educators and educationists do have a jargon of their own, just as for other professions. My second wife, following Lory's death, is a nurse who often speaks in terms of tissue forceps, sponge sticks, curettes, trabeculectomies, PDR and q,3h. Of necessity I often stop her medical talk to inquire into meanings of technical terms.

One of the education journals that landed on my desk contained an exception to the usual dry prose of such publications. In a box on about page fifty-seven of such a journal and entirely independent of the content around it was the following:

The parent of a high school student received a message from the principal reading, "Our school's cross-graded, multi ethnic, individualized learning program is designed to enhance the concept of an open-ended learning experience with emphasis on a continuum of multi-ethnic, academically enriched learning using the previously identified intellectually gifted child as the agent or director of his own learning. Major emphasis is on cross-graded, multi-ethnic learning with the principal objective being to learn respect for the uniqueness of any given person."

One parent's response read, "I have a college degree, speak two foreign languages and four East Indian dialects, have been to a number of state and county fairs across the United States and a Tulip Time parade in Michigan. I consider myself reasonably well informed, but I don't have the foggiest idea of what you are talking about. Do You?"

Despite this example, I found that most educators working in the actual school environment wrote in simple, accurate prose rather than high blown phraseology.

To me it appeared that the majority of the dense prose came from university educationists well insulated from the problems facing those actually doing the job in the classroom.

On another occasion I received a call from the father of a former student, indicating that the alumnus would be returning to Holland sometime in the future. The son had unfortunately lost an eye in an industrial accident, and the father  wanted to know if his disability would qualify him for housing in Holland at a discount. I patiently explained that although the schools serve the community in a great number of ways, such as draft registration, the issuing of all permits for under age workers, the conducting all of the area's driver education, they are not responsible for providing housing in any event.

Lory and I attended many student extra-curricular activities, dances, parties and club activities. Here we are at a senior prom.

Each year Lory and I attended the ceremonies of the National Honor Society during which juniors who qualified were inducted. The effort to perform academically to the level required for membership was considered to be an incentive to achieve

Parents and other interested adults were invited to attend this important program, to be held in the open area of the west classroom unit, where the lights were dimmed as the ceremonies began. A speaker, generally a leading citizen of the community, offered inspiring remarks. At the end of the ceremony, I would present membership pins to the new inductees. A portion of the ceremony involved members of the society lighting candles representing the ideals of membership, namely character, scholarship, leadership and service. Selected senior members of the Society advanced in turn with tapers in hand to light the candles, announcing one of the ideals, for example, *I light the candle of character.* On one such occasion the candle of character expired repeatedly, only to be relighted several times by succeeding participants until finally it continued to burn. Was there a message there?

Following the presentation of pins

Among the assorted papers and documents that survived in my collection for all these years is the program for the Society's Induction Ceremony dated May 9, 1971. Presiding over the affair was Jim Bradford, student president of the Holland Chapter. Each year, following the presentation of pins a reception provided an opportunity for parents, students and teachers to mingle. In the program below the outline of the ceremony is a list of members and those students to be inducted that evening, a list totaling forty-two students, with surnames beginning with most letters

of the alphabet ranging from Randy Alfieri to Kurt Zingle. I had a heart-wrenching moment as I noted the name of a niece, who took her own life a few years later by driving into a lake near the school where she was employed as a teacher. I wondered how many of those honor students are alive today and what they have accomplished.

Holland High had seemingly endless student activities, from athletic boosters and cheerleaders to language clubs and the various branches of student government, Many, if not most, held fund raising activities at various times to support their activities. I attended virtually all of these activities when invited, and was frequently asked to participate.. The picture at the left shows a part of the results of a custard pie throwing contest during which I was one of several volunteer faculty targets. Pie throwers were charged a small fee per pie and we targets had the satisfaction of knowing it was all for a good cause. The pies were more meringue than custard and were contributed by the students' mothers. We targets were at least allowed to retire to the field house locker rooms and change our clothes before the show and shower and don clean clothes after the pie throwing. Funny inexpensive prizes were awarded for accuracy, most effective shots and other perceived talents.

Pep rallies were a regular activity, particularly during the fall and winter basketball seasons. For the most part I didn't play an active role in theses. The cheerleaders, the coaches and the players were the normal participants. On one occasion I did bring back my old mentor, Prof Hanson to put on his razzle-dazzle performance as a cheerleader wearing a business suit as in the old high school,. The students loved it, but age had caught up with him and he could not be persuaded to do it again.

I don't remember who or what motivated me, other than to show our students that I, too, was human, but on one occasion before a most important game I was persuaded to don an outlandish wig, a borrowed cheerleader's uniform in every detail down to the patent leather boots. With pom-poms in hand I led the cheerleading performance in the field house.

Principal as Cheerleader

The field house was commodious, but never really finished during my principalship. The original design called for a foyer that would have provided facilities such that home games could be played there. The back doors opened directly onto a driveway, across which the clothes-less Tiger Teusink sped on a memorable evening when he   inadvertently locked himself out of the locker room and subsequently out of the field house, an event that is detailed in a later chapter.

Both my "In Basket" and "Out Basket" were constantly loaded with incoming and outgoing correspondence, together with a plenitude of teacher, student and parental requests, evaluation materials, requisitions, work requests and other documents involved in the operation of the school together with a deluge of professional papers, articles and brief commentaries.   Over the years of my principalship I became impressed by the consistency with which active educators wrote of the problems involved in educating *"all of the children of all of the people"*, a fine theoretical goal, but one that stressed educators in my time and does today as well.

The problems are easily identified and have been thousands of times in tens of thousands of educational treatises. At all levels prior to the college experience these problems include motivation, treatment of individual differences among both students and teachers, discipline, lack of parental involvement, lack of community interest, insensitivity of teachers, and the list goes on and on. I only wish I had a simple solution. Hard, consistent, dedicated work by all involved is the best suggestion I can make. Sniping from the sidelines is ineffective.

CHAPTER TWENTY ONE - ADVICE
"It's Not in My Job Description"

My notes don't reveal the background for one significant administrative foul-up on David's part, and memory fails me. Whatever it was, it required some communication on his part with the central office relative to the matter. David sought my counsel on how to respond to a letter from the superintendent requesting an explanation of his actions that could be presented to the board of education. By this point in my career as principal, judging from what I wrote to David, I was becoming increasingly frustrated and even cynical about my job. Fortunately I made a copy of my penciled sarcastic reply to my assistant's request for advice, written at home during a long sleepless night:

There are several alternatives for you in this situation. First of all, don't panic; much worse situations will follow should you pursue a career as a high school principal. The alternatives for you at present appear to be the following:

(a) Phone the superintendent, wherever he may be. Get and follow his advice. Get his hand on the "Tar Baby", and keep it there if possible;

(b) Since at the time you need his support, the superintendent is probably out of town, if you can't reach him wherever he is, pursue the same course of action with his sword-bearers, applying their hands to the "Tar Baby" as much as possible;

(c) Confer with your secretary; she may have some ideas, especially if she has been in her job longer than you have been the principal. She's seen it all before;

(d) Talk to the Director of Guidance, Pool Director and Director of Community Education and pool your joint ignorance— this is one of the better techniques available to you;

(e) Don't do a damned thing. Tell the board it didn't happen on your watch, you tried to counsel with the superintendent, but he was in Las Vegas;

(f) Discuss the matter with your wife and get her opinion. Her advice will lead you to one of two conclusions; either:
(1) You will believe you are married to Einstein's niece, or
(2) You will privately conclude you are married to the village idiot.

Now, if none of these techniques appears viable, it may be time to appoint a committee, one of the best obfuscating techniques in all of education. Since the problem you are facing is easy to define, but absolutely beyond solution, you are in a position to give all those noisy committee members a piece of the action. You can then write a charge to the committee that accurately defines the problem and gives the committee virtually total responsibility for arriving at an effective solution. This way, when the solution doesn't work, you can point to it and say, "They did it, and it doesn't work."

PROBLEM: In the meantime, the committee has been disbanded and the members have retired to the teachers' lounge where the individuals who comprised the committee have individually disavowed its actions.

SOLUTIONS: First line of defense is to blame the whole damned thing on your predecessor;

A possible second line of defense might be to file a grievance against the bastards! (Article VI, A, 1 of the contract _defines_ "grievance" as "A written claim of an alleged violation of a specific identified provision of this agreement.)

Since HEA members violate the specific provisions of the "agreement" in a ratio of about fifty to one to the violations by building administrators, it's time we started filing grievances under this provision. (Level One should be no problem, since the principal is the adjudicator --- beyond that there may be problems, but what the hell!)

The situation you are in is just plain "tough-titty"; you are the "bad guy" no matter what you do, so make your decision in each case to the best of your ability based on the best information available to you. Refer to the first paragraph of this missile, but anticipate that all central office personnel will attempt to waffle and blow smoke around the issue, at least until they can tell which way the wind is blowing. Following your decision, the following apply:

(a) Keep a tight sphincter;

(b) Keep a tight upper lip; no wavering now;

(c) Smile;

(d) Leave the campus for a time and smoke a big black cigar, or engage in some other more healthful but soothing activity;

(e) Forewarn your wife to prepare for a pleasant evening by:

(1) Placing a pitcher containing three double vodka martinis in the freezer;

(2) Sending the kids to the movies;

(3) Protecting the family pets by sending them to the kennel, and, finally

(4) Have her lady-in-waiting help her into the personal suit of armor that, hopefully, you have been sufficiently foresighted to purchase for her.

Occasionally the solution to a problem with a teacher may be to fire the S.O.B., but be sure to follow due process in doing so. If the teacher is on tenure, it may take upwards of twelve years, even though he/she/it may be the most flagrant incompetent since Icarus tried his sun shot. So, as your blood pressure recedes, remember the story of the young bull and the old bull. Since you are now the old bull, walk down and fornicate them all! In this particular instance, you have been screwed over once again, or, in more tender (and certainly more alliterative) language, you have been dicked by the dangling digit of destiny. Harry Truman put it approximately this way, "Make the best decision you can based on the information available. You will please about a third of the people, anger another third and astonish the rest."

At the risk of becoming repetitive, I offer the following:

1. Keep your cool;

2. Announce to your secretary you will be gone for an hour, and then do one or more of the following:
>   *a. Drive around , but be careful; don't take your frustrations out on any of the other drivers you might encounter;*

>   *b. Go to Kollen Park (a lakeside park in Holland) and either*

>>   *(1) Check on the growth rate of the lawn, or,*

>>   *(2) See if the waves are splashing water over the rip-rap rocks and onto the pavement;*

>   *c. Go to the Tulip City Airport and check on the landing patterns of local aircraft;*

>   *d. Attend a meeting of your service club.*

3. ABOVE ALL: Be patient and keep your own counsel. Don't shoot from the hip;
4. REMEMBER: Except for the superintendent, you are the SMARTEST employee of the district, or the powers that be would not have put you in this demanding job in the first place. Unfortunately there is another possible conclusion and that is that you are the STUPIDEST for having taken the job. You'd better keep your own counsel with respect to this dichotomy.

If at this point you have lingering doubts about continuing as a high school principal, consider one or more of the following:

1. Apply for any of the superintendencies open to you by virtue of your brilliant performance as a high school principal;

2. Attempt a lateral sublimation into the ranks of the sword-bearers and retainers of the superintendent's entourage;

3. Resign and go on the lecture circuit;

4. Retire, if eligible, or

5. Slash your wrists. (Before taking this action, refer to Point #4 in the previous paragraph; you might just be in the second category.)

Now, finally, remember these last-ditch defenses:

1. You can lose a lot of the piddley little battles and still win the war;

2. If you must fight the war, keep in mind that will have to fight it with the troops and weapons you have, and not the troops and weapons you wish you had;

3. Don't go to war over minor issues; save your strength and ammunition for the big ones;

4. In the meantime, "If you can't convince them, confuse them," thus blowing enough smoke around the issue until you can bring to bear overwhelming evidence that your position is the right one;

5. Ultimately, your best weapons are intelligence, <u>absolute</u> integrity, consistency and empathy. GOOD LUCK!

Other gems in my repertoire were brief and more direct, for example, the following:

Don't expect life to be fair; it isn't.

Give your children an allowance, but make them earn it by working at tasks appropriate to their ages; as a result they will become more careful with how their allowance is spent.

CHAPTER TWENTY-TWO
BEER, SMOKING, SEX, POT, CHEERLEADING & BIRTH CONTROL
"Sex Is Here \ to Stay"

Sex education or the lack thereof, was a hot topic among students, parents and he public in general during my days as principal, but there was little practical teaching of the subject in the classroom or elsewhere. I don't propose to take a stand, appropriate or otherwise on the subject in this work.

Such limited classroom presentations as existed were general rather than explicit, and were woven into such courses as Home Economics, Special Education, Biology and Physiology. Students at the time offered a humorous observation, *Teach Sex Education like an English course and the students will lose interest in it.* The practical aspects were taught "hands on" by the participants and fellow students in the school parking lots, in automobiles, on the sands of the local beaches, weather permitting, or other convenient or inconvenient locations.

Our cheerleading coach for a time was a girls' gym teacher in her fifties, Ginny Borgman, who with her husband Joe, one of Holland's laundry operators, were enthusiastic school supporters. Ginny generated for herself the idea that what the young women of the cheerleading squad needed was some instruction in newer, or at least different, cheers and techniques that might arouse more enthusiasm at pep rallies and sports events. She learned that there was to be just such instruction given during a three day period some weeks hence at a college in Missouri, and became determined that her team should attend.

Subject to the usual caveat that any expenses involved would be paid either by the team's fund raising efforts, or by the parents, and after consulting with the superintendent, I gave my approval for the venture. The team made the trip to Saint Louis in privately owned automobiles driven by parents, who also served chaperones for the three day event. All returned safely, having had, by all reports, a great time.

Our pep rallies were always enthusiastic events, held either outdoors or in the field house, the only building on the campus that was both appropriate and large enough to accommodate the entire student body . The rally held in the field house a couple of days after the cheerleaders returned from their trip had a special flavor, a few new cheers and an unplanned portion that was heralded for years thereafter as "The greatest of all pep rallies."

After a series of cheers supporting the basketball team for its game with arch rival, Grand Haven, that Friday evening, Mrs. Borgman strode to the microphone to comment on the success of the Saint Louis trip. After a few comments she said, *The girls worked out the whole time we were gone like a bunch of Trojans,* Her choice of words was unfortunate since "Trojans" was the well-known trade name of a brand of condoms. The field house risers, where the students were standing broke out in a roar of enthusiasm, much stomping of the seats and an uproar that lasted for several minutes. When the commotion had subsided, she said into the microphone, *Come, come, students"* The enthusiastic uproar resumed.

Unfazed by all of this student response, the speaker continued, although I was standing nearby, *I don't want to be misunderstood about any of this; the principal would have me in on the carpet....*

There was more uproar from the students body. She concluded, *Come on you guys, I just meant he'd bawl me out.* The stands exploded and the pep rally was over.

When Mrs. Borgman elected not to continue coaching the cheerleaders, her replacement, was Julie Keefer an enthusiastic young woman who set high standards both in her gym classes and in extra-curricular activities, which included her position as cheerleading coach. She was wise to prepare both her gymnasium curriculum and the standards for her cheerleading squad and distribute them in writing to her classes, and to the students trying out for cheerleading. In connection with the latter, she prepared a form addressed to each of the candidates' teachers requesting information relative to the student.

The form read *One of your students, (the student's name) is trying out for the Varsity Cheerleading Squad. Because we are looking for qualities in addition to spirit and gymnastic ability, your help is being asked in evaluating these other important qualities. Please rate this student in the following categories, with a "5" rating as the highest, and "1" the lowest.*
Julie Keefer

The qualities listed in a column on the form were: MATURITY, DEPENDABILITY, CLASS ATTENDANCE, CONSISTENCY, HONESTY, SHOWS RESPECT FOR OTHERS and DETERMINATION, each followed by a set of boxes in which the person rating the student could indicate a value for that quality. An added note beyond the box read *This information **WILL NOT** be seen by your student!*

None of this had come to my attention any more, for example, than had the football coach's standards established for selecting those chosen to be members of the varsity football team. I assumed the football coach knew more than I about the qualifications needed for success on the field. I did not think my two years of college football serving as a target during practice sessions for my much larger varsity team mates qualified me to interfere in the selection process. Cheerleading at Holland High was considered to be a varsity sport, and Julie had set the standards for participation. It would no more occur to me to interfere with this selection process than it would be for me to do so for any other varsity sport

At this point, the roof fell in so to speak The superintendent received a three page typewritten single-spaced letter from the parents of a student who had previously been a member of the cheerleading team, but who was not selected under the standards established by Miss Keefer. Mr. Ihrman, of course, bucked the letter to me for a response.

The student involved was a senior, Jane Leenhouts, who had been a reserve cheerleader while in junior high school and a varsity cheerleader for her first two years of high school. Her father was a well known Holland city office-holder, who was also active in local politics. By definition this was a delicate situation. I invited Mrs. Rogers to join me in my office for a discussion of the matter, and she came well-prepared, with all of the teacher evaluations of Miss Leenhouts, together with those of the successful competitors. One teacher rated her "average", with "threes" in all categories, a timid and not very helpful evaluation he used on the forms for all candidates. With that one exception, her teachers rated Jane in above average or average categories with fives, fours and threes in all qualities save one, *SHOWS RESPECT FOR OTHERS* on which her teachers rated her at the lowest or "one" level here with the one exception noted above.

My hand written notes from this conference say, "self centered"; "Shows lack of respect for others less fortunate than she", and "Stubborn and uncooperative."

Mrs. Rogers also brought with her the results of the observations of a six member faculty committee that judged a competition during which the candidates performed using actual cheers. Jean's performance ratings were average or above for all categories, but using a system of averaging all ratings of all members of the committee, she came out below other candidates seeking to become members of the cheerleading squad. Following my extensive investigation of the whole affair, I wrote a letter to the superintendent which essentially was a point-by-point rebuttal of the Leenhouts letter. This letter is also reproduced in Appendix___.(?) After all the effort and investment of time, I heard no more. I hope that if living, Jane has long since absorbed the learning experience and forgiven any slight she may have felt. Was the allocation of time that otherwise might have been used more effectively in addressing other challenges appropriate? I don't know.

In response to an action taken by a teacher involving alleged cheating on an examination, a student, remembering another teacher's definition of castration as *Removal of the testes*, he wrote, *The teacher castrated my paper and threw me out of the room.* I carefully filed this note too, preserved on a tiny scrap of paper.

Jokesters, humorists and exercisers of sarcasm are always a part of life everywhere and our high school was no exception. On a four page questionnaire relative to drug use by high school students submitted by the Holland Jaycees for completion by the students, the final item read *Your sex is: _____ .* I noted the varied humorous answers to this request on a blank copy of the questionnaire:

WONDERFUL!
GREAT!
INADEQUATE
NIGHTLY
SUPER
FREQUENT
PREDOMINANT

Another item on this questionnaire asked, *Where do you believe most drug abusers get their drugs?* Seventeen student answers read, *Christian High parking lot.* I interpreted these responses to be facetious, but never really knew. Another question, *Who is the best authority on drug usage?* received one answer of *Christian High students.*

Halfway through the questions was one reading, *What would you say to a person using drugs illegally?* One student wrote, *WHOAH!!*

On a follow up questionnaire, the Jaycees sought answers to questions generated from the first responses. The comments of one student impressed me most favorably and his mature responses continue to be applicable. To the question, *What is your opinion on the reasonableness of the laws which now govern the use of drugs mentioned in this questionnaire?* His response was, *Much change is needed. For first offenders, for example, laws are much too harsh; rehabilitation is needed rather than jail time, but no rehabilitation centers exist here. One is planned and oversubscribed, but has not been put into effect.* To a question, *Do you feel your school administration has any obligation to correct the use of drugs by students?* He appropriately responded, *Yes,* but added in his remarks, *As for education on drugs, we've already had more this year than necessary.*

Attempting to define what is and what is not responsible behavior posed many problems for me and for the dean. Likewise, the punishment to be awarded was a matter of judgment and depended upon the offense. The following is an example taken from the first couple of years of my administration.

Four girls, by their own accounts, ran to the student parking lot during a twenty minute break between classes, a break that was lunch time for a part of the student body. In the parking lot the girls became involved with a boy and a girl who were not Holland High students. Cigarettes and at least one opened beer were at hand, both violations of the school code of conduct. This much, including the names of the Holland High girls, was related to us by a fellow student.

The Dean called the girls to her office, and jointly and severally they acknowledged their presence during the incident but claimed, although they had joined in passing the beer between to two non-students, they themselves had not partaken of it. At this point Eddie, the dean, passed the buck to me, asking that I talk to the girls' which I did, leaving me with the question, *What is the appropriate punishment for students associating with non-students on school property when the non-students are in violation of the school's policies?*

Each girl acknowledged handling the beer and passing it between the non-students at some point during the period in question, but each denied having tasted of the beer or joining in the cigarette smoking. I decided that this was at least as much a matter for parental involvement as it was for the school, so I handed each one a tablet, assigned her to a student chair in the office area well separated from the other accused girls and directed each to write a letter to her parents explaining her involvement. Their letters were similar, and following is a composite of what they wrote:

Dear Mom and Dad,

Today during break four of us got out of Bonnie's car and went over to talk to Brenda & Ron, who were in separate cars. It just so happened that Brenda was drinking a beer, although at the time we didn't know it. When it was time to go to class Ron handed (me?) the beer to pass to Brenda, and I ran up the stairs from the parking lot to go to class.

Now Mrs. Dyk and Mr. Bertsch are mad at me, but they should be mad at Brenda & Ron and kick them off the campus. Now, after having had a little talk with him, I'm sitting in the Principal's office writing this to you as my punishment for using bad judgment .I know you're going to ground me. Do you think this is fair?

I made a copy of each letter and mailed it via registered mail to each of the students' parents, knowing that their reactions would probably have more effect on the students than anything I might do or say. As with so many things in the domain of discipline, it was a judgment call. Would this approach to discipline be effective today? I don't know, but in the raising of children it all depends on whether the parents want to be parents and consistent understanding disciplinarians or want to be contemporary friends of their children. I am convinced the supportive and understanding disciplinary approach is usually successful. I know from my experience the friendship approach is usually unsuccessful.

CHAPTER TWENTY-THREE - LIBRARY (1933-1978)
"One Of The Refuges"

As a thirteen year old high school sophomore in the old high school I learned that when assigned to study hall in the great assembly room, a library pass could be issued for those wanting to go to the library for study. I took advantage of this privilege at every opportunity and subjected myself to the scrutiny of Miss Lucille Lindsley, who presided over that sacred area located next to the principal's office.

Early that sophomore year I had had a confrontation with my world history teacher, Ed Damson, and the principal had arbitrarily given me the choice between expulsion or behaving in class. I wisely chose the latter, even though I didn't think I had misbehaved. The proximity of the principal's office, combined with the librarian's strict monitoring of her domain and my desire to avoid the study hall atmosphere as much as possible combined to keep my behavior well within the expected norms.

About the time I graduated from high school Lucille married Ed Donovan, the teacher of wood shop, and became Lucille Donovan. Both Lucille and Ed remained on the staff when I joined the faculty, but were seriously looking forward to a long and happy retirement. They participated in the great move to the new high school and served there for several more years, Lucille as a teacher of speech, and Ed in his role in the wood shop.

As a speech teacher, among the many things that received emphasis from Lucille was the importance of vowels in speaking. After a short presentation on the subject, Lucille, calling on a somewhat indifferent student, asked, *Mickey, why are vowels important?*

Mickey, aroused from a somewhat somnolent state, and mistaking the vee for a bee, responded, *All I know is that if they don't move, you sure get sick.*

On the occasion of Lucille's retirement, during a student assembly scheduled to honor this famed speech teacher and librarian, after a little skit and many words of praise from both students and faculty the honor of presenting the retiree with a gift from the student body fell to Jeff Padnos, the student mayor, whose father, Stuart Padnos, had graduated from Holland High many years before. After a long, carefully prepared speech lauding Mrs. Donovan, Mayor Jeff drew a retirement gift from beneath the lectern and offered a few more words as he presented it to the retiree on behalf of the student body. Lucille's response was characteristic. *Thank you Mr. Mayor. Your speech reminds me that when your father was in my public speaking class, and I was frequently having to say, 'Stuart, stand up and speak out, and now, with you, I find myself having to say repeatedly, 'Jeffrey, Sit down and shut up.*

With Lucille's retirement a new young librarian named Judy Mastenbrook arrived on the scene, to preside over the sparkling new library. She was a smallish, pretty woman with coal black hair and unfortunately a limping gait due to having been born with a deformed leg. While Judy didn't have the driving persona of Lucille Donovan, she presided over the beautiful library with skill and dignity.

In an effort to place the library in a central location available readily to all students it was assigned a place in what we called the administration building, although most of its space was occupied by activities other than administration, i.e., Home Economics, audio visual storage and offices for the counseling staff. The central passageway of this building was the principal route between the east and west academic units and had the added advantage of being under cover during inclement weather. As a result of this design, the passers by and occupants of the library had the opportunity to gawk at each other, sometimes displaying youthful antics disturbing the quiet atmosphere of the library.

The administrative offices and home economics area lay across this wide hallway. At the east end of the library, and connected to it was the media center presided over by Jack Aussicker, who distributed the films, tapes, recordings and audio visual equipment requested by teachers, delivering the to classroom where necessary as in the case of heavy projection equipment. Jack was also responsible for

Carol Van Lente

ordering new materials as requested by the teachers, always subject to the restrictions in the budget.

Jack stayed on top of his media materials, constantly checking his inventory and frequently writing short notes to teachers prompting them to return audiovisual materials they had drawn from his stock. One of his memoranda seeking to recover a movie that had gone as tray became a favorite of mine. It was addressed to Judy Mastenbrook the librarian, who passed it on to me as an addition to my collection. It read:

From: Media
To: Miss Mastenbrook
Subject: Sex

(1)Do you have this in your drawers?

The remainder of the space in the administration building was devoted to small cubicles in which counselors could interview students they provided shelter for the men counselors, Carey and Kempker, while Carol Van Lente used her office as head of the East unit in her dual roles as counselor and administrator.

CHAPTER TWENTY-FOUR - SURVIVAL
1971
"....This Honorable and Genteel but Threadbare Profession"

For the principals serving in the School District of the City of Holland, their personal fortunes were tied inextricably to the negotiations between the Board of Education and the Holland Education Association. In summary and practice, this meant that the principals were rewarded with raises that totaled whatever was left over from the planned amount budgeted for salaries after the settlement with the teachers was negotiated. This often meant that principals received raises smaller than those of teachers at the top of the salary schedule. Year after year this began to wear on the district's principals as a group and as individuals they communicated their concerns with each other on an increasingly regular basis.

In the fall of 1971 the strain of these discrepancies in our salary schedules became so great that the principals asked for an explanation for this perceived unfair position. At a meeting with representatives of the board, the principals received an explanation that was generally considered appropriate by the board, but unsatisfactory by the principals. This resulted in the dispatch of a letter to the Board of Education and addressed to the chairman, my friend from grade school days, Jim Lamb, a communication that expressed quite clearly the feelings of the principals:

"The results of the meeting last Wednesday....has left the principals with mixed emotions. The modest increases in conference monies, car allowances, payment of professional dues are all received as expressions of confidence in the middle management group. However, on two points the principals are deeply concerned:

(1) The discussion of contractual arrangements was delayed until long after the beginning not only of the fiscal year, but of the actual school year and even until after a negotiated settlement was reached with the teachers, and

(2) A salary increase offer of one percentage point less than that negotiated for by the teachers is universally viewed by the principals as disappointing to say the least; no principal wishes to receive a percentage increase less than that received by his staff. A review by you of this proposed inequity is solicited.

"Since the area of salary is the only one upon which disagreement exists and since we have agreed not to negotiate, it is the conclusion of the principals that further meetings would not be productive at this time."

Although cleverly worded, the scarcely veiled threat of the editorial reproduced below was *Examine what goes on in the public schools and if you disapprove of anything at all, vote down the proposed ad valorum millage.* Ad valorum millage was the measure of the tax to be imposed on real estate, and thus it taxed only the owners of real property. The very idea of taxing only real estate for the funding of education, while providing education for those who pay no such taxes at all is a broad subject in itself, and I don't propose to examine here whether or not there are better or fairer ways to finance public education. The hard boiled fact was that funding for education beyond readin', writin' and 'rithmatic was obtained through special millage elections.

Saturday, June 10, 1972

School Election Monday

The problem of our schools today is ever with us. The most important part is trying to find the correct answer to furnishing the money to keep the schools in operation.

We, the people who pay the taxes, are finding that our tax dollars do not reach far enough to cover all of the expenses.

There are many people who have some questions about the operation of our school systems today. Our legislature and our Congress are finding that there are more and more needs for the tax dollars.

We therefore should take a close look at all of our educational problems. Some of the graduation programs we find were not very well attended.

So remember to take a few minutes of your time and go to the polls and vote. We think that voting is important. We hope that all of our readers are of the same opinion.

The ying and yang of the whole situation is evident from this editorial that appeared in the *Sentinel* a few months later.

In fairness to the Holland Board of Education, it must be observed that the amount of millage that could be expected realistically to be approved by the majority of the electorate in any given special millage election was limited by the stranglehold to which the board was subjected. The stranglehold consistently included the following:

The size of the special millage proposed

The stated purpose of the proposed millage

The constituency that might receive benefit from the use of the money, a variable which changed from election to election, and the state of the general economy at the time of the election.

The major constituencies expected to support public education consistently included the following, among others:

Public school enthusiasts, notably parents;

Community leaders who saw the public schools as necessary to carry out the ideal of providing education for all of the children of all of the people;

Community leaders who saw education as a key to improvement of the economic welfare of the area;

Voters who believed that the education of the children of this generation should be better the one they had received as children.

The major constituencies that frequently composed the opposition to providing additional millage included the following:

Those voters who supported the parochial or private schools, particularly parents whose children attended those schools;

The elderly, many of limited means, who frequently viewed the millage as "providing frills;" a mind set that included, "What was good enough for me is good enough for our grandchildren";

Those who simply didn't like paying taxes in any form or any purpose, noble or otherwise.

It was also during this period we encouraged Buck to enlist in the naval reserve, it was through this enlistment that he qualified to apply for a naval reserve appointment to the United States Naval Academy. He was accepted, although his high school record indicated he should be enrolled for a year in the optional naval academy preparatory school, his SAT scores were very high, and he was allowed to enter the naval academy as a plebe. Future events proved that declining the opportunity to attend the prep school was probably a mistake. In a further fateful decision, he elected oceanography, generally regarded as the most difficult, as his major. The combination of these two choices took him to the spring of the year, dismissal as a midshipman and a return to civilian status, but with his inactive naval reserve enlistment still be served in his rating as a quartermaster second class.

Buck elected to enter the Reserve Officer Candidate program designed to give reserve enlisted men an opportunity to become commissioned officers after completing thirty days of special active duty for training each year until graduation from college, followed by a period of educational active duty at the end of which he or she would be commissioned as an ensign and ordered to an initial period of regular active duty as a reserve officer.

Each of those years Buck worked at factory jobs while not on active duty, one year as a slitter operator in a Northern Fiber Incorporated plant and another year at a different company unloading box cars. These jobs convinced him that he never wanted to work in a factory again and motivated him to be successful in the Reserve Officer Candidate program. At the end of his junior year in college he asked Cindy Marlink to marry him. After another of our "extravagant" receptions at the beautiful Enterprise Lodge serving a wonderful dinner prepared by the two sets of parents they moved into a tiny basement apartment in our newly acquired Enterprise Building, the former Steketee-Van Huis Printing Company, near Holland's downtown and just a block from the campus, thus facilitating their senior year at Hope College.

At the end of Buck's efforts extending over a period of four years to become a naval officer, Lory and I, together with the extended Marlink family were proud to attend his commissioning at Newport, Rhode Island. Significantly, the group included Cindy's Uncle Lornie, the family sobriquet for Lawrence Veldheer the chief of the Zeeland police department and his wife, Wilma. They had long since forgiven Buck for running into their new family car when he was seeking to pick up Cindy for one of their early dates. All of us shared a sense of pride at his achievement.

At the end of the program Buck stood off to the side of the stage commission in hand and beckoned me to join him. When I came to his side he had a most serious expression his face, and asked *Dad, do you think I should request flight training?* As a former naval aviator recognizing the hazards involved in military flying and recalling the many instances in his short life when he demonstrated he was accident prone, I could offer no other advice than recommending that he apply for duty in destroyers, where responsibility comes early in the career of a naval officer.

When the ceremonies were concluded, we all went to a celebratory dinner at a beautiful restaurant on Newport's waterfront, during which, after cocktails, we were all properly impressed when Cindy's mother demonstrated her ability to tie a knot in a maraschino cherry stem with her tongue.

In compliance with the young officer's orders, the couple drove across the country and established themselves in a small apartment in National City south of San Diego Bay and just north of the U.S.-Mexico border. Buck then reported for duty aboard the *U.S.S. John S. McCain* a destroyer whose home port was San Diego but scheduled to depart for a rotation the Far East. Following that tour and the ship's return to San Diego he was ordered to the pre-commissioning detail of a new ship under construction in the Norfolk area and after another cross country drive they found a place to live in Virginia Beach.

Not long after reporting there, he began to lose weight, spit up blood and see fresh blood in his stools. While he sought medical help and was referred to the various naval medical facilities in the area, he kept all of these matters from Cindy, who felt quite naturally the isolation into which Buck projected himself as he considered his undiagnosed disease and, no doubt, his own mortality. Cindy began to suspect that her husband might have some attachment on the side.

Meanwhile, he was tested for every possible cause, including tuberculosis which was rampant in the areas where he had served. Nothing was established from all the testing, but his symptoms continued. His secret had to come out eventually and it did when he arose one morning and the bed clothes were filled with blood. We received this news with shock and concern and concluded that we should make a fast trip to Norfolk to give support to both Cindy and Buck. We elected to take a day of sick leave on a Friday and then drive all night to Norfolk in my little Ghia. There was nothing we could do other than lend moral support to both Cindy and Buck, which we proceeded to do for a couple of days and then returned to our duties in Holland, fearing that our son was in his final illness.

Some time after our departure Buck's primary care physician at The U. S. Naval Hospital, Portsmouth, advised Buck he would lead a medical team to repeat an examination of his lungs one final time using a device that would enable the doctor to see any abnormalities, but the doctor also informed his patient in advance there was little reason to believe he had anything other than cancer of the lung and he should plan on living no more than six months.

The examination revealed a small lesion at the bottom of the left lung and further study showed a sample to be a rare form of tuberculosis found only in the Far East, and which in Buck had escaped detection for so long. The disease was readily treated with modern drugs and Buck made a complete recovery over the ensuing months, running many miles every morning, and suffering only a collapse of the previously infected lung in the process. His diagnosis affected the entire family as we had all been exposed to the disease and were required to have a Schick test periodically and a lung x-ray each year for several years.

Following this episode, the young officer was assigned to limited duty in the Norfolk area for a considerable period during which he would normally be on sea duty, a situation which he properly saw as a threat to his career. He considered resigning his commission, but fortunately consulted with me before taking that drastic action. I was sensitive to the fact that I had exposed our family to considerable financial risk only a few years before by taking a similar action. I pointed out that as long as he was on active duty, even though limited, the navy would provide for his medical care until he could be restored to full duty. He took my advice, completed his recovery and served most of his thirty year naval career in destroyers.

CHAPTER TWENTY-FIVE - LETTERS
1964 -1978
"Restore the Fine Spirit and Prestige...."

One thing I did early on in my tenure as principal was to establish a file folder into which I dropped items I thought might have might have some significance such as letters I either received or sent, notes on happenings of the school day, board meetings, reactions of faculty, townspeople and students, and so forth. Some of these concern matters serious and important at the time; others are amusing and trivial.

Not all of our efforts to guide the student body in the ways of democracy and the enjoyment of individual freedom while acting responsibly within a structure of law and order were successful. We had initiated an effort, scheduled for late May, to orient the junior high school ninth graders to what they could expect the next fall when they became sophomores on the new campus. Our team to accomplish this mission included a knowledgeable and supportive teacher, two of our better senior students, and the duly elected student mayor, who was not exactly a model student either academically or by virtue of exemplary behavior.

According to some who were there as home room teachers for the ninth grade students, the presentations went well, except that of the mayor, whom they identified as a poor representative of the high school. One of the home room teachers whose classroom assignments were Latin and English undertook to commit her comments on the presentation of the student mayor to writing in a letter addressed to me. While I was not happy that the student mayor should make such a poor impression, I also thought that the letter to me contained many anti-democratic observations or suggestions, and for those reasons I made some notations on it and tossed it into my folder of autobiographical material. The letter was written by a highly structured individual, one who thought the idea of giving students freedom and responsibility was a bad one. Excerpts from her letter, with a few of my penciled notations made at the time:

I have a few comments about Dave Lauridsen's appearance before the ninth graders yesterday. His gum chewing, his stance, his dress and his haircut all gave a miserable impression, and instead of sounding like a fine student leader, he sounded like a delinquent. Dave was a dismal character in junior high. There seems to be nothing positive in his record, then or now....

Are we the victims of such a hoodlum? Is there nothing we can do but stand helplessly by and say, "He was elected by the student body?" There are dozens of ways by which he could have been prevented from running for office. The error, in my opinion, was not made in his being elected; it was in his being allowed to run. (Nazi talk; no democracy here!)

Is there enough supervision in this process of election? For all the wonderful leadership a Holland High, why can this election process not be directed so that one of the highest type of leaders emerges as Mayor. If only the finest young people are allowed to run for office, this would automatically result. (This is the way all dictatorships operate, from Nicaragua to Moscow!)

To think that the mayor won an election by boasting that he was made of common clay and was experienced ...having hob-nobbed with all types of people! (John Adams, Andrew Jackson and Abraham Lincoln all made similar claims.).

In the spring of 1976, another letter from Mr. Buter on Holland Motor Express stationary complained about a failing grade his daughter received in an advanced placement English course. It concluded, *My sincere request is that you just forget she was ever enrolled in this course. Cordially, Harvey J. Buter.* This was neither the first nor the last parental request for a change of grades. My policy and that of the high school was that grades given by a competent teacher, if not prejudicial, would stand as the record.

Immediately ollowing my appointment as principal, I received a flood of letters from people of influence in the community. Stuart Boyd, president of Holland Furniture: *I know you will ... restore the fine spirit and prestige of this school.* Bill Vande Water, executive secretary of the Holland Chamber of Commerce: *Congratulations. We know you will do a god job!* Henry Maentz, president of the First National Bank, he who had insured that no Holland Bank would lend Lory and me the money to continue with the development of Baywoodlands, only few years earlier: *All of us at First National are pleased that you have been named to one of the most important positions in the community.* There were many others from prominent local citizens,

From former residents, now living elsewhere came a smaller batch of mail. From Chuck Wurmstedt, previously the manager of the Holland Sears store, but now the president of Sears, Roebuck: *I suppose that with this promotion and being commodore of the yacht club, we can expect your picture on the cover of Time magazine by January.....* Elizabeth Lichty, Dean of Women at Western Michigan University, formerly at Hope College and long-time cheerleader for both Lory and me: *I am very proud of you and know you will do a grand job. ...* From Douglas Tjapkes, General Manager of WGHN, the Grand Haven radio station, and former manager of WJBL, Holland: I *can't think of another man in the Holland School System that I'd rather see get the job. I know you are going to provide some needed leadership..."* This comment was particularly significant for me, as Doug's former position had made him a strong voice for the Christian Schools, sometimes mildly derisive of public schools. The letter that came the farthest was from W. S. Beinecke, postmarked Summitt, New Jersey. Bill was at that time president of the now mostly forgotten S&H Green Stamp Company, a family business. His was a friendship established when we were midshipmen in the same company during officer training in 19 41.

United States participation in the Viet Nam war was expanding, as was criticism of that effort when I received a letter with a return address, Quan Loi, written by a recent graduate that read, in part, *Dear Mr. Birch, I'm writing now in the hope that in some way I can express my 'appreciation' for all that you and the faculty have done for me. The three years I spent at H.H.S. were the happiest I have ever known....In the four months that I have been in Viet Nam I have grown to understand a lot of things about life and the complexity of living....We are in Viet Nam to help an embattled people preserve the right of freedom and security....They say that freedom isn't really free, each generation has to win it all over again. Well, after having over here, I believe that my generation is doing it in style! Arvie D.McCauslin.*" I choked up a bit on this one. Our daughter, Susan, was serving a year as a nurse in Viet Nam and after thirteen months there was flown home on a litter only to be spat upon when deplaning in San Francisco. She was flown to Fort Knox for a period of recovery there. It was a relatively easy drive there for a visit and later she was allowed to come home with us and spend a couple of weeks of leave.

A few years later there was this one neatly hand lettered on a lined sheet of notebook paper: *I am writing this letter for the concern and safety of myself and the other students who ride bus number 16......* The letter then enumerates a number of safety issues before concluding, *I'm not the only one who notices these things, and I'm positive I am not the only one who dreads riding that bus this winter. I don't see how this maniac ever got hired, but for the safety of all the students I think we should get another driver....If this letter doesn't help, I'll get a petition signed by all the students on our bus. Sincerely, Laurie Vande Vusse.*" I had nothing to do with the hiring or firing of bus drivers, but I passed a copy of Laurie's letter to those who did.

Another letter from Mr. Buter concerning his daughter, Jane was dated April 23, 1976, in which he expressed concerns about his having received reports of Jane's absences from a class taught by a Mr. Vande Bottom*, an English teacher who, as a volunteer devoted a great deal of extra time in support of our theater program. Having read the letter thus far, I was wondering why a parent was objecting to receiving such reports, when most parents expressed appreciation upon receiving them. When I read onward in the three-page letter it expressed concern about the teacher's objectionable conduct which was outlined in the letter as a veritable shopping list of characteristics that might be tagged onto a homosexual male. The letter concludes, *If Mr. Vande Bottom has not attained tenure, I would hope that you would consider initiating steps to drop him as a teacher from the Holland system. Cordially, Harvey J. Buter.* The fact was that homosexual or not, Mr. Vande Bottom was a talented teacher, and a great volunteer contributor to our widely acclaimed theater and music programs. I had no other evidence or testimony concerning his sexual orientation.

One letter I received several years into my tenure as principal was hand written on lined school tablet paper; it touched me sufficiently to be included it in my file: *Thank you for the excellent ay you are educating the youth of Holland. I am constantly amazed....at the way everything is so organized....I received a complete schedule of all of my son's classes several weeks before the start of the school year...parents night was beautifully organized....Finally, thanks for the notices of truancy about Marty...without them I could not confront him. Thanks for all this.* The letter is -signed, *Grace Novak.*

An envelope postmarked April 15, 1970 reads: *a bomb placed in Holland High School to go off Thursday, April 16. 10 A.M.* I told the secretary, who hurried into my office when she opened the envelope, *Tell no one. We'll hold a fire drill at 9:50 that day,* and that's what we did. No one else knew there was a special reason for the fire drill at that particular time. I was sure on this and other similar occasions when I had ordered the school evacuated, the result would be a series of "copy cat" alarms that would seriously jeopardize the school's educational program. I wonder whether my strategy would be effective today, although it did remove the students from any possible danger. In this and subsequent similar incidents, Holland High did not have follow-up threats induced by publicity. There is no question that a highly publicized incident in one institution triggers others in other domains, and sometimes in the same domain.

In an undated letter hand written on a printed letterhead of a local proprietorship, including the writer's name, Peter den Blocker*, I received the following: *"Dear Fritz, This letter is to inform you that I have removed Verne DeWitt from our home and he is presently staying with his grandmother on 16ʰ St,*

"My investigation into the matter has shown that Verne has been physically abusive to my wife Gloria (his mother) and on several occasions has attempted to sexually assault her. Gloria was reluctant to involve me, as she felt she could somehow cope with this mess and that given time his attitude would change. She also was afraid because of my violent nature at times I might do something unpleasant.

"Verne's allegations are fantacys (sic), or whatever you might call them, are an obvious attempt to get back at her or hurt her,. I am convince (sic) that he is

incapable of normal feelings toward any female because of his own mother's past. I also feel he has shown sadistic tendencies both toward Gloria and myself. He needs phycological(sic) help. We will be no further involved with this case and will not discuss it further. I appreciate and value your friendship. Sincerely, Pete. P.S. – I have written also to Jack Plakke, his probation officer in Grand Haven informing him of his removal."

Communications from parents who had been drinking were just part of the game. We fielded phone calls, occasional personal visits and written communications from intoxicated people, not all complimentary. A letter written in an apologetic vein addressed to both me and she school secretary was written by an alcoholic father following a phone call to my office in which he poured out a volume of obscenities to my secretary, who, in turn, passed the call to me. In many ways it was typical, although different from most, it was written in grammatically perfect English:

...during the two weeks involved I was continuously in a drunken stupor...For the life of me, I do not know why I would have any reason to call Holland High School, since I have only one daughter attending there....

As a result of the drunken stupor I was under, (Here he inserted a paragraph of his various violent actions during the time period about which he was writing.) Continuing, the letter read, *For what it is worth, during that time I drank eight quarts of Kessler's eighty-six proof bourbon and two quarts of another brand. I have stopped buying bourbon by the quart, and have started buying it by the half gallon. I always had to buy enough for the weekends, shall we say for moral support?*

Now I am paying for it dearly; I am a disgrace. This well written description, apology and cry for help goes on for two typewritten single spaced prose. It ends, *...please accept my sincere apology for the trouble I have caused. God bless you and God help me.*

As a teacher I had attempted to improve student health and social behavior. In the latter category, for instance, I stood at the doorway to my classroom with a small toy bucket of the kind used by children when playing in the sand and collected the gum many of the students were chewing. As a principal I campaigned against smoking with little success, although I may have dissuaded some from starting the use of tobacco. However, the most effective message was delivered by Olin Van Lare, an outstanding English teacher, but also a heavy smoker. Olin would retire to the teachers' lounge and smoke a cigarette between every class and constantly during his free periods.

Several years after we moved into the new high school, Olin's doctor advised him to quit smoking, and remarkably he did so cold turkey. However, the damage had been done. It was only a short time later that he died of lung cancer. This did make an impression on the student body.

In an incident that reinforced my belief that all parents will lie in what they perceive to be defense of a son or daughter, the parents of a boy had been enrolled in a small local private sponsored by a church, transferred to Holland High. It appeared that the reason for the transfer was that the boy had failed a course in mathematics the previous year. His mother called and requested that I change the recorded grade from an "E" to a "D" so the boy could be enrolled in another private church related school in another state. To my repeated statement that we would not consider changing a grade from another school, the mother ended her plea with the question, *Who would ever know?*

Christmas vacation and spring break brought floods of requests from parents to allow their student son or daughter to accompany them on an extended visit to Florida, California, Arizona, Aruba The Amazon or Timbuktu. One family was awarded a trip to Venezuela as a reward for the sales achievements of the father, who was an insurance salesman. The two week trip was scheduled for mid semester.

The parents requested that their son be excused from school without penalty for that period. I denied the request, but conceded there was little I could do about such an absence, but noted that his grades would undoubtedly suffer.

The son was a star performer in the choir and in an adjunct play to be presented on two consecutive evenings during his proposed absence. The young man took the trip. The choir director and theater instructor gave him failing grades for the marking period.

What, if any, action should I take as the high school principal in attempting to improve the effect of these situations? I don't know the answer to this day, but these situations constitute a short list of examples of what the day might bring.

I kept on my personal bulletin board the old wheeze about school administrators, *Success as a principal is the art of dealing with institutional problems in such a way that, although you are constantly under pressure, you can still give the impression you are leading the parade, even as you are in fear of being run out of town.*

CHAPTER TWENTY-SIX - FINE ARTS
1958-1978
"Blah, Blah, Blah..."

Jeane Visscher was not only the head of the art department at Holland High, she was the leader and shaker for Holland in the fine arts, while her husband, Bob, at several critical moments in the art and educational life of the community was the city's mayor, and thus in a position of some influence.

A small slice of local history as background is necessary for one to understand this phase of the story of my connection with Holland High School: Ray Herrick had been a student at Holland High School early in the reign of Jock Riemersma, Jay Formsma's hard-nosed predecessor. Ray crossed swords with Jock for some now long forgotten misdemeanor and lost in the ensuing confrontation.

Ray was expelled from school on the permanent basis popular in those benighted ages. Ray departed from Holland, and as a young man founded, or otherwise procured control of Tecumseh Industries, manufacturers of small gasoline engines, a firm that since its inception had powered everything from lawn mowers and log splitters to chain saws and garden tractors. Along the way, although he was barely remembered in Holland, Ray became the multi millionaire chief executive officer of Tecumseh.

Mayor Bob and a few others were conscious of this story of a local dropout making it big in the world of business and conceived the idea of enlisting Ray Herrick as the honorary grand marshal of one of Holland's major Tulip Time parades. Mr. Herrick must have felt honored that his former hometown was offering him an olive branch, for he accepted the offer after considerable persuasive efforts by the mayor, his wife, Jeane, and several other prominent local citizens. Tulip Time in Holland at that time was a major event, ranking just below California's Rose Festival and Mardi Gras in New Orleans. Mr. Herrick enjoyed the experience of serving as grand marshal, the accompanying accolades and notoriety. During all of this, and afterward, Jeane and Bob continued to cultivate their friend and increase his respect for the culture of the City of Holland.

The city's governmental functions were scattered across a wide area with the offices of the mayor, city clerk, city treasurer, city engineer and board of public works, which ran the city's utilities, including electric power all crowded into the building designated as "city hall", as was the relatively limited Holland Public Library. City council meetings were held in the library, so when occupied for by the council, the library had to close. The police and fire departments were likewise scattered around the growing city. There were other complications not necessary for an nderstanding of this tale; For many reasons, the need for a new Holland Public Library was apparent.

The mayor saw a possible benefactor in the person of Ray Herrick and suggested that a library named after the Herricks would be an appropriate reminder of Mr. Herrck's association with Holland. Jeane was a significant player in this effort, as were several other prominent Holland citizens, including Walter Scott, the then superintendent of schools.

A committee formed from this group was appointed to approach Mr. Herrick with the idea of building the library, and ultimately gained his approval subject to his examination and oversight at every step in the process of designing and building the new library. The Visschers were included in many of the planning sessions with the architect for the new library, and thus were in regular contact with Mr. Herrick. The net result of this phase of the story was the building of the beautiful Herrick Public Library which remains an attractive cultural center in use today.

When planning began for the new Holland High campus, Jeane, still meeting with Mr. Herrick in connedtion with the building of the library, began a another personal campaign to convince Mr. Herrick to build an art center for the new school. She was successful, once again, in persuading him to benefit the Holland community. Jeane was pretty much given carte blanche for the design of Holland High School's Herrick Art Center to be built in a location overlooking the slope to the northeast of the campus and lying between the industrial arts building and the east academic unit.

A year or so after we occupied the new campus, including the newly completed art center, the man who donated the art center and had given so much to his native city, gave the commencement address and was presented with an honorary Holland High School Diploma. We teachers snickered that the man who had given the school a million dollar art center was rewarded with a piece of paper, an honorary diploma with his name on it. In a move that struck me as a further bit of irony, Jock, now long retired, was present at the dedication of the new art center a few months later and shook the hand of the intransigent kid he had kicked out of school.

Jeane was now the prima donna, the queen, the dictator and the major domo of the art center and thus, in some ways a problem to me, although we were always on friendly terms. It was just that I couldn't necessarily get her to do things my way, or in compliance with the standards of operations that were needed to make things go smoothly.

Our scheduling system was similar to that of a small college, in which students were exposed to the nature of the offerings in the various departments at an assembly in the spring, and then, during a week of the summer vacation, allowed to select for themselves the courses in which they intended to enroll. The assembly was intended to be limited to one hour, and thus each of fifteen presenters would be limited to three minutes, allowing a bit of time for shuffling speakers, and so forth. At a teachers meeting in advance of these presentations, I would exhort the speaker for each department to be brief, practice their presentations in advance and sit down at the end of their three minutes. Each year I would give Jeane some special attention for a week or so before the assembly, emphasizing the need for brevity.

All these efforts were for naught. Once Jeane took over the microphone, there was no stopping her. With no consideration for the staff to follow, she would pursue her special interests until I rose to interrupt, and even then would continue her presentations as I wrestled the microphone away from her in an effort to protect her colleagues. Finally, I conceived the idea that solved the problem; I scheduled her to be the last staff member to speak. When her time was up most students fled the auditorium and let her continue speaking to a dwindling audience.

Jeane particularly liked working with metals, and let both staff and students know it. One year her description of one of the advanced art classes read, *Art 7 – 8 Metals – Studio class in metals. Students desiring to work in advanced metal for studio must be assigned to Mrs. Visscher, as the other instructors are incompetent.* Although her meaning clearly was that the rest of the art staff was not experienced in working with metals, it appeared to be a snub with just a touch of ego.

CHAPTER TWENTY-SEVEN-ATHLETICS
1964- 1978
"Or Is It Athuh-Letics?"

Of all the Holland High graduates on the staff who served as coaches of the variety of athletic team sports offered, Ken Bauman, Don Piersma and Tiger Teusink symbolize for me athletics during my time as principal. There were others, Tom Carey, Roger Plagenhoef, Dave Kempker and Ed Damson, for example, among the men; and Virginia Borgman among the women. All were positive contributors to our athletic programs, and most are featured elsewhere in this chronicle.

"Zeke" Piersma and "Fuzz" Bauman had been given their sobriquets by a friendly neighbor early in boyhood, and the names stuck. I always think of them as Zeke and Fuzz; and rarely do I use their Christian names in speaking of them. They had lettered in football and basketball at Holland High and in the same sports at

Hope College. Each at one time or another coached these sports at Holland High and each served a period as athletic director while teaching physical education during my time as principal.

With an athletic program encompassing twenty team sports, varsity and reserve, there were plenty of memorable incidents to recall beyond the scoring, and the victories and defeats of the various teams. During my tenure, Holland spent several years in each of three conferences, and was independent for at least one year. While quite successful overall in basketball, tennis and swimming, our athletic teams were largely of the type that made the upper third of the competing high schools possible.

Ken Bauman, aka "Fuzz"

Zeke, the longtime basketball coach, longed to have a state championship on the record, a feat that had been accomplished by a Holland team many years before either of us became a part of the scene. His dream was shattered in an unfortunate misplay at the end of an otherwise successful season. Piersma-coached basketball teams had won a number of district championships but usually lost in regional competition, a second hurdle en route to the statewide competition among the regional winners. I had been attending the meeting of the North Central Association of Colleges and Secondary Schools in Chicago one year when Holland had won the district championship followed by wins in the early games of the regional competition being played in Kalamazoo. I had hoped to make a detour to Kalamazoo while driving from Chicago to Holland, a move that would permit me to attend that final regional game, or at least part of it, but my departure from Chicago had been

Another district championship, with the team holding the trophy aloft. Coach Donald "Zeke" Piersma looks on with pride and approval as does Superintendent Ihrman.

delayed making that impossible, so I found myself listening on the car radio as soon as we got within range of the a.m. station that carried a broadcast of the game.

Victor Amaya, a huge student, almost seven feet tall as I remember him, was the center on the Holland team during his high school years, and he dominated the opposition in most cases with his enormous height. There were, however, drawbacks. Despite Zeke's most diligent efforts to get him to change his habit, on receiving a pass Vic would either dribble and run with the ball, or, if unable to shoot or run, he would hold the ball chest high rather than hold it above his head and thus beyond his opponent's reach. On several occasions during the season the ball had been knocked from his hands by a shorter but quicker opponent, usually allowing the opposing team to score.

As I tuned in the game, the announcer was saying, *With that basket, Kalamazoo Central has tied the score and Holland will put the ball in play..... here comes Holland down the floor.....there are fewer than thirty seconds left to play, and now Holland will take a time out.*" At the end of the time out, following Zeke's careful coaching, the ball would be passed out from the midcourt sideline to Vic Amaya, who from that point could easily out run his opponent and either dribble to the basket for a lay up or pass the ball to a team mate.

At the end of the time out, the announcer said, *And here we go for the last thirty seconds of play. The ball goes to Holland's Amaya. Holy smokes! The ball is knocked away by Kazoo's Thompson.* Thompson goes in for the lay up and Kalamzoo Central is the regional champion*" I could hear the squawk of the horn signaling the end of the game. Vic had taken the inbounds pass and held the ball at his chest rather than over his head out of reach of the opposition. The smaller but quicker man had knocked the ball away and was gone for the lay up. I think that Zeke is still weeping over this loss.

Vic Amaya was much more successful on Tiger Teusink's conference winning tennis teams. By virtue of his towering height, Amaya could serve downward to his opponent with ball speed that almost no high school opponent could match. But Vic was not at all adept on the return as his feet seemed to cling to the court surface; he won his matches on his serve. After graduation he was somewhat successful as a doubles player on the professional circuit where his partner could be counted on to play any successful return, but he couldn't compete in singles, where his serve was often returned and he would not be able to reach it.

Both Tiger and Zeke were honored by their fellow coaches in the Lake Michigan Athletic Conference and later honored with well deserved life achievement awards by the Michigan High School Athletic Association. In a private discussion with me during my final visit to Holland some years after all of these events, Fuzz Bauman, a former HHS athletic director, heaped praise on both coaches, but concluded his remarks with, *In their eyes, the accomplishments become greater year by year and defeats are somehow minimized.*

As the Latino population grew, athletic aspirants from among their student offspring were more evident. Mike Bos, coaching the reserve football team, called the unalphabetized roll of the sophomores lined up before him in the fall of 1974, *Gonzales, Mendoza, DeLuna, Rodriguez, Vasquez...*Mike paused, looked up at the assembled group and remarked, *Say, you guys ain't all Dutch, are ya?"*

Holland High teams had often been referred to as "The Big Dutch." A local observer commented, We'll have to change it to "The Big Latino, or the Big Mex." By the time my principalship was over, something like half the starting line of the "Big Dutch" was, in fact, Latino.

The funniest thing in the athletic arena that happened during my tenure was contributed by Tiger, generally thought of as among the most sober-sided of the coaching staff. It was a Monday, and Tiger's tennis team had completed a tough practice session. All retired to the locker rooms in the field house, where Tiger, as he often did, spent some additional time with his team members as they showered and dressed.

Members of his and the other teams sharing the showers dressed and disappeared from the scene. Tiger retired to the coaches' dressing area, separated from the students' area only by a cage-like screen and entry door, all made of expanded steel.

After undressing and carefully placing his keys next to his watch and wallet, he discovered that all of the coaches' towels had been used, so he decided to retrieve a clean towel or two from a stack in the student area from which he had just come. He was reminded that the expanded metal door to the coaches' area was equipped with an automatic lock only when the door closed behind him and he heard the familiar cluck of the lock. It was now about six o'clock and Tiger was keenly aware that he, as a deacon, had a meeting of his church consistory at seven.

He grabbed a towel and raced up the stairs to the athletic director's office, hoping to use the only telephone in the field house to obtain communication with the outside world and somehow extricate himself from the situation. He tried the door; it was locked; everyone had left. What to do? The clock was running. Tiger decided that clothes or no clothes he would have to get to a telephone and call a fellow coach who lived only a few blocks away and thus obtain his release. He went to the south doors of the field house overlooking the thirteen acres of practice field lying between him and Twenty-Eighth Street, along the south side of which were the nearest houses. As he stepped outside that door, wrapping his towel about him, the panic bar on the door behind him snapped and reminded him that he was now locked out of the field house.

Tiger made the run across the intervening thirteen acres in record time and rang the door bell on the nearest house. There was no response, so it was onward to the next house, where a youngish housewife responded to his ring. While attempting to explain his plight, the voice of the husband came from the living room, *Who is it, Honey?* I don't think Tiger got any dinner that night before attending the consistory meting, but the homeowners did let him use the telephone after an explanation of the situation.

While their other accomplishments in the athletic and physical education areas were considerable, Zeke and Fuzz made a major contribution to the athletic program in 1967, when they compiled a document titled, "Recommended Outdoor Facilities for Holland Senior High School and the Community of Holland at Large." As is often the case during the construction of many new school facilities, more development was planned than could be completed within budget and the net result was a failure to develop the planned outdoor athletic facilities. This was certainly the case in Holland

Following an introductory description of the land area recommended by national studies for a school of Holland's enrollment, a total of thirteen acres, their report noted that this area, designated for development of outdoor athletic facilities was already included in the new campus site. The report was divided into four sections;

      I. Existing outdoor facilities;
      II. Facilities needed in the immediate future;
      III. Priority list of needed facilities, and
      IV. Recommended outdoor facilities based on the existing site plan.

Section I begins, *At the present time, our existing outdoor athletic facilities are practically nil. We have one playing field the size of a normal football field across the street from the high school. It is used only for girls' field hockey and band practice. It does not have adequate turf for it to be used for football practice. Other than this field, we have <u>nothing</u>,* and goes on to describe the hodgepodge of facilities owned and operated by the city, and shared with other schools for both practice and competition. Referring to Riverview Park, the site for football competition, having spectator stands rescued from the previous fairgrounds when usage of that area was changed to cemetery, the report stated. *Facilities have deteriorated so badly that it is not advisable to continue using them, both from the standpoint of the spectator and the athlete.*

Section II is divided into the needs for outdoor athletic facilities and the needs for physical education. Athletic needs included football fields, baseball fields, golf driving range and running track, with a rationale for each and how it would be designed and used. Physical education needs were listed in detail for both boys and girls, together with possible community usage.

Section III recommends a priority list for the completion of the recommended facilities in each category, and Section IV details how the design could be accomplished within the thirteen acres available at the high school, and includes a site plan for the entire project, to be accomplished over several years. It was a job well done, and the effects became visible as time went by. The Board of Education was duly impressed by the work of these two, and by the early seventies we had all the facilities recommended by Zeke and Fuzz, despite the ever-pressing shortage of funds. As a by-product, I learned the meaning of the word, "berm" as one was bulldozed into place alongside a portion of the running track to separate it from a football field.

Coaching football attracted newcomers to the staff, and competition for the position of varsity coach was always intense, but, with the exception of Milton "Bud" Hinga, an almost legendary coach back in the early thirties whose team one year compiled a six and three record, the best ever of any Holland High football team, there never was a coach who kept the job for more than a year or two. Hinga left to coach at Hope College, where his teams performed in the "above average" category. Among his former players, his won/lost record, both at the high school and the college improved markedly over the years as they polished up his image.

Despite the competition among the high schools in conferences in which Holland participated, former college football players appeared to believe they could be the spark that would radically change the future of the sport at Holland High. Consequently competition for the position of head football coach among the applicants was intense. On one occasion a candidate not selected came to my office in tears to decry the decision after our committee selected another teacher-competitor for the position. Two years later the crying coach became the successor coach. He had two average seasons and left the position, only to serve as a varsity assistant for years. There apparently was something humbling about being the head honcho.

In each of these cases the coach left the job voluntarily, having proven to himself he was no miracle worker. Departure was sometimes with grace and sometimes with bitterness, but in every case the ex-coach regained his equanimity as time proved his successor to be no more successful than he had been. Most continued to coach in some capacity.

The most successful football coach during the time I occupied the principal's chair was Dave Kempker who was a member of our counseling staff. His best season, and as far as I know, the best record of any of Holland's football teams was six and three. Buck had been too busy with hunting and other fall activities to become involved with football, but when he transferred from West Ottawa to Holland High he decided that one way to make some progress on the social front was to go out for football. In his junior year he played a few minutes in several games but not enough to letter. It was that year, as he describes it, *I got my thirty-two seconds of fame against Muskegon Heights, the powerhouse of the conference, when they were beating us by some unbelievable score and pretty much everyone else on our team had been injured, so the coach sent me in. It was that year also that Holland instated a swim team. Imagine my surprise when I became the third best swimmer on the team and lettered both as a junior and a senior.*

Our son became seventeen that spring and enlisted in the naval reserve at my insistence. He was promptly sent to both boot camp and a two-week training period at Detroit. When not on reserve duty, he worked at Jesiek Brothers Shipyard as a gopher. A frustrating experience for everyone involved was when he filled the gasoline tanks of a motor yacht with diesel fuel, necessitating the draining and thorough cleaning of the tanks.

Continuing his description of his high school athletic career, Buck said, *As a senior on the football team Coach Kempker assigned me to all of the special teams, and I was used for punt returns and so forth. I learned to use the pursuit curve after a receiver ran right past me when I was briefly on the punting team. I played enough to earn a varsity letter as a senior.*

Historically, Holland High's school colors had been maroon and orange, and a dwindling number of letter sweaters, athletic jerseys and cheerleaders' outfits are still hanging in closets somewhere, but sometime during the period when I was serving in the navy, that, too, had changed, and, as with so many things, the motivation was the hiring of a new coach. The new coach had played on a Big Ten team, Wisconsin, whose colors were red and white and he believed that a change in school colors would help to improve performance on the field. His perception was that maroon and orange were somewhat passive, whereas red and white were active colors. Holland High's colors became red and white, and despite any influence color might or might not have, his teams recorded average performances, and he left for some coaching nirvana, leaving the colors behind.

In a similar series of events, a year when there were no staff seeking the position of head football coach, there appeared on the scene a youthful applicant for a teaching position and one who had excellent football credentials. Dan Porretta was a graduate of Ohio State University, had lettered as an outstanding lineman in football for three years, and honored in the Big Ten. There were trade offs in the negotiations surrounding his accepting a contract to teach, most famously for me was his insistence on having a seven-man sled. Prior to this time I had thought of a sled as a vehicle used for transportation in the winter months. I found out that a seven man sled was not a down-hill bobsled that held seven people, but rather a device used to give resistance in the training and conditioning of football linemen. Another stipulation was that Coach Porretta would be allowed to select his assistants from among the available staff. In the event, no former Holland High varsity football coach was selected for his staff.

Announcements of each of these decisions received headlines on the sports pages of the *Sentinel* and there was much enthusiasm for the projected program among sports fans in the community. Dan proved to be rather good at public relations as well as football, and he helped Zeke put together a brochure advertising the sale of season tickets for all sports, but with the emphasis on football. The reverse of the brochure displayed, among other items statements by me and Coach Porretta. Mine, in part, states, *Holland High is proud of its athletic program. Football is a sport that combines excellent physical fitness and a high order of mental alertness.*

Dan's section reads, *Holland will be playing the best schedule in the state, but with the impressive team turn out, improved coaching staff, and the ability to put the ball in the air, Holland High School can truthfully say, "We respect all teams, but fear none."*

The enthusiasm of the football parents and other Holland High football fans in general was such that collections were made for the purpose of firing rockets and other fireworks after each Holland score at home games, now to be played in the newly-built Hope College stadium. The only problem was that Holland won only one of its home games and went on to a one and eight record overall that year. The following year was a great improvement when the record became three, five and eight. A year later, at his request, Dan was transferred to the junior high school staff, where he coached freshman football for a number of years.

Several years later, following a long wait during which he served in various assistant coaching positions, Mike Bos satisfied a life-long ambition when he became the varsity football coach. It was my last year as principal. The team's record that year was four and five. Mike, as with most of his predecessors found that a winning season was a hard goal to reach when competing with schools like Benton Harbor, Muskegon and Muskegon Heights

HOLLAND HIGH DUTCH
RESERVED SEAT TICKETS ARE NOW ON SALE

REGULAR PRICES

Admission at Gate (Adult) $1.25
Students at Gate 1.25
Student Season Ticket 2.50
Children under 12 at Gate .... .75

All Purpose Ticket — Includes over 30 Athletic Contests
All home games for:
1 - Football   (5)
2 - Basketball   (10)
3 - Wrestling   (9)
4 - Swimming   (10)

Adult Price $12.00
Student Price 7.00

VARSITY FOOTBALL SCHEDULE 1972				RESERVE FOOTBALL SCHEDULE 1972			
September 15	7:30	West Ottawa	Away	September 15	4:00	West Ottawa	Home
September 22	7:30	Niles	Away	September 21	4:00	Dowagiac	Away
September 29	7:30	G. R. Godwin	Home	September 28	7:00	G. R. Godwin	Away
October 6	7:30	Benton Harbor	Home	October 6	4:00	Benton Harbor	Home
October 14	7:30	Muskegon	Away	October 12	7:00	Muskegon	Home
October 20	7:30	Portage Northern	Home	October 19	5:00	Niles	Home
October 27	7:30	Grand Haven	Home	October 27	4:00	Grand Haven	Away
November 3	7:30	St. Joseph	Away	November 10	4:00	Mona Shores	Home
November 10	7:45	Mona Shores	Away				

Please fill out and mail today

APPLICATION BLANK FOR RESERVED SEASON TICKET

TYPE OF TICKETS
Adult General Admission (4 games) $4.00
Reserved Seat Admission $6.00
Reserved Box Seat Admission $8.00
All-Purpose Ticket (Adult) $12.00
All-Purpose Ticket (Students) 7.00

Name..
Address.....................................

Check type of ticket:
General Admission ☐   Season Reserved ☐   Box Reserved ☐
All-Purpose Ticket ☐   Number of tickets desired ....

• Make check or money order payable to:
HOLLAND HIGH SCHOOL
ATHLETIC DEPARTMENT
• Mail application with check or money order to:
DON PIERSMA
Faculty Ticket Manager
Holland High School

Attention! Please check your preference:
1. I desire the same seats I had last year. Mail my tickets.   Yes ☐   No ☐
2. I shall select my own seats by coming to the ticket office.   Yes ☐   No ☐
3. I will allow the ticket manager to use his own discretion and have tickets sent by mail.   Yes ☐   No ☐

my last year as principal. The team's record that year was four and five. Mike, as with most of his predecessors found that a winning season was a hard goal to reach when competing with schools like Benton Harbor, Muskegon and Muskegon Heights

For many years, the football team's designated physician was Dr. Van Raalte, a direct descendent of Holland's Dutch founder. He was of the "old school" in many ways, loved football, and sat on the bench with the players and coaches at every home game. While I was not able to attend all home athletic events, I did try to make some in each sport. One evening at a football game, a Holland player sustained a deep laceration of his lower left leg. Dr. Van Raalte attempted to stop the bleeding with the handkerchief from his him pocket ad then loaded the player in his car, and I accompanied him to the doctor's office. Once there, preparations were made to address the player's needs, i.e., the doctor lit a cigarette, sat down on his stool opposite the player, swabbed off the wound and proceeded to stitch up the edges of the laceration with a needle lying on a table already threaded with cat gut.

I was hardly in a position to criticize a physician attending a patient, but I was horrified that all this was going on without the doctor even washing his hands. The patient, however, was in school on Monday, displaying a slight limp, but apparently without infection, and otherwise in good shape. He was back on the practice field by Thursday, preceding the next game.

FINANCIAL SUPPORT

Principal Bertsch says:

"Holland High School is proud of its athletic program. Football is a sport that combines excellent physical fitness and a high order of mental alertness.

To maintain and improve our present athletic program, it is necessary that adequate financial support be provided by the people in the community.

You can help this worthy cause by filling out and mailing the attached order for reserved seats for all the Holland High home football games. You will be assured of an enjoyable time during each thrill-packed football game on the Dutch schedule."

The Reserves in '72!

The junior varsity football team for 1972, in the opinion of head football coach Dan Porretta, promises to be the best sophomore class in the six years that he has been associated with the Holland Public Schools. "There is no doubt that we will enjoy the largest numerical sophomore class and the physical size and maturity of this group far surpasses anything that we have seen in many years. At this point about 56 boys have signed up for junior varsity football and I sincerely believe that a great portion will remain with the team once they have a chance to be associated with our program."

There will be a dramatic change in the roll of the sophomores in this 1972 season. In order to allow the sophomores a chance to feel part of the Holland High School football team they will be included into varsity drills where they will receive more individual attention by varsity and junior coaches alike. Also, approximately six to eight deserving sophomores each week will be allowed to dress with the varsity. Hopefully the result will be a better coach-player relationship that will establish a highly motivated, highly skilled football team.

The Dutch will have two new coaches at the junior varsity. However, this new combination reflects unusual experience for junior varsity coaches. Lynn Post, a graduate of Holland High School and standout player at Hope College, will assume the duties as head junior varsity football coach. Lynn has been head coach at Wyoming Lee for four years and has been a varsity football assistant at Seattle Public Schools. Lynn will also help the varsity by coaching ends and wingbacks.

Terry Catron will assist Lynn as a junior varsity mentor. Terry was a standout player at Warren High School and was a football player and wrestler at Wayne State U. Terry has coached at Warren High School for one year.

HOLLAND HIGH DUTCHMEN
Independent for 1972
Record Last Year 5-4

The coaching staff representing the Dutch in 1972 will be almost entirely new. However, according to head coach Dan Porretta, the staff reflects rare experience for a high school football team. All of the coaches have had college experience and every coach has had at least an assistantship in varsity football.

Jim Wilson, who is a Bay City Central and Hanover College graduate, has served as assistant varsity football coach at Monroe High School in Middletown, Ohio. Jim is a Math instructor at E. E. Fell and will be coaching the line with Dan Porretta.

Don Johnson, a graduate of Colon High School and Western Michigan University has served as head football coach at Colon High School for the past four seasons. His last year's record was 7-1-1. Don will be teaching English at Holland High and will be coaching the backs. Don will also be working with Coach Porretta towards developing a passing attack.

Season Outlook

In evaluating the coming season Coach Porretta feels that Holland will be playing the best schedule in the state; but with the impressive team turn out, improved coaching staff, and the ability to put the ball into the air, Holland High School can truthfully say we respect all teams, but fear none.

PREVIEW

HOLLAND HIGH FOOTBALL 1972

Holland's "ALL NEW" Coaching Staff:

Back Row: Don Johnson, Varsity Assistant; Lynn Post, Head Reserves; Terry Catron, Assistant Reserves; Jim Wilson, Assistant Varsity

Front Row: Head Coach--Dan Porretta

To:

Head Coach:
DAN PORRETTA

Line Coach:
JIM WILSON

Backfield Coach:
DON JOHNSON

During my final year as principal, the girls' swimming team won its third straight conference championship with a thirteen to one record, and sent ten swimmers to the state finals. The cross country team also went thirteen to one and had competitors in both regional and state competition. The girls cross country team had a very successful fifteen and two record, losing only to Portage Northern. Varsity basketball had a disastrous two and seventeen record. The women gymnasts went ten and three. Wrestlers posted a record of eleven, four and one. Many participants, some successes and some defeats marked a successful athletic program, with good experiences for all participants.

As athletic director, Zeke was often at the lectern in the field house during student assemblies held to recognize student athletes, and was effective in his presentations honoring those who were particularly outstanding in their performances. One of his favorite words before these gatherings was "accolades", but some trigger in Zeke's mind repeatedly caused the word to come out of his mouth as "allocades." Try as he might to correct this tangled version of the word, at the lectern it would be something like, *This student athlete deserves all the allocades we can give him.* As I was writing this word came that Zeke, ten years younger than I, has gone to his reward in the great athletic arena in the sky.

****** ****** ******

Our adventures in Baywoodlands and the environs continued unabated. Our second subdivision, a replatting of the land Mrs. Sulkers had sold us some years after her unfortunate call to the Park Township Fire Department we labeled Bay Forest. To the north lay a parcel of low land, essentially swamp, owned by one Michel Thorgeysky and extending to Ottawa Beach Road. Earlier he had married the widow of August Landwher, one of the founders of the highly successful Holland Furnace Company, a manufacturer that once was dominant in Holland but by this time had fallen into bankruptcy. Count Thorgeysky as he wanted to be called, purported himself to be a member of the Polish aristocracy, although Poland had been a communist puppet since World War II and between the two World Wars was an independent democracy. The area residents called him "The Count."

The Count's pets were peacocks and guinea hens, both of which uttered loud unpleasant sounds that disturbed the neighbors' composure and further disturbed the tranquility of the neighborhood by escaping his pens and subsequently littering the area with droppings and feathers. Periodic efforts to recapture these birds was a further distraction to the populace as the count and his minions trespassed on and trampled down the properties along Pine Creek Bay, many of them within our subdivisions.

Other senior executives of the company lived on our side of the bay, and we had ample contact with them both at social affairs and in connection with education. One of the wives, Mrs. Albert Klomparens, taught with Lory for many years at Lincoln School in Holland.

CHAPTER TWENTY-EIGHT
EVALUATION 1964-1978

(I) PROGRAM EVALUATION
"....Endless Hours....."

As a staff, we were constantly reviewing and evaluating the Holland High School program of "Freedom With Responsibility"' At the same time we were constantly being evaluated by the public and by the students we served. Most external evaluations were heavily weighted to emphasize negatives, while our own, I'm sure, were weighted to emphasize success.

One survey requested by a doctoral candidate in 1973 is a representative sample of the many time-consuming requests we received, together with my responses:

NAMES(sic) & ADDRESS OF HIGH SCHOOL: Holland High School
600 Van Raalte Avenue
Holland, MI 49423
RESPONDENT'S NAME & TITLE: Fred S. Bertsch, jr., Principal
1. What is the population of the community...?: @26,000;@50,000 in the area
served by the high school.
2. What is the student enrollment in your high school?: 1215
3. How many certified staff members in your high school?: 62
4. Is your school a three or four year high school?: 3
5. Is it possible for all students to participate in the open campus program?:
YES
*(Added note in my writing: "Sophomores require considerable counseling.
In my opinion, ninth graders would be too immature, generally speaking.")*
*6. Would your school district allow me to administer an "Open Campus"
Survey" to the students, teachers, and administrators and board of education
members of your district? YES__ MAYBE_X* NO__*
**(Added in my writing at the end of the document: "We are 'surveyed',
'questionaired' & 'opinionaired' so much that it is difficult to maintain a positive
attitude toward another one, particularly if it is for the benefit of a private individual.
Frankly, we would prefer you come and see us as we are.*
*We have been operating this way for nearly twelve years and thus feel quite
comfortable with a program that many consider to be "radical".)*
*7. Please write five comments that you feel reflect a positive attitude toward
the "Open Campus" program: (a) The "open campus" and "Freedom With
Responsibility" philosophies provide a better analog to a free society than the
traditional, or "concentration camp" atmosphere. (b) Our basic belief is that each
citizen is deserving of all of his rights and privileges in a free society as long as he
does not abuse them. (c) Our philosophy is directly opposed to the notion that
students are no good and thus should be restrained. (d) We believe that students can*

be responsible for their own actions, and thus do not require constant surveillance. (e) The program provides a good background for life in a democratic and free society.

8. Please write five comments that you feel reflect a negative attitude towards an "Open Campus" program: (a) Students are no good, and therefore should be restricted; (b) Students should be "forced to study" and therefore should be restricted. (c) Students are thieves and therefore should be restricted and carefully observed (d) Students are careless drivers and therefore should be restricted from driving, even after completing driver education, and are licensed by the state to drive (e) The program is no good because "it wasn't that way when I went to school."

It is obvious, even though more than thirty five years have past since I wrote those answers, that I was getting tired of the constant prying, evaluating and judging by others who had never seen our school in session.

Another and more effective series of evaluations were those of the University of Michigan and the North Central Association of Colleges and Secondary Schools which evaluations usually were scheduled for the same year, as they overlapped in many essential details. Holland High School had been certified by these prestigious organizations for many years prior under the aegis of Principal Jock Riemersma and Superintendent E.E. Fell, all of this long before the arrival of Walter Scott and his plans to reorganize the high school program upon moving to a new campus. Qualifying for these periodic evaluations and seeking approval required a time-consuming effort on the part of the staff in completing an extensive volume of searching questions, followed by the visit of an examining team made up of teachers and administrators from other school districts, organized in a manner similar to the visiting teams conducting materiel or combat readiness inspections during my naval career. This team was charged with the responsibility of verifying the veracity of the written materials school personnel had completed.

I had been through the process of preparing for a visit from the accrediting organization as a teacher under my predecessor and suffered the imposition of time and effort that was required to satisfy the team of visitors. My attitude as a teacher, and that of most teachers in previous times had been positive toward these evaluations.

However, as a result of the increased strength of the education association turned union following the successful conclusion of the strike, some teachers rebelled against devoting their time, mostly beyond the scope of the school days, to the tasks involved in obtaining recertification of the school by the North Central Association. In anticipation of this possibility just prior to the Christmas-New Year holiday, I wrote the following on decorated paper for distribution to each member of the professional staff:

Dear Colleagues,

As you leave for a well-earned holiday period, I want to thank you all for the generally professional way in which you have approached the evaluation by the University of Michigan and the self-study which we are undertaking as a responsibility of an accredited member of the North Central Association of Colleges and Secondary Schools.

I am confident that each of these studies will help bring about improvements of our educational system both in our primary mission of helping boys and girls and in the circumstances under which we provide this service. Your professional attitude is fundamentally necessary in bringing about these improvements.

Certainly it is appropriate at the Christmas season that we be involved not only in personal reexamination and evaluation, but in the reexamination and evaluation of our professional attitudes and performances as well.

Merry Christmas and a Happy New Year!!

Fred S. Bertsch, Jr.

For the most part, the dedicated and well-qualified teachers on the staff willingly undertook the tasks at hand. Roger Plagenhoef, a leader in the strike and subsequent leader of the union in various capacities, represented the exceptions, who insisted either that they could not be directed to comply with the evaluation requirements, or, if they did so they should be paid at an overtime rate based on their salaries. Roger was a well-qualified and dedicated teacher, but he also was one of the most recalcitrant of union members. He personally complied with every element of the North Central and University of Michigan evaluations affecting his department and his functions as a teacher, while insisting that those who refused to comply were well within their rights as members of his bargaining unit.

This, quite naturally, imposed a considerable leadership burden on me in seeking the cooperation of the entire staff. In this situation, and many others, Roger and I spent what seemed like endless hours attempting to reconcile differences, solve perceived problems and settle grievances.

At about this time in my school career (January 1975) I wrote an analysis of some of the problems in the administration of public schools and shared it with Mr. Ihrman. He was impressed enough that he asked me to present it at a combined meeting of the district's, principals, assistant principals all other administrative staff and the board of education. The only copy I have of this set of observations from the high school principal's point of view is hand written on lined yellow tablet paper. I'm not sure it was ever published, or even presented verbally more than once, but it makes some cogent points.

A CALL FOR UNDERSTANDING AND CORRECTIVE ACTION
Who is Running This Show, or Who Is In Charge Here?

By Fred S. Bertsch, jr.
Principal, Holland High School

1. Teacher organizations are openly reaching for absolute control of the public education process. This effort is made, not by a majority, but by a vocal, militant and dangerous minority which has had too much success.

2. In grasping for power, this minority is blatantly tramping on the rights and obligations of others, notably:

a. The right of the lay public to control through democratic processes the educational programs paid for with the taxes they pay;

b. The right and obligation of boards of education to control the process on behalf of the electorate;

c. The right and obligation of the duly appointed administrators to control the process. While this affects all administrators, it is particularly agonizing at the high school level, where principals are trying to cope with the militancy and stubbornness of teachers;

d. The right of serious, dedicated teachers to teach without interference from the radical representatives of organizations to which they either feel they must belong because of loyalty, or are required to belong because of a negotiated contract;

e. Principals have become increasingly isolated at the very time when, as the immediate first-line management within the school, they are constantly being confronted with these issues and, as a result of legislative, executive and judicial actions at the federal, state and local levels, the educational task has been made more complex to a degree unimagined fifteen years ago; specialized staff had been added in everything from Special Education to Multicultural Education and from Reading to Physical Education

I could not resist a temptation to include a sarcastic remark, *That small group of radical teachers will apparently not be satisfied until they are responsible for nothing other than coming in every other week to pick up their pay checks, and then they will want to "negotiate" until the checks are mailed to them.*

My rather lengthy dissertation ended by quoting in full an article by the then executive secretary of the **Michigan Association of Secondary School Principals**, Robert F. Hall. The following is an excerpt from his article:: *The staff that formerly worked with you in the education of students and in interpreting curriculum to the community is now following the leadership of (Unions) at the local state and national levels to make it more difficult to administer the school.*

Refusal to show up for an open house program designed for the parents; refusal to allow communication between teacher and administrator; by setting the time period beyond which they will not remain in the building; an hour free lunch period without regard for the welfare of students; the continuing harassment of principals with grievances over matters beyond their control; the refusal to support worthwhile programs or activities for fear of evaluation and accountability are all indications that that the radical's perception of his job is to make yours unpleasant.

My frustrations accompanying the composite of problems thrust upon the high school principal were expressed in a humorous bit:

Get up, you have to go to school, she said.

From beneath the pillow where he had sought refuge came the reply *I'm not going to school; I hate school. The students hate me and the teachers hate me. Everyone hates me. I'm not going to school. You can't make m go to school.*

The response was *You must get up and go to school. After all you're paid to go to school. You are the principal.*

(II) TEACHER AND STAFF EVALUATION
"What Goes Around Comes Around"

Evaluation of the effectiveness of individual teachers is a duty prescribed in the employment contracts of most principals, and strongly emphasized in mine. In many cases it was a difficult task, particularly when it involved inexperienced teachers or older teachers worn out over a lifetime of teaching. My position with the latter group was made more difficult and painful by the fact that many in the latter group had been my high school teachers a few years earlier.

It is not necessary to name the individual teachers and thus possibly offend their surviving family members, but with a sense of honesty, fairness and integrity in this narrative I recite these nameless examples. Both of these teachers had been evaluated for years as competent, but now the years had worn them down and it was my contractual obligation to deal with their weaknesses. All are now deceased.

A teacher of history, whose classroom presentations consisted largely of reading from the textbook in a droning voice, had been one of my teachers. He had volunteered to serve as coach of the reserve football team during my first year as principal to fill a position no one else wanted at the moment, and I appreciated his contribution, but my evaluation of his classroom performance was necessarily, "unsatisfactory". He was eligible for full retirement benefits, and he took advantage of them after a couple of such evaluations. We both suffered under the strain created by this relationship, but he couldn't change. After being forced into retirement, he later admitted privately to me that he enjoyed the opportunity to travel, both for the broadening experience and for the opportunity to visit his grandchildren, all of whom lived far from Holland.

Another had been an outstanding teacher of both English and Latin, but by the time I became the principal, something had worn out. Her voice was weak and lacking in emphasis. Students were falling asleep in her classroom. Parents were complaining about her performance, and something had to be done to rectify the situation. She also was qualified for full retirement. At the end of our final evaluation meeting, she broke down in tears, whimpering, *What am I going to do with my time? Teaching has been my whole life.* I tried to assure her that there are many worthwhile and interesting pursuits in life in addition to teaching. She was retired at the end of the year. A few weeks after school began the next fall she came back for a visit to her former domain and spent time with her longtime colleagues. She even dropped into the principal's office to greet me and the staff there. Her remark to me was, *I'm having the time of my life and I don't miss teaching at all.*

A strikingly different case involved a friend whom I had known since school days. Bob Chard had taught English Literature at the school ever since his graduation from college. I enjoyed visiting the classes of this well-qualified teacher. He was vibrant, enthusiastic and well-prepared. The students liked this charming man, although some were said to whisper, *He lives with his mother; I think he's a fairy.*

Several times a year Bob would take long absences and his mother would call in for him, stating he was sick and confined to his bed with vaguely described symptoms. On some of these occasions he would be hospitalized. I eventually came to realize that Bob was an alcoholic and that his absences were caused by this disease.

Bob Chard

I met with Bob toward the end of the school year in 1967 and confronted him with his problem. He freely admitted he had a drinking problem, but that he could refrain from drinking to retain his beloved teaching position. This meeting brought forth a note, *Dear Fred, Thanks you so much for your consideration at this time. My prose may be prosaic, but my thoughts of you go far beyond the ordinary. Most sincerely, Bob.*

Prior to the opening of the school year, in August 1968 I once again confronted him regarding his drinking and he agreed that his it was a problem, but insisted he could overcome it. My letter documenting this meeting included the following:

My comments and our conclusions during our recent meeting centered around the fact that you have a serious drinking problem....that has been a problem for many years....I have suggested that it might be advisable for you either to resign your position on the staff, or take a leave of absence....It was your decision not to accept either of these alternatives....

Your long service and many contributions to Holland High School and its students are noted appreciatively; however, the intent of our conversation and of this letter should not be misconstrued. If your personal drinking problem cannot be eliminated, you must be removed as a Holland High School teacher.

It was not many weeks later that Bob's mother called once again to explain his absence. The next day, shortly before classes began, my secretary announced, *Dr. Kuipers is on the phone.* Walter Kuipers and I had been classmates in college and he also served as our family physician. *Good morning, Fritz, this is Walt,* and then, abruptly, *Well, you won't have to worry about Bob's drinking any longer. He just died in a drunken stupor here at the hospital.* Two days later I stood next to his mother at a burial service in Graafschap cemetery. Including the pallbearers and the minister there were nine people present

There were others, particularly among the new and inexperienced teachers and those teachers who came to us, having served in a succession of different school districts, a characteristic that I learned was often a clue to unsatisfactory service and sometimes drunkenness, drug use or serious behavioral problems.

Many administrators found it easier to assess a teacher as satisfactory without revealing the underlying problem and then sending him or her on the way without too much concern for where the individual would teach next.

A textbook example of the latter group was a last minute hire to fill an unanticipated need for a teacher of English. When we sifted through the accumulated pile of applicants we found a man named Weyman Helton who appeared to fulfill all of the desired requisites for the position. We interviewed him and found him to be a pleasant well spoken man and hired him to fill the position.

Mr. Helton proved to be a problem within a short time after he entered the classroom when a student complained to the assistant principal that both in his classroom and otherwise he frequently referred to students, particularly athletes, as *smart asses, smart assed jocks and assholes,* etcetera. A week or two after this initial complaint a student came into the office to complain that Mr. Helton had ordered him out of the classroom for some perceived offense, with the directive, *Get your ass out of here.*

In another confrontation the teacher ordered a student, Doug Sage, to take the assigned but vacant seat of another student, Jeff Martin, who was absent. When Jeff returned he was surprised to see his assigned seat occupied and complained to Doug, who replied in a low voice, *That's tough Martin I didn't put myself here.*

The teacher, who observed the interchange but could not hear the actual words used, asked Doug what he had said and the student replied, repeating exactly the words he had used. The teacher responded belligerently *Get the hell out of here.* The incident was verified by several students who complained about the language used and verified by Helton when confronted with the complaints. As tenure was not involved he was not offered a contract for the following year.

Not all student complaints were legitimate. A typical example of an invalid student complaint involved a tall handsome young male art teacher well liked by his students, one of whom idolized him in dreamlike visualizations that led her to believe he had responded in ways that any responsible parent would deem inappropriate. She confided her dreams to several other girls and inevitably several of her confidantes described some or all of these confidences to their parents, one of whom was a member of the board of education. The board member, doing what she saw as her duty, called and demanded I do something about the situation, which I did. When I interviewed the art teacher and confronted him with the allegations, he denied them with considerable vigor. When I confronted the student, she quickly recanted the whole scenario. I invited her parents and the teacher to join us in the conference room to give the girl an opportunity to explain to them what had happened. The parents were stunned at what this meeting revealed about their daughter. I concluded that this meeting was sufficient punishment for her indiscretion. My experience was that some girls in their teens are prone to such fantasies.

As the cooperative training program expanded, more teachers in the industrial arts and coordinators of the program were required. Particularly sought were teachers who had come into the profession after years of practical experience in a particular trade. They often came with the baggage of poor English grammar, and common usages such as, *It's me...* rather than *It is I...*, or incredible mixtures such as *They gave him and I sandwiches,*" which struck my ears like verbal brickbats.

Miss Doane, my grammar school teacher had us repeat little instructive sentences such as *It is I, said the little red hen,* and *It is I, it is you, it is he, it is she, it is we, it is you, it is they.* In teacher evaluations I noted these deficiencies, and expected corrective action by the staff members whose English usage was so deficient, but with scant success. Today, as I listen to the talking heads on television, they who influence English usage by millions of people are guilty of the same or similar misusages, so how can our students be expected to do better? Is it important? The counter argument is that it doesn't matter as long as the user is understood. Perhaps this is true, but my perception is that in many circumstances it may be that precise use of the language is as important as precise measurement in the composition of the medications we ingest. How often have you heard a television personality say something like *There's two of them,* rather than the correct *There are two of them?*

The television gets more of a student's time in most homes than an English teacher gets in a week. Furthermore, despite my best efforts, I found most English teachers of the generation following mine speaking in such patois. This was a disturbing development, to say the least and apparently one it is impossible or at least extremely difficult to reverse. Should TV announcers and other public speakers be required to pass a course in syntax? The language continues to evolve as it has for generations and I have not been able to staunch the flow of change. .

Then there was the case of Wilber Johnson, the chemistry teacher whose letter requesting schedule changes had been the first piece of paper handed to me during my first few minutes on the job. Mr. Johnson had taught at Holland High for many years, succeeding Rex Chapman, the veteran teacher whose classes I had immaturely disrupted when as a student I blew air into the gas system, snuffing out all the Bunsen burners in the lab. Webb, as Mr. Johnson preferred to be called informally among his colleagues, was in a category all by himself.

When I sat down in the principal's chair on that fateful morning in August, fully in charge and responsible for everything that went on at Holland High School, one of the first things to which Mrs. Veeder invited my attention was a three page, single spaced typewritten letter addressed to Mr. Scott, the now-departed superintendent. Hand written at the top of the first page was a note from Webb: *Betty - - No doubt you are now doing the Principal's job, so this copy is for your decisions. I hope you can make these changes without too much trouble. Much Luck, Webb.*

When I asked Betty for the files on teacher evaluation, she told me there really were none but that my predecessor had kept notes on the performance of some teachers, After a search I did find a file almost an inch in thickness containing extensive and frequent letters and numerous notes on three-by-five cards written by Mr. Johnson. Included in the file were a few letters from my predecessor addressed to the chemistry teacher and several from the superintendent. All of the teacher's writings contained complaints about his teaching schedule, room assignments and the role of chemistry in the high school curriculum as well as personal complaints and/or suggestions, only a few of which were constructive in nature..

The letter Betty handed me called for extensive changes in class assignments, room arrangements, and several physical alterations to the classrooms and laboratories involved. It was less than two weeks before the planned opening of school, an interface with the teaching staff was looming, and I and the superintendent were new in our jobs! I wrote to Mr. Johnson that we could not consider his recommendations at that time, but could consider them for the following year.

One file from the period prior to my appointment as principal, written from Wilber's home town of L'Anse in the Upper Peninsula of Michigan, and dated just after the end of the school year, caught my attention. The letter was typical of the many I would receive during the following fourteen years. It was a diatribe that decried the design of the new school as being obsolete, and demanded a separate building for the teaching of science to include separate laboratories and classrooms. Mr. Formsma's response was essentially a refutation of everything about which Mr. Johnson had complained, including the fact that the nature of school financing would preclude such changes.

In February, 1965, in a lengthy letter addressed to me Webb wrote a recommendation for an advanced chemistry program that by his calculations, after all the extraneous rhetoric had been excised would cost $3,500.00 in capital outlay, plus the salary of a qualified teacher. Just above his signature block, *Wilbur J. Johnson, Chairman, Chemistry Dept.., Holland Public Schools,"* he typed, <u>*ALL THESE THINGS, I DO BELIEVE!*</u> I began to believe that handling Mr. Johnson's requests was going to be anything but easy.

A year later, Webb was invited to attend an advanced institute for teachers of chemistry to be held at Hope College during the summer, but he declined in a long letter to the college, largely self-congratulatory, based on his need to return to L'Anse for a long rest following a demanding year of teaching.

At about the same time, a student teacher under Mr. Johnson's supervision gave a failing grade on a six-week report card to the daughter of a mother who considered herself to be an expert in all educational fields. Responding in a two-page single –spaced letter addressing her complaint Webb used a great deal of gratuitous and condescending language to invite the mother to observe one or more of the student teacher's classes, and then to meet with him, the principal and the student teacher. He went on to inform the mother the student teacher was available on a daily basis to help students outside of regular school hours; to provide the mother with the spread of grades in all of the chemistry classes, and, finally, to have the daughter transferred to another section of chemistry under another teacher. Much of this was beyond Mr. Johnson authority.

The mother's response was another tirade of criticism and rejection written in a sarcastic vein rejecting all that had been offered. Stapled to the letter was a typed memorandum addressed to me decrying the poor teaching of a specified teacher, a situation I was monitoring with considerable care. Her screed began, *If I seem a bit sanctimonious over having made the attached criticism, I would like to have you know of an incident which pricks my conscience for NOT having made a criticism. Last year my daughter was taking second year Latin…The situation was rather reversed in that if they hadn't had a student teacher, those kids wouldn't have learned a thing….* As a professional among all these bits of information, how could I assure her that I was doing the best I could to deal with a worn out tenured teacher? When, the next year, I had persuaded the teacher to retire before being evaluated once again as unsatisfactory, she came back to school for a visit to her old haunts and made a special effort to come into the office and thank me for my actions in light of the fact she was having the time of my life in retirement.

As school opened in the fall of 1967 Webb's letter to me announced that he was *having pains, and would be consulting with his doctor relative to gall bladder problems.* A follow-up letter ten days later indicated he might make it to Holland by the end of September. He finally did appear to resume his duties, and a year passed with only a half dozen note cards inscribed with his thoughts and signature.

In March 1970 he wrote an extensive complimentary letter to me approving of my insistence that all students including seniors be required to take final exams for the semester. I was appreciative of the support, as I believed that promising no exams would relieve many students of the motivation to do well in their studies. Webb further noted that *It is our duty to contain those rebellious students …if we let them sleep in rather than take exams…it doesn't make for good public relations.* All well and good; however, in the same document, he felt constrained to suggest schedule changes for his next year of teaching, a request I was in no position to fill.

A letter to me dated May 16, 1972 is largely one of defensive self-admiration together with a rationale for not developing an advanced chemistry course in light of another forthcoming millage election needed to keep the schools running for another year. There followed in the file a series of lengthy letters, interspersed with file cards addressed to various administrators and teachers.

His letter of May 17, 1972 was addressed to the superintendent, the assistant superintendent, the high school principal, both assistant principals, the director of guidance, the chairman of the science department, the chairman of the millage campaign and the chief negotiator for the Holland teachers in the Holland Education Association, now an affiliate of the Michigan Education Association. A half page opening paragraph complaining about his being assigned to teach two sections of general biology, a course designed for average students not planning on careers in science, is followed by several paragraphs asking for letters of recommendation in case he must seek another job; support for the millage campaign, and a final statement of appreciation for administrative support of him in light *of ....the large amount of criticism heaped on the administration on my behalf.*

A letter addressed to me two days later on May 19 starts, *I discussed my assignment for next year with Mr. Shufelt, assistant principal,......If you confirm his decision to give me two sections of general biology next year, I'll accept this as being final.* This statement is followed by two single-spaced pages of complaint relative to staffing, chemistry laboratory safety, potential lawsuits in connection therewith, the assignments given to fellow teachers, his assessment of the Christian Schools, prospects for the approaching millage vote and, finally a paragraph announcing his resignation in a few days, followed by a closing statement, *And all this hub-bub because of two lousy chemistry sections.* Such hub-bub as there was had come entirely from him. I was determined to allow the teaching assignments to stand as prepared

In a hand-written note in red ink dated May 23, 1972, Webb threatened to speak publicly against the impending millage vote, and included the imperative, *Just juggle the schedule some other way –it has been done before!!* Not only would it be difficult to juggle teaching assignments for the next semester at that time, it would be unfair to his colleagues, who already new their teaching assignments.

On June 1, 1972, Mr. Johnson wrote a lengthy letter to the superintendent repeating much of what he had written before, as summarized above. Mr. Ihrman forwarded the letter to me and requested that I respond. My letter to Webb included the following:

You have written several letters and memoranda on these subjects and have talked at some length with me in regard to your concerns. The following are specific areas listed in your most recent letter upon which I do have comments:

In your letter of May 26, 1972 to Mr. Ihrman, you say,

'All I am doing is making a very simple statement, as I have done for the past twenty years...

   (1) My schedule of classes must be in writing and signed by the principal before June 5.....;
   (2) Five chemistry sections will be assigned to Mr. Johnson for the next school year.....;
   (3) No other classes will be assigned to the chemistry lab.....'

This, of course was an ultimatum to me. My letter continued, *Regardless of the terminology, these terms are unacceptable and, barring unforeseen circumstances that would change the assignment, the master schedule will stand essentially as it is presently prepared..... Your assignment to teach two general biology classes .....gives you the opportunity to have contact with the entire spectrum of normal human performance. The proposed schedule gives you the opportunity and challenge for what it is, and to cope with it successfully.*

In your letter of May 17, addressed to Mr. Ihrman, myself and a number of other addressees you request a brief typewritten letter of recommendation relative to your character and past performance record. If you will provide me with the names and addresses of the party or parties to be addressed in this letter, I will be pleased to write it. He did not deliver a proposed addressee for a letter of recommendation, life went on, and he was scheduled for five sections of chemistry for the following year. His performance was interspersed by occasional memos on cards.

The finale was another long letter of self-approval which included in a next-to-last paragraph, *The president of a Minneapolis manufacturing company drove over from Minnesota four weeks ago Sunday to see me. He made me an offer I cannot refuse, to be a manufacturer's representative in this area.* The end of the school year was just a week or two away. At the close Webb left the area and I never saw Mr. Johnson again.

Those who had long thought Webb to be too easy on his students and had also urged the superintendent and board of education for years to seek a more stringent and better qualified chemistry teacher were delighted. They had their way, and a chemistry teacher with the qualifications they demanded was found and placed under contract. Her name was Karla Spence.

Mrs. Spence

Mrs. Spence had all the qualifications sought by the group that had campaigned for Webb Johnson's ouster, and then some. She was good looking, well groomed, articulate and she had been awarded a doctoral degree in chemistry by a prestigious university. She promised to preside over a rigorous course in advanced chemistry for those who elected it. Her qualifications were just exactly those sought by the dissident group.

What they did not know was that Karla had political and labor organization convictions well to the left of those who sought her as a teacher. She was also seen as a fiery left wing agitator who was ready to join Roger or anyone else on the staff in fomenting problems with the Board of Education and its representatives, including me.

Just as her teaching was rigorous, so were her grading standards. No more Lake Wobegon where all the students were above average; she relistically graded on a curve that included grades "A" through "D-", graciously omitting the deadly "E".

At the end of the first semester some of those petitioners who insisted on challenge found that in advanced chemistry courses their sons or daughters received grades not always acceptable to their parents. Some of Web's former students who received grades of "A" or "B" in his regular chemistry classes now were awarded "C" and "D" grades in the more rigorous course. Parents of these students now regrouped and formed what amounted to an anti-rigor group, active almost to the extent of wanting to draw and quarter the very person who was carrying out their previous demands.

Principals, teachers, boards of education, superintendents and other staff are constantly being evaluated at the dinner table and other venues by parents, students and other citizens of the community. All of these constituencies are human and subject to human weaknesses. There are always differences and disagreements among these people, but all can best be addressed around a conference table rather than the dinner table where negative criticism of the schools can undermine a student's confidence in the school and destroy his or her eagerness to learn. Parents should arrange a conference with the teacher if there is a serious breakdown in communication between teacher and student. Total education is a cooperative enterprise in which parents, teachers and many others including both the helpful and the negative characters on television who influence the student, whether for better or for worse. Parents and teachers in combination are charged with keeping students on the right track, a responsibility that should never be abandoned.

In the case of Karla Spence, although I had rated her well above average on her evaluations, the parental clamor for her head resulted in a vote by the Holland Board of Education to deny her tenure and her realistic appraisals of student performance were replaced once again by those of Lake Wobegon and all of the students subsequently were appraised as above average.

(III) SELF EVALUATION 1964-78)
"If It Were Not for You, I Wouldn't Be the Man I Am Today"

Superintendent Scott had established a committee entitled *The Curriculum Council* composed of the district's elementary and secondary principals, the central administration and the counseling staff, together with selected teachers. Don Ihrman decided to continue with this arrangement. While it did deal with curriculum matters, the council made studies and recommendations on many matters. One of these, a matter of considerable concern to me was teacher and staff evaluation.

On my instigation and pressure, by the early 1970's the council had designed an instrument, largely patterned after the navy's fitness report form, for evaluation of administrators, teachers and support personnel. It specified who was to be evaluated, and by whom. Unfortunately, in explanatory instructions were some directions that left the impression that every three years all principals were to be evaluated by all teaching staff, rather than by the superintendent and central staff. As a result, while all teachers got to evaluate the principal, they were not required to sign the form. Some strange anomalies occurred, and the evaluation process, to my disappointment, was considerably compromised.

I kept in my files two of the teacher evaluations of me as a display of the wide variations of evaluations due to the perspective of the evaluator. The first of these evaluations was completed by our teacher of business and bookkeeping, who was not only a teacher under my supervision, but also a chief petty officer attached to a naval reserve unit of which I was the commanding officer. Not surprisingly, I was marked "outstanding" in most categories, and "strong" in the rest. He wrote extensively in the *Evaluation Summary* praising my functions as an administrator, my efficiency, my honesty, my humor and my command of the English language. In his summary he stated, *When I compare Mr. Bertsch with the previous principal, I see Mr. Bertsch standing as a giant. He has done an excellent job of leading the staff and students back to sound educational standards that were so lacking under his predecessor.*

By contrast, a teacher relatively new to the staff and who was a union agitator in the Holland Education Association marked a few items "strong", a majority of blocks "average", and the remainder as "weak". He made no comments in the summary blocks on the last page of the document. Understandably, I preferred the evaluation of the chief petty officer/teacher.

The most meaningful evaluations of my performance came from above, as is the case in most organizations. Mr. Ihrman in general ranked me as outstanding. Where he or the board perceived a need for improvement or change in policy, they so advised me in private, and, when appropriate, the changes were made.

One copy of a self evaluation prepared in January 1974, after ten years of my service as principal has survived in my file. I consider it to be fair in both my comments, and the check marks where the range from "unsatisfactory" to "outstanding" offered eight levels of evaluation for each quality or characteristic. In the check marks I was perhaps a bit harsh on myself in light of the marks given me by the superintendent in parallel evaluations. The marks I gave myself were all in the two "strong" categories; none in the "outstanding" blocks. One could say I left that opportunity to others. Where I made comments, they appear below in italics.

The comments:

I. PERSONAL CHARACTERISTICS.

"Appearance:

I do not consider myself to be a "clothes horse," but I do try to dress in a manner that I consider to be appropriate to my professional position.

"Health and Vitality:

However, I find that I am wearing down under the frequently grueling physical and emotional demands of the position.

II. LEADERSHIP CHARACTERISTICS (Willingness to make decisions and accept responsibility; forcefulness; ability to effect desirable change; enthusiasm and initiative shown in work)

I consider myself to be among those in this school district most willing to make decisions and/or recommendations and to accept responsibility for the results thereof. Likewise, I am forceful and straightforward in both expression and deed.

III. SUCCESS IN PROBLEM SOLVING (judgment, logical thinking, creativity, imagination)

I believe that I exercise good judgment and logical thinking both in my day-to-day administration of this school and in my recommendations to higher authority. I find that I am less inclined toward creativity and the 'imaginative,' as I become older, but I do not believe that I restrain such activity unreasonably. Further, I believe that I am more foresighted in predicting and perceiving social change than all but a few of my colleagues nationwide.

IV. PROFESSIONAL KNOWLEDGE AND UNDERSTANDING (Keeps current on educational trends)

I am as well informed as, or better informed than, any principal in this system.

V. SUCCESS IN SUPERVISION (Evaluating and improving teaching; developing a strong instructional program.)

Here I marked my self in the upper half of "strong."

VI. ABILITY TO BUILD MORALE. (Democratic in interpersonal relations; delegates; Listens to other points of view)

I made no comment, but marked myself in the upper half of "satisfactory."

VII. RELATIONS WITH COLLEAGUES (Includes professional ethics)

I believe that my standards of ethics in dealing with colleagues are second to none. The fact that I expect similar standards to be maintained by others sometimes strains relationships with colleagues. I have generally good rapport with individual staff members." I marked myself in the lower half of "strong.

VIII. RELATIONS WITH PARENTS

I made no comments, but marked myself in the lower half of "strong"

IX. RELATIONS WITH COMMUNITY

I made no comments, but marked myself in the upper half of "strong."

X. RELATIONS WITH STUDENTS

I made no comments, but marked my self in the upper half of "strong."

XI. ATTENTION TO DETAIL AND ROUTINE (Aware of use of district facilities, services, reports, orders)

I marked myself in the upper half of "strong, with the following comments: Further, I believe that Holland High School has the most accurate, detailed and current set of policies, procedures and philosophies in existence for any school in this district.

XII COMPOSITE RATING

I made no comments, but marked myself in the upper half of "strong."

EVALUSTION SUMMARY

AREAS OF STRENGTH

(1) I am honest. I make decisions on a basis of professional rather then personal considerations. I am forthright with all;
(2) I am loyal to the local educational system and to both my superiors and subordinates;

*(3) I have a basic and continuing interest in youth, and have a generally
youthful and optimistic outlook;*

*(4) I have the ability to analyze situations and trends and to make appropriate
decisions and/or recommendations for dealing with them;*

*(5) I have the ability to deal with a great variety y of people with generally
excellent success;*

(6) I have a high order of idealism tempered with a sense of reality;

*(7) I have a respect for the need for economy in operations and a good
understanding of business procedures;*

*(8) I have a broad background in both education and experience in the real
world.*

AREAS IN NEED OF IMPROVEMENT (Or areas of relative weakness):

*(1) I am inclined to see all sides of a question, problem or personal
confrontation. Hopefully, this helps me to be fair in making decisions, but,
unfortunately, the fact that I cannot satisfy all parties ever is extremely
frustrating to me, and delays the decision-making process at least somewhat;*

(2) I tend to trust people too much;

*(3) I do not propose to seek additional post-graduate work unless it would be
in one of my academic majors;*

*(4)Once I have considered a matter, I'm fairly confident that my conclusions
and/or attitudes about the matter are correct. This is not necessarily so, of
course.*

SUMMARY AND/OR RECOMMENDATIONS:

*I am effective in administering an extremely complex program under
circumstances that are frequently frustrating.*

*Approximately a year later I noted on this evaluation form, I have reviewed
the detailed comments on my self-evaluation dated 1/25/74 and they appear to be of
continuing applicability.*

Some years after my retirement in an envelope addressed to me in a penciled
scrawl came the most meaningful evaluation of my performance, and one that helped
to make me feel that it was all worthwhile, a former student typed, *I had a
conversation with a classmate recently that brought back a lot of memories of the
backbone you gave me when I was a student at Holland High School. If it were not
for your influence in my life, I would not be the man I am today. I needed to say,
Thank you Fred."* It was signed, *"Mark Williams, 1972 and Gary Strabbing, 1972,
deceased."* These were two of several thousand I helped get onto the path to
success, and I appreciated the acknowledgement.

(IV) TEACHER EVALUATION OF STUDENTS
"The Place Where All Students Are Above Average"

Holland was not exactly Garrison Keilor's Lake Wobegon, but with regard to the school's evaluations of students it came close. The expectation of most parents, and particularly that of most mothers was that their sons and daughters were "above average" in all things, both academic and non-academic, in defiance of the generally accepted idea of the word average which to most people in most situations means there would be equal numbers "above average" and "below average." Then and now, any distribution curve representing numbers of grades from "A" to "F" awarded, in the Holland schools as elsewhere, would be badly skewed toward the "A" end of the curve.

The Curriculum Council decided that the grading system, about which there was not then, or even now, anything like an objective system, because of the uncontrollable variety of elements involved in the "affective domain", as educationists liked to label them. The efforts of the Council did almost nothing to affect the distribution curve, but it did have an effect on grades that disturbed parents in many cases. Two incidents can illustrate the sensitivity of parents to grades:

The first incident resulted from a decision by the curriculum group based on the idea, particularly popular at that time, insisting that the educational system should strive to educate and train the whole child, a rather amorphous conclusion that could be interpreted in a variety of ways. It followed in the eyes of the council, in one of its apparently minor decisions, later approved by the Board of Education, that physical education grades would be included in a student's grade point average as weighted on a pro-rata basis by the number of hours the class met each week. That this was a recipe for trouble in certain circles was not really foreseen.

I had known Jim Prins, English teacher extraordinaire at Hope College, since our college days when we worked together at the Holland Heinz factory, the largest pickle factory in the world. Our job was filling retorts, large steel vats on wheels, with boiling hot pickle jars coming off the capper. The final gesture as the bottles came out of the capper just before we picked them up two at a time to set them in the retort was to spray them with live steam to insure sterilization. With our hands, protected only by thoroughly wet canvas gloves, themselves now at a temperature just below the boiling point, we picked up the bottles, one in each hand to place them in the steel vat.

In that world Jim at six feet six inches and I at five feet three inches in height presented a comical Mutt and Jeff appearance. Jim wore of his Heinz-prescribed blue-striped overalls, the largest available, with the straps let out to their very ends, while I was fitted out with the smallest size available and had the straps taken up until the bib of the overall fit tightly under my chain. Our careers had taken us on different paths, but as I glanced through the window of my office, a couple of days after the end of the first marking period following the installation of the gym grade as a minor element in the calculation of students' Grade Point Averages, I could see the distinguished professor, friend and parent, approaching with a look on his face that portended trouble.

There were no introductory comments. Professor Prins went directly to his position which was that physical education, which was a required course in the Holland High curriculum, should not be included when calculating a student's grade point average. I tried to placate him with such ideas as that a comprehensive high school should include a broad spectrum of experiences for all students and that physical education was one of those experiences. Jim would have none of it.

Grades in courses such as home economics, wood shop and typing were included in our grade point average calculation, why not a course in physical education that could have an influence on the health of the student for his entire life? There were different skills involved. Jim would have none of it. This parent-principal conference, as many others, ended in a Mexican stand-off, and not much later I learned that my friend Jim was running for the Board of Education. He was elected, and did a good job, so results are not always as anticipated.

Example Two: In a subject previously discussed, a small group of parents, including the even smaller group of parents who had engineered the release of Webb Johnson as the chemistry teacher, further insisted that he be replaced by a *fully qualified teacher who could challenge the more advanced students*. Karla Spence was hired as just that teacher. She provided challenges all right, but the grades didn't compare with those awarded in home economics or woodshop.. All of this, of course, argues for a grading system less judgmental; perhaps "satisfactory" and "unsatisfactory".

Most teachers are discreet in dealing with parents, but some are brutal, particularly in written communications. Here are a few examples:

This kid just doesn't have it.

This young man is a good citizen, but a poor student.

This kid just can't do it.

Life adjustment is at least as important as preparation in course content, but this student neither adjusts nor prepares.

IQ is the key here; your daughter is simply below average. .

Your son needs special consideration; he's sick.

Most of these should be handled by direct personal contact involving parents and the teacher. In some cases a staff counselor can help. A person to person conference between teacher and parent or parents is almost always better than involving third parties, but when teachers take on a prejudice against a particular student, intervention by a counselor or administrator may be necessary.

Should there be a grading system? How do you compare physics with music (although there is some commonality)? Mathematics with history? One teacher's standards with those of another teacher? Should effort be recognized as well as accomplishment? Some studies show that a system of pass/fail grading causes a decrease of motivation in students, many of whom might conclude that enough work and study to achieve a passing grade is sufficient. Many colleges prefer to see actual grades, even though they may be based on criteria that are highly subjective.

If there are no grades, how do we calculate grade point average and rank in class? Should there be a valedictorian and salutatorian or salutatorians? Many educators and educationists believe these should be eliminated for reasons outlined in the previous paragraph. Surprisingly, parents in general favor a grading system that is weighted in some way to recognize the differences in difficulty of the various course offerings, but no one has devised a system of weighting the grades that is fair to all concerned.

In a personal example of these difficulties, our daughter, Susan, who attended a neighboring high school, pursued a college preparatory course heavily weighted in the sciences and advanced English courses in literature and writing beyond the minimums required for graduation. She was awarded "A" grades in all of these courses, with the exception of a course in advanced physics in which she received an "A −". A classmate obtained a perfect "A" average by taking beyond the minimum requirements only courses such as home economics, cooking, sewing and dress-making and was declared the class valedictorian. Susan became salutatorian. Was this fair? All are created equal, it's just that some are more equal than others.

I could not conceive a system for use in Holland that would be fair to all, but wrestled with these questions for twelve years and never found a satisfactory answer. The then-prominent proponent of educational reform, B. Frank Brown, proposed theories on evaluation that could only be implemented by accepting his proposals as a package, a proposal that in Holland would almost certainly be rejected by the populace. (See Appendix A.)

(V) STUDENT EVALUATION OF TEACHERS
"The Teachers Have It In For Me "

I was familiar with many aspects of student misbehavior, as I was not always a paragon of virtue myself during my school days. This often helped me in the disciplinary aspects of my job as principal, as I knew all the tricks, deceptions and other devices of the miscreant or at least thought I did. Nevertheless, in any school there are examples of unfair treatment of students, and I tried to cope with them where evident. One of my methods was to collect student input by making myself available to students during breaks between classes, lunch periods, and, in general, maintaining an open attitude. Another was to encourage written anonymous communications from students. I don't have a record of the verbal comments made by students, but I have a collection of the anonymous notes.

Not surprisingly, these notes are largely negative, and often aimed at a particular teacher or situation. Many reflect the desire of all teenagers to change the world.

In many cases we attempted to change teaching methods in the directions students suggested. In other cases our judgments were that the general populace was not ready to accept radically new concepts. Overall, in recalling all of this, I'm reminded of the father who sarcastically says to his son, *Why don't you quit school and fix everything that's wrong in the world while you still know it all?*

Here, written in italics, are some examples of responses to my invitation to students to write me about their school experiences, good, bad or indifferent, selected as typical from among those collected during the fourteen years of my service as principal:

*Don't judge people until you know them. Don't show favoritism. (*This is a theme that pervades my collection. Unfortunately, many teachers do generally favor the brighter, cleaner, neater students particularly those from locally prominent families.) *Grade each person on a different scale because everyone is different.*

We should all learn in our own way and not be forced to learn or even come to class so long as we pass the subject. (While this might be the ideal, in my time, at least, it would have been a hard sell with parents and the general population.) *Teachers should get to know every student as a person and not just as a dumb kid over whom they have control.* (Amen!)

1. Don't place yourself above the level of the students;
2, Be the kind of teacher you want to be; not just a stereotype;
3. Don't judge a student by his or her dress, or their family's reputation – You learn the most about someone by their actions;
4. Be fair and don't condemn just for the sake of comparing;
5. Know your subject matter – be up to date;
6. Let the students know you have feelings too; don't be so hard.

Perhaps this high school student should have been instructing in a college offering teacher accreditation.

I think all teachers should try to make the shy and quiet people talk because when they get out in society they will remain that way, and the loud noisy person will push them around. I also don't believe in grades. If a person is doing the best he can, he shouldn't fail or get a low grade just because he can't think as well or as fast as others in the same grade.

GET OFF MY BACK! Stop getting on kids for having dope because you use it too (At least some of you do anyway.) I'm sick of you teachers getting on our backs! You should teach like Miss Keefer, except when she gets mad! (I don't mean anything by that!) , When it comes to picking kids for stuff, the same ones get it. (Is this by now a familiar theme?) Teacher shouldn't have favorites; they treat them different than other kids.

TEACHERS – I think your (sic) doing a far out job.

Listen to kids' opinions without telling them they're wrong just because you think you're right. Be open, don't hide behind your job or your desk. Be helpful, not a demander. Try not to be boring. Learn what you can from the students. Don't show movies all the time. (These are four points I re-emphasized during numerous staff meetings.)

I hold a great deal of respect for teachers and the way they keep their cool in tense situations when most people would have lost their temper(s). How teachers can go to school and listen to all the troubles of the kids in their classes and still seemingly stay calm *is* amazing.

I wish they would treat every body equal!

Don't be so closed up and afraid to open yourself up to kids. I can't learn from someone I don't know. Maybe I won't agree with how you think, but I respect it, because you've been honest and said it. So please respect how I think. Don't try to change me if I don't want to be changed.

These comments were written on pieces of paper, large and small; pieces or whole sheets of notebook paper; blank areas of newspaper advertising; lined school tablet paper; sheets of advertising brochures, and one even written with care on toilet paper (the school kind of paper that's rather hard and non-porous.) Most, but not all, are complaints. Several themes predominate:

Teachers are too tough, too demanding and too arrogant;

Teachers should treat us all alike, whether we're white or black, Mexican or Dutch.

Students whose parents are either wealthy or prominent receive preferable treatment.

Teachers choose favorites and give them special attention.

The grading system is too arbitrary, too tough or unfair, and does not consider individual differences.

Students should not be held responsible for class absences and tardiness.

Here are a few additional and potentially helpful gems:

Dear Administration: This school is as good as any except for one thing. If you don't put doors on the bathroom stalls, I'm going to personally blow this place sky high, I think we're old enough now that we won't swing on them and break them off, Just think if the stalls had doors on them, you could (1) paint them a pretty color (2)Hang the morning announcements on the inside and (3) Provide individual private study quarters. Thanks for listening, your fellow student.

The teachers in this school have all been very nice to us students, and I think that is very nice.

Teachers shouldn't be allowed to smoke in the lounge if the students who are also dumb enough to smoke can't. Practice what ya teach. (Amen!)

Most teachers will do almost anything for the jacks, (or what ever you want to call them) and the cheerleaders. What about those of us who want to go to the lower parking lot and smoke pot? Are we supposed to take all this crap from the teachers?

Some women teachers put down boys who play sports, especially football and basketball.

Some teachers are around when you need help with problems you have or other things on your mind. They are willing to listen to you and help you out. They get involved with the things that are happening around them. (This comment points out a part of what teachers should be doing. Read on.) *Some just don't care how students feel.*

Grading scales that are too tough are like expectations that can never be met. Is this some latter day Aristotle? *A cheerful voice brightens up the school day.*

We're all the same; treat us all alike; don't pity us.

Some teachers walk around glaring at you like they're going to bite your head off and they shouldn't condemn kids if they don't know the answer to a question.

There isn't much I can say about teachers, because there are some really nice ones, but I think some teachers shouldn't act like their subject is the most important one when it comes to homework, because kids don't like to be cooped up in the house all night studying and I'm sure when they were in school they didn't like it either.

I'm class we can sit and talk about the subject, but then the teacher starts picking on the kid he likes or shows favoritism to. It's not fair to the kid, and not fair to the rest of us.

And finally one that expresses succinctly so much of what is written in the other communications:

Don't play favorites!!!
Show us the same courtesy that you expect us to show you.
Authority should be respected by students and teachers alike, not resented by students and used as an instrument of intimidation by teachers.
Respect is something one earns, not demands.
Don't judge students by their mode of dress or speech, or their nationality..
Students are people, not just names on the attendance slip, just as teachers are people, not teaching machines.

Why does the teacher have in for you, Jim?

She just dont like me.

Are you always cooperative in the classroom and courteous to the teacher? Do you come to class prepared?

Nah, she just calls on me when I'm not ready to answer, She's got it in fer me.

How do we motivate all students?
How can we really treat individual differences?
How can we be fair to all students?

These were questions that constantly plagued me during my time as principal and have frequently come to mind as I observe the challenges confronting educational professionals today.

CHAPTER TWENTY-NINE
PARENTS
AND THE BOARD OF EDUCATION
"Unions Are Caused"

The official canvass of the votes cast in the school board election of 1972 showed the following: Charles L. Bradford, Jr. 3,651

Wilber Johnson	1
Dale Van Tongeren	1
Sheldon Wettach	1

Could this have been the result of an election in an African or Central American dictatorship? Chuck Bradford was en effective and foresighted member of the board, reelected repeatedly. It was he who observed to me, about the time of the Holland teachers' strike while standing at the yacht club bar late one evening, that unions are caused. This was an eye-opener that helped me gain some understanding of events that occurred during my years as a high school principal.

Parents are electors, and are to be soothed, aided and abetted to keep them as happy as possible with the performance of the schools. This was both appropriate and necessary, but sometimes led to frustrating or amusing situations. I became involved in efforts to aid parents, and was frequently at some pains to do so. One Ciro Cardena had a son, Jesus, who had somehow managed to break his neck and was wearing a plaster cast to immobilize his neck while it healed. The father, who worked at a local bank, called to request that someone pick up his son each school day during his recovery so he wouldn't get behind in his studies.

This seemed a bit presumptuous, but as the Cardena house was not far off my route to school, I offered to pick up the student each morning shortly after seven as I was en route to the high school. One morning after a few such trips, I casually asked the boy what his father did for a living, and he told me his father worked in a bank as an assistant cashier, and wouldn't get up to go to work until about nine thirty. I forthwith decided the Cardena family could very well arrange to get their son to school, even if Mr. Cardena had to get up a couple of hours earlier then had been his practice.

Another of my notes, written during a particularly boring school board meeting noted that, *The board debated for fifteen minutes whether or not to eliminate the word 'snowball' in the student code of conduct.*

In my envisioned competition for interesting things board members said, first prize would be awarded to the to the man who left the position with the comment, *This district sure has growed a lot since I was first elected.*

The board of education, as it was comprised during the final period of my principalship is pictured at the left. In the foreground are Deanna De Pree, a supporter of the fine arts; Marilyn Feininger, one of the parents seeking the ouster of Webb Johnson and Jim Prins, my partner in pickle making days, and my disputant

over the matter of awarding grades for physical education. In the back row are Carroll Norlin, an elementary school principal; Charles Bradford, who much earlier had given me the insight, *All unions are caused,* late one night at the yacht club bar; William Coupe, an attorney and former law partner with Jerry Roper with whom I had had some previous association; and finally Robert Gosselaar, owner of several local grocery stores and a strong supporter of Holland's cooperative training program.

Just as I received letters advising me of my personal weaknesses and our performance shortcomings as a school, I received letters of appreciation for my services. I retained several in my file. One of them, dated the day after my resignation was announced, read, in part, *I want to tell you that I was saddened by the news of your retirement...I have appreciated knowing you and want you to know that my two sons have always had the highest regard for you and your dealings with them during their high school days. May your decision bring you joy in the future days and your service to all mankind be glorifying to God, our Creator.* The letter was signed by Mrs. Annagene Webber, a person I knew only slightly.

Another letter of even date, came from my friend, school board member, and fellow member of Macatawa Bay Yacht Club, *I'm writing to let you know how much I personally appreciate the years you have served as principal of Holland High School. I've never before written such a letter, but in this instance I feel compelled to do so. I have been greatly impressed with the way you have administered the high school. You have demonstrated sound, calm reasoning in many, many instances which would have completely unnerved most people. I know with certainty that Holland High School is a better place as a result of your leadership and I equally sure that your leadership will be missed.*

I am also aware that this service has been a great personal sacrifice to you – to a greater extent and in more way than anyone can fully realize. I have highly valued our relationship over the years, both "in school" and out. You have my heartfelt thanks for a job well done.

These letters gave me some reason to believe my service had been for the good of the students at that time.

CHAPTER THIRTY-INSTRUCTION IN PERSONAL DISCIPLINE

"I'm Here to Learn, So Learn Me"

Three years of teaching under the aegis of the open campus philosophy had brought me and many others on the staff to believe that while we approved of the concept of freedom and responsibility, our school during those first three years unduly emphasized the value of freedom, but placed little if any emphasis on the need for the students to act responsibly in all of their activities, whether or not on the school campus, just as responsible adults throughout society are expected to operate within the acceptable norms of human behavior, whether they are at work or leisure.

There were staff members who freely voiced their objections to even trying to operate a school under such a philosophy, often in terms that were variations of the ancient themes, "We've never done it that way before," or "If it's not broken don't fix it." There were staff members, not surprisingly, who took a wait and see attitude, and of this group, some were willing to try new efforts in education, and some were not.

The dilemma was, and is, that there are many problems with education as identified by a host of critics over the years. Few, if any, of these critics, and particularly those not actually performing in the field of education, provide solutions to the practical problems in public education. There are the vast ranges of individual differences found in any cross section of the population, and the staffs of the public schools are charged with coping with them every day. It's easy enough to criticize from the sidelines, but it's far more difficult to be successful on the field.

I decided, as seemed apparent to all staff, that there was a need to put some teeth into the responsibility aspect of the open campus. After considerable personal interaction with individual teachers and students, small groups of each and discussion in staff meetings I decided to institute what we dubbed, "Instruction in Personal Discipline", or IPD as a regular class assignment for those recalcitrant students who did not use their free time profitably or at least responsibly. For example, it was acceptable to be idle in free time on the campus or elsewhere, but unacceptable to smoke or drink beer on the campus in violation of either or both school regulations and/or state law. We would prefer students to study while on campus, but if not studying we expected them to live within the law and school regulations. In the cases of some students, particularly sophomores, individuals did not adapt readily to their newfound freedom, and failed to pursue their studies. We included "failing grades" as one of the criteria for assignment of a student to Instruction in Personal Discipline.

Some teachers volunteered to accept an assignment to teach or supervise these IPD sessions; many did not for a variety of reasons. Teachers of the old school who believed in hard boiled discipline of the *Straighten up or leave*, philosophy prevalent in the days before schools were mandated to keep all students, no matter how ill adapted they were to the school atmosphere, how unruly or how rebellious, honestly believed that the entire school philosophy was wrong, and that no good could come from IPD. Some teachers simply felt they personally were not suitable for the task, while still others, no matter their thoughts on the subject, were involved with schedules that simply would not permit them to be so assigned.

When those omissions had been made, there remained a group of teachers who were anxious to fill the roles of teacher and counselor in an experimental situation which might or might not be effective, and which could probably be molded to become more effective with experience. From this group we selected seven who would supervise the periods of IPD.

As with so many things in education as well as elsewhere in the human experience, the challenge was always present and there were successes and failures. At least we tried, modifying our techniques as time went by. Some of the teachers who supervised IPD were natural counselors and had corresponding success. Others, although sincere in their efforts, were not so successful. Some students refused to help themselves, no matter how hard we tried to help them. A few put their heads down on the desk or table and refused all efforts to help them. Initially, virtually all students assigned to IPD expressed resentment at being so assigned, but eventually most accepted the assignment and made the most of it.

One young man who had come to Holland High from another school marked as a recalcitrant offender was assigned for a year to IPD, and later became, as related in the following chapter, a local youth hero for using his initiative in hijacking a police cruiser for a brief but exciting period of time while working as a cooperative training student at a local automobile agency.

A senior student, assigned to IPD for having an excessive number of absences from a class he had elected said to the supervising teacher, *I'm here to learn. So learn me.*

Some among the student body perceived the institution of IPD as a threat from the administration and a prediction of a possible move back to the highly structured past. One of our better students, not a candidate for IPD, nevertheless saw a threat in the move, and wrote a poem on the subject. I found it on my desk one morning shortly after the establishment of IPD:

THE ROTTING IVY
There Is No Joy Among Underclassmen

What's happened to our ivy halls?
They're turning back to stables
All the 'sacred cows' are back;
They're sitting at our tables.

We're back in junior high once more,
Next year we have eight blocks.
They put the pressure on old Fred,
So Fred dragged out the locks.

We're going to have those study halls
And different hours for lunches;
Fifty-five minute classes again'
No breaks no snacks, just lunches.

We'll probably have those bells again
And with them, 'the ninth hour'.
It's not the kids that make the flack,
It's the town that's going sour.

Holland's elected a new school board,
Most of whom are 'Goody' –
All think about the same of us:
We're big and bad and hoody.

There was a little hope, we thought,
But that was yesterday.
Today they changed our system again,
And as guinea pigs we pay

Next year we have no freedom;
The 'Goodies' brought this about.
Look away, oh hallowed halls I knew
Mighty Holland has struck out.

The rebellious nature of all youth is evident in this bit of doggerel, a characteristic that we dealt with every day.

There were many situations unrelated to IPD in which teachers found it necessary to exert or even exceed their authority, sometimes throwing me into difficult situations. Four such teachers were Ed Damson, my nemesis many years before; Zeke Piersma, athletic director; Tiger Teusink, tennis coach, and Carl Dephouse, band director. Each within one short period of time displayed his authoritarian approach to discipline.

In the first of these incidents, a student was eating his lunch in the west commons area with his lunch in his lap and his feet up on the table. With the comment, *Where were you raised, in a barn?* Ed kicked the back leg of the chair, spilling its occupant onto the floor and scattering the young man's lunch on the floor around him. This maneuver did effectively remove the student's feet from the table, but I thought the method was not entirely appropriate. Neither Ed nor the student was injured, but the boy's parents were on the phone with me the next day demanding an explanation of the unseemly behavior of a teacher.

The second confrontation involved two long-time friends and fellow coaches, Zeke Piersma, the basketball coach, and Tiger Teusink, the tennis coach. Zeke's daughter was on the tennis team coached by his friend Tiger. The mildly rebellious daughter came into conflict with Tiger when she announced she would not play in the regional tournament that year. She had what she considered an irreconcilable conflict. Although she had played in every dual match of the year, Tiger's understandably brief response was, *If you don't play in the regionals, you don't letter.* As to the outcome, my memory fails me and my notes don't indicate how the two highly structured and generally uncompromising friends settled this one.

Tulip Time in Holland was a major event during that period of time; the third largest festival in the United States, ranking third in attendance after New Orleans' Mardi Gras and Pasadena's Rose Festival. The schools were major participants in this four day celebration of the blooming of Holland's signature flower, with all elementary students and school staff marching in the parades in colorful Dutch costumes. High school girls performed a Dutch dance several times a day and involved the majority of highly motivated high school girls who wouldn't consider missing either an after school practice or a performance.

Bands at all levels, elementary and secondary marched in all of the parades, and provided additional color to the parade of bands on Friday, an event featuring bands from all over the state, and a few from other states. Holland High School's band, outfitted in wooden shoes and executing dance-like patterns intermittently during this big parade was recognized nationwide for its unique performance.

This was all "well and good" except for the fact that seniors and a few other members of the band could count on being employed during Tulip Time, and were reluctant to give up the resulting money in order to march in the parades. Carl Dephouse, the band director pronounced his dictum, *If you don't march, you get an 'E' in band.*

The counterpoint to this came from some of the employers, who said, *If you don't work, you're fired.*

CHAPTER THIRTY-ONE
COOPERATIVE EDUCATION
Car 89 in Holland

Cooperative education, or cooperative training had its roots in the old industrial arts programs which included courses such as wood, metal and print shops, auto mechanics, mechanical drawing, business and restaurant operation. Co-op was an extension of these courses into the practical world, where responsible students worked for half of the day and were involved in the classroom for the other half day. Initially, Don Gebraad, who joined the faculty the same year I did, and Myles Runk were the directors and supervisors of this program. They were later supplemented with additional personnel as the program grew into the multi-district educational effort described, in part in the chapter on Special Education. Myles and Don (and later the other coordinators) spent about half their time on campus and about half the time on the road checking with employers on student performance, resolving student-employer problems and seeking additional employers willing to take on the responsibility of having a student involved in their business in an educationally-significant way, and not just bagging groceries, pumping gas or washing dishes.

"Cookie" Gebraad was an avid supporter of every aspect of Holland High, often alternating with me as a cheerleader in preparation for "the big event." He later was invited to join the staff of the Ottawa Area Intermediate School District and was instrumental in developing its vocational programs and the vocational center of the district. He retired in 1985 as Director of Vocational Education for the district.

At the beginning of my tenure as principal, we had students assigned to employers in the Holland and West Ottawa areas; by the mid-point in my time these programs extended to the entire area from the southern boundary of the Grand Haven School District, fifteen miles to the north to and including the Allegan District twenty miles to the south and inland to include the Zeeland School District, seven districts in all. All of these high schools had students in the Co-op program, and all had cooperating employers; the coordinators were kept busy covering all this territory.

These circumstances provided plenty of opportunity for interesting, humorous and sometimes frustrating developments in connection with the inter-personal relationships involved. Differences between student and employer in age (and thus maturation level), work ethic, philosophy and degree of responsibility were all in the mix. The coordinators were charged with keeping all of this on an even keel, but occasionally things got out of hand, usually due to circumstances beyond the control of the coordinators.

Sam Van Klompenberger* was a sophomore student, already eighteen years old who came to Holland High after having been ejected from Holland Christian

High for lack of cooperation, failing grades and a number of other perceived character flaws. After a semester out of school, Sam's parents decided for him that he should be in school and brought him to my office toward the end of the summer. We were obligated by law to accept Sam as a student, at least until he became so recalcitrant that we had to follow the example of our fellow high school, and expel him for cause. We scheduled him for classes in which he would not be seriously challenged, to determine, if possible, his native abilities. Because he came with a record of uncooperative behavior and numerous absences, he was scheduled for all of his otherwise free time into Instruction in Personal Discipline, or IPD, where an experienced teacher could observe his behavior, and, if possible help him to adjust to an educational environment quite different from the highly structured one he had previously experienced.

Sam's reaction, initially, was to put his head down on his arms, folded on his desk or table during both his classroom time and IPD. Eventually, through the cooperative efforts of the classroom teachers and IPD supervisors, by the end of the semester, he was persuaded to lift his head, unfold his arms and sit up. He was even awarded passing grades in gym and typing. This was an example in which all those pat phrases that are batted around in educationist circles and society in general didn't apply. Talking about *affective education, education of the whole child* and *no child left behind* couldn't change the outcome of this young man's prognosis. It was up to his teachers, IPD supervisors and counselors to get him onto the right path. I'd like to think that I played some part in doing so, as well. It took a lot of one-on-one counseling to get this young man to cooperate in his own education.

By the time Sam had completed his junior year, he was doing much better and getting improving grades in more challenging classes, including his shop classes. He was particularly interested in auto mechanics, and after completing the advanced version of that course, applied for enrollment in cooperative training during the first semester of his senior year. When school opened in the fall, Sam was assigned to work half days with the mechanics in the repair section of the local Chevrolet dealership, at that time still downtown in Holland; it was before the time they all fled to the outskirts, where land was more plentiful and vehicles for sale could be exhibited more enticingly. I continued my special interest in Sam's progress, although I had no direct involvement in it

I was seated at my desk, idly looking out through the big glass windows overlooking the oval, trying to collect my thoughts on some matter among my manifold responsibilities and listening to a siren somewhere in the distance. The siren grew louder by the second, and shortly a police cruiser with its siren wailing and its "bubble gum machine" flashing alternate red and blue lights, entered the oval and stopped. This grabbed my attention immediately, and I started toward the window for a better look. Three doors on the cruiser opened, and five of our students climbed in. This did involve my responsibilities.

The police car left with its siren screaming, lit up "like Charlie Davis on Saturday night," and turned to the right out of the oval toward thirty-second street, at that time a through street all the was to U.S. 31 the principal Western Michigan north-south highway. Our switchboard went into overload, and Mrs. Smith, my secretary, who by nature became tongue-tied any time there was even the smallest

hint of emergency was unable to respond appropriately on the one line she answered. I was unable to take any action that might change the situation, so I turned on our police scanner and monitored some of the action.

The adventures of the two comic cops in the popular television program, "Car 89, where are you?" were minor compared with this. The Holland students' cruiser with Sam at the wheel was talking to the Michigan State Police in Lansing, and several of its road patrol vehicles, as well as the Holland Police and several of its vehicles. The Ottawa County sheriff's patrol chimed in as it became apparent that Sam was on his way to Saugatuck, but reversed course and came racing toward the campus on thirty second street with a string of police vehicles in pursuit, but not close enough to prevent him from making a full turn around the campus for a drop-ff of his passengers at the back parking lot and thence back to the Chevrolet garage without being intercepted. At the very least, it was an astonishing feat of driving in eluding all those law enforcement vehicles, a demonstration of poor judgment on the part of the young man, but an even more egregious display of poor judgment on the part of someone at the Chevrolet garage.

The service manager at the Chevrolet garage was Sam's direct supervisor, and it was he who handed the keys to the police car and said, *Here, kid, take this car for a post-repair check up and let me know if there are any discrepancies.* Well, who was a fault here? In my mind it was like inviting a qualified pilot the opportunity to fly the Navy's newest and hottest combat aircraft. What would you expect the pilot to say? He is not likely to say, *I can't today; I have an invitation from Lady Ashley for tea at three o'clock.*

Sam was fired. I thought if anyone was to be fired it should have been the service manager, but he had seniority, tenure and a family, so it was Sam who was fired. We found him a job at another dealership, and he graduated, not at the head of the class, but with an acceptable record, and one that was improving as he made his way through Holland High School.

Sam started his own business a few years after he graduated, became very successful and moderately wealthy. When I last encountered him it was in the bar at the Macatawa Bay Yacht Club. He described his family, including his wife who was also a Holland High School graduate and their several children. Although he acknowledged that his experience at Holland High was helpful, he expressed no memory of arriving at the school as a virtual basket case mentally and I was careful not to remind him.

Toward the end of the school year, amongst all of the dinners, celebrations and other special events was the Co-Op banquet. It was never a banquet, but more like a big church event, the usual chicken, mashed potatoes and peas with chocolate cake for dessert. The Co-Op banquet was a little different from most in that the students did everything in connection with it including selecting one from their group to act as master of ceremonies, another to give the principal address, a student to introduce the speaker and others to provide music and/or entertainment.

Employers of Co-Op students were invited by the students and ex pected to sit with their trainees. Spouses were included in the invitations. School superintendents, principals and school board members together with other significant figures from the various participating districts were also invited, so the number of invited guests formed quite a group spread out among the students and parents. It was expected that a proportion of the invited guests would not be present, but no provision was made to identify which among them might be absent. One year, with Lory me present, the function of introducing the guests fell to Nelson Dyke, a loquacious and quick-witted young man, the son of a prominent area contractor.

Don Gebraad

Nels gave a nice little humorous speech explaining his function at the affair and then started in to introduce guests in some unidentifiable order, requesting that each individual or couple rise and be recognized. He began, *Mr. and Mrs. Robert Gosselaar, employer.* No one rose. The next was *Mr. and Mrs. Lloyd Van Raalte. Mr. Van Raalte is the superintendent of the West Ottawa Schools, our hosts for this evening.* No one rose. Continuing, but sounding a little unsure of himself, Nels said *Dr. and Mrs. Walter Kuipers.* Still no one rose. Not losing his cool, he said, "*Well, folks, I'll give it one last try. This guy's got to be here; he's everywhere all over the place; Mr. Fred Bertsch, principal of Holland High School, and his wife, Lorraine.* We rose and gave a wave to the crowded room. Nels said, *Boy am I ever glad to see you. I was starting to think I was at the wrong banquet.* His remark brought down the house.

Don Gebraad, a likeable and effective leader, as described before, was the chief coordinator of the co-op program. He had one irritating flaw in his otherwise excellent English: he would say, *I could care less* when in fact he meant *I couldn't care less.* I tried on numerous occasions and evaluations to get him to understand that *I could care less* means *I care more*, which he didn't mean to say. It was a lost cause. *I could care less* popped into his verbal expression, possibly even as he was saying *Good bye*, at the end of my almost twenty year association with him.

CHAPTER THIRTY-TWO
SPECIAL EDUCATION
"Execute the Chairs"

The educational needs of children and adults who are physically or mentally handicapped are an aspect of the educational spectrum that both fascinated and frustrated me over my years of direct involvement, and it does to this day. Where does it begin and where does it end? Who gets the benefits, and who does not? To what extent are monies in effect taken from those of "normal" students (those who do not have measurable handicaps) and spend it on those who are never going be able to earn a living? Who gets to go to the circus or other entertainments and be treated to an ice cream cone or other treats during school time, the whole being labeled *an educational experience*? By contrast, what about those students who, although having "special needs", get to stay in a regular classroom and struggle with concepts beyond their comprehension?

This conundrum is emphasized in a little bit of anonymous poetry that hit my desk one day:

> *Johnny Jones has lost a leg;*
> *Fanny's deaf and dumb;*
> *Marie has epileptic fits,*
> *Tom's eyes are on the bum.*
> *Sadie stutters when she talks,*
> *Mable has T.B.,*
> *Morris is a splendid case*
> *Of imbecility.*
> *Billy Brown's a truant*
> *And Harold is a thief.*
> *Teddy's parents give him dope*
> *And so he's come to grief.*
> *Gwendolyn's a millionaire;*
> *And Gerald is a fool,*
> *So every one of these darned kids*
> *Goes to a special school.*
> *They've extra special teachers*
> *And special things to wear*
> *And special time in which to play*
> *And a special kind of air.*
> *They've special lunches right in school,*
> *While I - - It drives me wild;*
> *I haven't any specialties;*
> *I'm just a normal child.*

Holland schools had long had elementary level programs for the education of such children housed at Jefferson School, just a block south of the new high school campus. Older handicapped children were cared for at home, or if severely handicapped were cared for by the state in state run facilities.

My insights relative to special education were influenced by several factors. Perhaps the most significant was that the first child of the superintendent, Don Ihrman, and his wife, Lynn, was a girl who, while not as handicapped as some, definitely needed the benefits of special education and training. Their two younger children, David and Clair were well above average in intelligence and were excellent students, (albeit that occasionally David was a bit of a problem both to me and to their family.

During my tenure as principal of the high school, special education in the county expanded rapidly to include education of the deaf, education of the blind and a cooperative training program in which special education students eighteen years old or older, were given an opportunity to demonstrate their ability to become self supporting citizens. One descriptive phrase often used by defenders of special education in general, was, "Make them taxpayers rather than tax recipients." All of these programs were funded to some extent by the state, but never enough to cover the burden on the local taxpayers.

All of these problems, challenges, and opportunities were stirred into the mix called *"special education"; "education of those with special needs,", "education of the handicapped", or "exceptional education."* The latter term was intended to include those above the norm in intelligence as well as those below, but in a practical sense any available funding was used only for the latter. When I first heard the phrase, exceptional education used to identify special education programs for the mentally handicapped, I sarcastically remarked, *I had many fitness reports during my navy years that said I was an exceptional naval officer and recommended for promotion, but I didn't understand that what they were really saying in those reports was that I was a dumb bunny.*

During the time when I became the high school principal, Holland Public Schools had classroom courses taught by designated special education teachers to educate and train special education students in basic skills needed for them to survive in society, such as personal hygiene, sex, interpersonal relationships, preparation for the world of work, and so forth. Sometimes a bit of humor emerges unintentionally as in this note from Jack Aussicker, our audio visual man, who wrote to Mrs. Brownson, *The film strip on excretion has not yet been returned. Would you check through your drawers to see if you still have it?*

Insofar as possible or practical students were integrated into regular courses in wood shop, machine shop, printing, auto mechanics, home economics and restaurant management. Some employers already involved in cooperative training agreed to employ special needs students who had learned enough in those courses to qualify. Laurel Ihrman, daughter of the superintendent and his wife, was one of these, starting at a "hands on" manufacturing job at Kandu Industries, a program established to train the handicapped. After her high school years she continued to be employed, securing a job with Herman Miller, using and further developing the skills learned in the program.

One problem that loomed large in my mind was the differential between the grading of students in the regular classes and those assigned primarily to special education where classes were aimed at teaching the students social, health and behavioral subjects. At about the same time, the legislature passed legislation that effectively required students' records to be accepted as written, or as marked regarding grades. Most, if not all, special education students received grades of "A" or "B" in all of the health and behavioral subjects. Such students were awarded a certification of completion, but this designation clearly indicated the student was a product of the special education program.

After the passage of this legislation and four years of special education as described here, at the insistence of the special education teachers and as approved by the board of education, students were awarded a regular Holland High School diploma with no indication that the person to whom the diploma was granted was a special education student.

While I worried about the possible consequences of such activity, there was, as far as I know, only one serious casualty due to these practices. Gerald Vander Heest* gained admission to Ferris State College based on his Holland High School diploma and his grades in special education. Apparently no one determined that these grades didn't reflect actual academic proficiency. At the end of the first marking period at the Big Rapids school he had a nervous breakdown, having failed all subjects in which he was enrolled. He was consigned, at least temporarily to Kalamazoo State Hospital, and I have no record or memory of him after that time.

By agreements involving the school districts lying to the north, east and south, Holland became a part of a Planning District that would eventually have its own building as a base for some of its operations, but depend on several of the districts involved to provide hands on education and training in specialized areas for all of the districts involved, such as education of the deaf and education of the blind, two specialized areas assigned to the Holland schools.

My first involvement with either of these special areas was in the effort to find a qualified and socially suitable candidate for the position of teacher of the deaf. During the summer following the designation of Holland as the school district responsible for education of the deaf, several women, but no men, applied for the job and were interviewed by a committee composed of Mr. Ihrman, Helen Brownson, one of our special education teachers, an assistant superintendent and me. From the group of applicants for the position we unanimously, but mistakenly as it turned out, chose one Irene Van Dousen*. Mrs. Van Dousen had been profoundly deaf since birth, and I remember feeling strongly that she was a natural choice for the position. The fact that she was deaf, I reasoned, as did the other interviewers, would make her more empathic with the students, more understanding and better able to communicate with them. This assumption proved to be almost totally wrong.

When classes began that fall, there were eight students assigned to her small classroom opposite the vending machines in the East academic unit. All of the students had serious hearing disabilities and most had hearing aids, but none was totally deaf as was the case with the teacher, who preferred to express herself by signing rather than by using her limited speaking vocabulary as that was how she was taught from birth to communicate. The students, with their limited hearing much preferred to turn up their hearing aids and through listening vastly improve their vocabularies, their knowledge and their English usage. These were not Irene's strengths. Never having actually heard the words, she would frequently mispronounce them. Many erroneous uses of words were pointed out by students, and overall scant learning in the classroom resulted.

Perhaps an example will demonstrate the quandary in which we found ourselves.

There was scheduled a large group gathering of all students assigned to the east academic unit. There would not be enough chairs in the wing where the event was to be held, so teachers were requested by a memorandum distributed earlier, to have classroom students use their own chairs for the event. Mrs. Van Dousen attempted to communicate this message by signing, but the students couldn't comprehend what she was trying to say. She finally, in a state of frustration shouted, *Execute the chairs to the commons!* Execute to her was one of the word's dictionary definitions, *To carry out.* There were many such communication failures, together with much continuing frustration. I had numerous meetings with this young lady in attempting to resolve the problems in her little class of eight students.

I finally came to the conclusion after three semesters of such frustration and inability to communicate that she should not be rehired for a third year. Too late, I realized that having a teacher of the deaf who herself was profoundly deaf was a bit like having a football coach who had never played the game because he had no feet.

The organization of special education was being altered almost day by day. Although I was responsible for the supervision of special education teachers on the high school staff, and could make recommendations with respect to special education teachers, final decisions in all matters and especially staffing and evaluation of teachers lay with the "Director of Special Education" on the staff of the intermediate school superintendent housed fifteen miles from where all this activity took place.

My two page letter to the director with a copy to the teacher outlining the reasons for not rehiring her brought forth a letter from the director to Mrs. Van Dousen requesting a meeting to discuss my recommendation. It also brought forth from her a seven page, single spaced typewritten letter of rebuttal that in my opinion simply confused the situation. Ultimately the director decided to keep her on the intermediate district staff to be reassigned elsewhere. This, in my opinion was not a good decision.

While having a strong desire to give the eight deaf students involved an education that would be of use to them over their lifetimes, I found that the number of hours devoted to attempting to solve Mrs. Van Dousen's problems was totally inappropriate, and that my time should be used in a more equitable way to pursue the interests of the other approximately eleven hundred students enrolled in Holland High School.

We were more fortunate with education of the blind. The new instructor was proficient in Braille and well educated and trained for the job. This transition went well.

The role of special education was expanding rapidly, and when Ottawa County assumed major responsibilities in the field of special education, Mrs. Brownson became a coordinator in that broader program. I received a letter from her that read, in part, *"I feel I owe a great deal to you and the opportunities for growth and service I gained in working these years with you as you encouraged me to work freely in efforts to develop programs and try innovative and creative ideas....In periods of frustration and even tears, you had a listening and supportive ear.....and provided a wisdom and political awareness in relating to the community that weathered us through many a storm. I know it hasn't been easy....we love you and thank you...."*

I evidently had opened the day's mail at that point, for I wrote in a memo to myself of even date, *All we ever get from the federal and state governments is more paperwork, mandated programs, bureaucracy and administrative demands. Little or nothing has filtered down to the student.* Obviously, the pressures of the job were getting to me.

CHAPTER THIRTY-THREE
PROTESTORS, MAYORS AND EDITORS
(1968 and 1977)
"A New Voice; A New People; A New Life"

It was the beginning of a new school year in 1968. Teachers were rested and ready for new challenges. Most students were anxious to prove their worth. We were all looking forward to a peaceful and fruitful academic year. Edna Dyk, although wearing out on the job, was at her pleasant best, although still determined to set the standards of dress and grooming that has been in effect for decades. While adhering to the principle of freedom with responsibility, we did insist that a part of a student's responsibilities was to live within the law, meaning within the rules of conduct as laid out in the student handbook, a copy of which was given to each sophomore or new student as he enrolled for the first time. Boys were to keep themselves neat and clean, clean shaven and with reasonably short hair. While these rules later gave way to more liberal notions as time went on, those were the rules at the time. When a student was called in to see Mrs. Dyk for some now forgotten minor offense, spoke to the students, cautioned them not to repeat their misconduct, and then told them to go home that evening, shave and get a haircut.

The world is full of surprises, and we had had our share of them, but how could we anticipate what happened next? I was not even aware of Eddie's directive to the students, and if Eddie recalled it at all, it must have been stored in a remote file in her brain. The following Wednesday, when I finally went out to my little Ghia after a long day, there was a mimeographed flyer clasped under the windshield wiper. This is what it said:

FREEDOM

Thursday, September 12ʰ, 1968, two Holland High School students were called to the office of Mrs. Edna Dyk, the dean of students. They discussed a slight matter, and then the boys were told to get a haircut and a shave, or else they would not be allowed in school. This is what this flyer is all about. We think it is wrong to deny a student the right to an education because he has hair on his upper lip or chin. Unfortunately, one student alone does not have the voice to help decide school policy, The individual student only has the power when united with other students, This is not a democracy and what is the purpose of our public school system other than to prepare us to live usefully and maturely in a democratic society.

We appeal to the students of Holland High to unite to protest the tyranny of our administration whose idealism supports individualism and tries to emphasize independent thinking and decision making on the part of the student, but in reality will n0ot even allow students to make decisions concerning their own appearance.

We ask the students of Holland High to open their eyes and see what is being done to their minds and independent selves. We are only a few years, and in some case, a few months from adult responsibilities. It is about time that our educational system started to live up to its own responsibilities. We object that we should not be allowed to wear beards and long hair if we so decide, and have our parents' consent and good will concerning this matter, and we firmly believe that the school should not object as long as we stay neat and clean.

A NEW VOICE, A NEW PEOPLE, A NEW LIFE.

The document ended, *Watch for the new student newspaper of the students by the students and for the students.*

I gave this all some thought over night, wondering which of our students had originated this well written document, and considering what might be a suitable response, since I personally agreed with virtually everything it said. There were few options if the student body in general responded positively to this ringing appeal. Fortunately, before I had the opportunity to do anything, when I parked my Ghia the next morning a student with an armload of flyers approached me and handed me another flyer titled *FREEDOM WITH RESPONSIBILITY; An open letter to the student body of Holland High School.*

On Wednesday, September 25, a group of Holland High School students distributed a mimeographed sheet protesting the issue of beards and long hair. In this article they appealed to the student body to help them protest the "tyranny" of the administration and to open their eyes to the "atrocities" committed to their individual selves.

However, to deny them the right to print and distribute their article and their future newspaper would be contrary to the beliefs on which this school and the United States have been founded. Yet the line must be drawn somewhere. An enlightening and well planned dissident newspaper would be an asset to out school, but if the editors choose to fill it with libelous remarks and slanted views without chance for rebuttal, this we cannot tolerate. We must not condone slurs and mud-slinging against those whose careers belong to us the students. Dissidence is necessary to a healthy society, but rebellion is a mark of a society in decay.
Signed, *A Concerned Student*

As I read and re-read these two documents, I couldn't help feeling a sense of pride and identity with what these students were saying. Their ideas were the heart and soul of our educational efforts. Specifics, as in the last sentence of the second epistle, I could disagree with, but not with the spirit of these two students.

What action should I take? I decided to call a student assembly at the time when the protesters were planning their gathering, and invited them to join in a discussion of the matter. Virtually all students attended this assembly, which I opened by reading Ecclesiastes III, *For everything there is a season, and a time for everything under heaven. A time to be born and a time to die......What gain has the worker from his toil?*

I read through verse ten, and then added *There is a time for protest and a time for reconciliation,* plus a few words of invitation to the students who wished to speak on the subject, asking them to alternate sides on the question of whether Holland High's society offered an appropriate degree of student freedom, or was the degree of freedom too much or too little?

The ensuing discussion brought forth little that had not been proclaimed in the two handbills distributed to the student body, and with time the whole matter disappeared into oblivion, although I remained keenly aware of differences within the student body, as differences are present among sections of the entire spectrum of human existence. The period of my principalship coincided almost exactly with the period of United States participation the Viet Nam War, 1964-78., and the effects on the student body were not largely different from those experienced elsewhere.

Lucille Donovan, who had taught a course in public speaking for many years and who was, more lately, our librarian, was retiring, and accolades were being showered on her from all sides and from all the local institutions upon which she had had so much influence, not the least of which was Holland High School. The student council decided that a student assembly would be the appropriate venue for honoring Lucille, who was herself an institution. In addition to the skits, short speeches and other activities honoring the retiree, the student mayor was to present the retiree with an appropriate gift from the student body.

Our student mayor at the time was Jeff Padnos son of Stuart Padnos and grandson of Louis Padnos, founder of Louis Padnos Iron and Metal Company behind which lies a "rags to riches" story of some note. During her lengthy career Mrs. Donovan had had considerable contact with both father, Stuart, and son, Jeffrey, in either her capacity as a teacher of speech in the case of Stuart, or as librarian in the case of Jeffrey, the son.

Mayor Jeff stepped to the microphone at the appointed point in the program and asked the honoree to join him. With Lucille at his side Jeff started a lengthy speech filled with words apparently selected from the dictionary, for many were not in his normal vocabulary, although his normal vocabulary was extensive enough. Mrs. Donovan stood patiently at the mayor's side, shifting her weight occasionally from one foot to the other. Finally, Jeff ended his remarks and reached into the lectern for the gift from the student body, which he delivered with a flourish, followed by an invitation to the retiring teacher to say a few words.

Mrs. Donovan stepped to the microphone and said, *Thank you all, and thank you Mr. Mayor for those kind words. I would now like to add, Mr. Mayor, I've enjoyed having both you and you father as students during these forty years. I recall directing your father in speech class, "Stuart, stand up and speak out," and lately, in dealing with you in the library, I find myself saying "Jeffrey sit down and shut up."* The student body erupted with laughter and applause.

As with the press in general, the editors of the *Holland High Herald* varied in personality, quality and political persuasion. Editorials were usually aimed at dissatisfaction with school policies, actions of the administration or the board of education, and were generally well written. One notable activist editor was David Ihrman, the son of Superintendent and Mrs. Donald Ihrman, who regularly attacked the policies of the board of education, his father, the superintendent, and, of course, my administration of the high school. David is now a tenured professor at Grand Valley State University, living in Holland and caring for two young children after the death of his wife in a tragic automobile accident. When I spoke to him briefly on the phone during the writing of this book, he announced that he is still an activist, and likes to "stir the pot" in order to challenge students and others to consider alternatives. I agree, although his role at Holland High was a bit trying both to me and to his parents.

Fast forward to February, 1976. The war in Viet Nam was grinding to an end with the United States withdrawal of its troops. Suddenly, once again, handbills were being circulated by a student group closely allied with David Ihrman, son of the Holland superintendent of schools.

The first of several new student protests started with an assembly of a large part of the student body in the school parking lot across Van Raalte Avenue. Hearing the noise of much shouting, I went to the window and viewed the scene, following which I requested Alice Beukema, then serving as assistant principal, to proceed to where the students were gathered. She was joined by Carol Van Lente, the girls' counselor and several other volunteer teachers.

Mrs. Beukema and her cohorts gained the attention of the leaders and assured them that I would join them in the theater building to hear their complaints. Recognizing that the group of protesters comprised only a portion of the student body, while they were making their way into the auditorium, she dispatched one of the teachers to arrange for the rest of the student body attending classes to join the assembly. Some of the student body could not be reached because they were off the campus on co-op jobs, attending college classes or taking time off campus during a free period.

With the assurance that their grievances would be heard, the student leaders persuaded their assembled fellows to adjourn to the auditorium, where I and my colleagues took the stage accompanied by the leaders of the student "strikers". It took some time, of course, for the entire group, strikers and non-strikers to file into the auditorium and quiet down.

This gave me an opportunity to reflect on what approach to take in dealing with this situation. For some unidentifiable reason, the thought behind *Ecclesiastes Three* jumped into my mind, *For everything there is a season, and a time for every matter under heaven.* I noted that one of the students seated below me in the front row of seats had a red Bible with her, no doubt the text for our elective course, *The*

Bible as Literature. I leaned forward and asked her if I could borrow it. The table of contents led me to page six hundred ninety-five and the passage I was looking for.

As the last of the students straggled in Alice Beukema, the well-liked assistant principal, went to the lectern and spoke a few words of assurance that there would be an opportunity for all reasonable complaints to be addressed, and then asked forbearance to allow the principal to say a few words.

I knew that the day's events and particularly a report on this assembly would be the subject of discussion at many dinner tables in just a few hours, so I decided to suggest something for them to talk about, *Is it appropriate to interfere with the educational process to air complaints that could be resolved without this interruption?*

I added that perhaps the answer lay in *Ecclesiastes,* and with that I proceeded to read: *There is a time to be born, and a time to die...a time to kill and a time to heal; a time to break down and a time to build up....a time to rend and a time to sew....*In conclusion I offered the comment that the protesters should go home and talk to their parents about whether educational time paid for by tax dollars should be spent in advancing protests that could be settled in some other manner.

With Alice serving as moderator, we then listened to the student protests, most

PROTEST AGAINST
PERSONAL SUPPRESSION
BY, THE ADMINISTRATION
U. CO.   DETAILS
      WILL
      BE
      GIVEN
WE NO LONGER WISH TO
BE CARBON COPIES PRODUCED
BY ARBITRARY RULES

PROTEST
AGAINST
PERSONAL SUPPRESSION
BY
ESTABLISHMENTS
THURSDAY FEB. 6
12:10 LOWER PARKING
LOT OF H.H.S.

of which were trivial, and a few of which, when presented, were booed by the assemblage. The most significant of the complaints involved a decision I had made to block off the U-shaped driveway lying to the south of the east academic unit, to the east of the principal's office and to the north of the performing arts building. My rationale for taking this action involved a need to overcome student abuses of the restrictions on the "circle" as we called it, including student drivers racing through and revving up their engines, some of which had no mufflers (I had been unsuccessful in numerous attempts to obtain authorization to install speed bumps); student parking in restricted spaces, which were few, perhaps ten in total, that were intended to be used for brief periods by vendors and other short time visitors; at the beginning and toward the end of the school day parents wanting to pick up sons or daughters had a tendency to stop in the circle and wait for their children, thus blocking the circle and leading to a cacophony of disruptive horn blowing. I agreed to re-open the circle with the stipulation that students violating the rules for its use would be assigned to IPD. We had no standard way to identify the speeders, but did our best. After my retirement the much needed speed bumps were installed at very little expense when requested of my successor. By and large the parents did their jobs and this whole event ended.

The second confrontation, also led in part, at least by the superintendent's son, David, was, to say the least, a delicate situation apparently having something to do with the pregnancy of a female student who happened to be the daughter of a school board member. The girl left school, birthed the child, a boy, and then returned to finish high school. I have been told that the father was a Mexican-American student enrolled in the Holland Public Schools who disappeared from the scene as soon as the girl's pregnancy became known. As far as I know, I never set eyes on the young man who impregnated the girl, but the young mother was well known to both the faculty and student body.

In an interesting sequel or conclusion, my informant tells me the girl moved away from home, took a job to provide for herself and kept the child. She was aided in her efforts by a Holland High School graduate who later married her, and with whom she bore another son, a brilliant person who became a star student at Yale.

The Ihrmans' son, David, was a brilliant young man, and a non-conformist of the first order. He was non-violent, but in constant confrontation with what was generally viewed as the norms of society in Holland. He frequently and unabashedly embarrassed his parents by expressing his views in handbills, the *Holland High Herald,* and through letters to the editor of *The Holland Evening Sentinel* until the editor was implored to stop printing them. At one time or another he held forth on a seemingly endless collection of opinions on controversial subjects, including his opposition to the grading system, the calculation of grade point averages, (despite the fact that most colleges weighed GPA heavily in determining whether or not a student should be admitted), establishment of rank in class based on grades and required class attendance. He argued that grade levels, i.e. sophomore/junior/senior, be eliminated. He favored pass/fail grading, although research of the records of students across a broad group of schools seemed to show that such a system where used tended to reduce the quality of student achievement. All of these matters had long been argued by school people without resolution, and I, my Holland colleagues and educators across the country continued to wrestle with solutions. David wanted all these matters to be settled immediately.

Shortly before he left school, to his parent's consternation, he distributed to the student body a document expressing his views on education, the world situation, the evolution of thinking, sex and morality. His thesis was carefully written and duplicated from a typewritten original. The title page reads, V.CO. in large hollow hand-drawn letters, the meaning of which, if I ever knew, has long since been lost to me, and then:

"WHOSO WOULD BE A MAN MUST BE A NONCONFORMIST- R. W. EMERSON

Here are a few excerpts from that document:

There is much discussion and controversy on the subject of sex, a subject we know about in the biological sense, but fail so completely to understand in regard to emotion.

*I am an advocate of free love, but only under certain circumstances...including mutual respect.....*His paper goes on to give several examples which to him support his views, and then with respect to sex in marriage, *They take such a vow, but all too often the fondness was not sincere and either divorce follows, or a tragically unhappy marriage continues...*

This was a very well written paper, remarkable in that it was written by a seventeen year old high school student. It was accompanied by a questionnaire requesting answers to a number of questions related to the text.

David's parents, Lynne and Superintendent Don, while supportive of their son, were not supportive of his ideas. Neither was the community, and my phone began ringing as soon as any of this reached a few parents' homes. It was a delicate situation. My time was occupied for a period with trying to placate both parents and students while others sought to collect as many of the flyers as possible. Once again I scheduled a school assembly and appealed to the student body to exercise some restraint in the implementation of their right of free speech.

After most of the furor in the community had calmed down, I received a very gracious letter of appreciation from Lynne Ihrman for my efforts in what continued for some time to be a difficult situation: *I would like to take this opportunity to express my appreciation to you for taking a valuable block of your time and efforts to respond to a group of young people of which our son was a leader, regarding a survey, the results of which they wanted to publish in the Holland High Herald. We are sympathetic to the negative reactions to the flyer and the survey in the community. Our son, being suspicious of "the establishment"....elected not to consider our suggestions...*This was followed by several paragraphs of comment on the nature of protest and their counsel to their son.

Concluding that neither Holland High School nor our advanced placement arrangement with Hope College had anything further to offer him, David Ihrman left school to pursue his further education at a prestigious eastern university. The son of the superintendent never received the Holland High School diploma that was so coveted by others.

CHAPTER THIRTY-FOUR
VEHICLES 1964-1978
"If You Want to Buy a Nice Present for Your Son's Last Birthday, Buy Him a Motorcycle."

One of the sobering and saddening facets of school life, both then and now, is the rate at which young people are killed, maimed, or suffer a hospital stay due to injuries suffered in automobile accidents. Holland High School was no exception; every year we sustained the loss or severe injury of students in motor vehicle accidents resulting from the inexperience of young drivers,

The Bertsch youthful drivers were among those contributing to these statistics, but fortunately we did not have a death or serious injury within our immediate family. Each had an accident, arrest or both within a year after being licensed to drive and thus automobile problems were played a significant in our lives during the entire period of my principalship.

As an addition to our 1953 Ford Country Squire station wagon, we managed to eke out the funds to buy a red and white Jeep, the second and last motor vehicle we ever bought new. We didn't like the idea of dropping the hundreds, or even thousands, of dollars that are lost the minute the new car is driven away from the dealership. This Jeep was another station wagon basically the World War II Jeep chassis, but enclosed with a body that started immediately to rust out, giving it at least the illusion of having received heavy use over a long period of time. The intent of this purchase was to provide Lory with independent transportation to her job as a teacher at Lincoln School, but when Susan was licensed to drive, she was often allowed to drive the car to some of her many extra-curricular activities, and later provide transportation for both of the older girls. Almost immediately after given permission to drive, Susan attempted to back out of the garage with the door on the passenger side open, a feat that crumpled the door rather impressively. The door was tied in place with a piece of rope until we could get it back to the dealer for replacement.

It was not long after the Jeep was repaired that Sue, once again backing out of the garage, crashed into a visitor's car parked in the driveway causing several hundred dollars in damages to the visitor's car, making a considerable dent in our family treasury. The jeep was essentially undamaged, but getting tired. When Martje got her driver's license and authorized to drive, she managed to be awarded two traffic tickets in a single evening of driving, a feat that I thought should have some considerable publicity, but thought better of it after a day or so of contemplation.

I don't recall the disposition of the Jeep, but somehow we came into one of the first of the black Volkswagens manufactured in Germany for export after World War II. It was essentially a wreck when we procured it and because of deficiencies, either built in or acquired, the vehicle required some knowledge of its peculiarities and a few basic skills to operate it. The battery was under the limited back seat area, and access was difficult. The ignition switch was frozen in the "on" position, so power could be applied only by connecting the battery to the whole system, requiring that two electrical leads in the engine compartment be twisted together so the car could be started, and power applied where required for ignition, lights and any other electrical application that happened to be operable. We felt is was secure from theft because no one would really want it, and further no stranger to its configuration would be able to get it started.

The VW did have running boards, a feature that allowed youngsters to hang on the sides of the car for surfing rides through Baywoodlands. It did not have a fuel gage, but instead had an emergency fuel reserve that would keep it going for about thirty miles after shifting to this source of gasoline. When Martje started driving, it was in this car that she regularly ran out of gas, despite the fact that she had an adequate allowance, and gasoline during that period sold for about twenty cents per gallon.

It was in this car that Martje achieved the distinction of receiving tickets for two traffic violations issued by the same policeman in a single evening. We considered that this achievement should receive some sort of award, but didn't pursue the matter. I don't recall, but believe this vehicle died of natural causes.

With respect to discipline, Martje was a handful for Lory and me, always in trouble or skirting trouble, and not only with motor vehicles. She developed a friendship with Vickie Venhuizen a relationship that has endured to the present, despite all the difficulties, marital and otherwise, that have plagued them over all these years. The two girls were of a similar rebellious nature, and the combination seemed to accelerate their penchant for adventurous and sometimes illegal activities.

Due to my restless sleep habits, I am often awake and out of bed at the crack of dawn. Arising one summer morning just as it was getting light after fixing myself a cup of coffee to carry with me, I thought I should walk down to the dock to admire the new Lyman power boat we had purchased from Jesiek Brothers Shipyard only a few weeks before. As I stepped out on the patio a glance toward the lake told me the cherished water craft was gone. Only after I had recovered somewhat from the sinking feeling at the loss and the astonishment that accompanied it did I look up and scan the part of the lake that was visible from our dock. Coming around Pine Point across Pine Creek Bay from where I stood the gleaming white Lyman with its engine idling to avoid detection was the Lyman. Martje had filched the ignition key from the cabinet in which I stored all keys, and taken an all night cruise on the inland lake. On questioning, it was revealed they had considered taking the boat out through the shipping channel to Lake Michigan for a ride on the big waters, but postponed that diversion for some future date.

Pine Point and forty or more acres of wooded property on its land side was a resort named Pine Lodge, occupied by Bob Horner, a retired University of Michigan professor, and his wife Charlotte, who either did the work around the resort, or hired it done. I learned later that it was her inherited money that had allowed her to purchase the property.

Bob was an adjunct to the place but held no proprietary interest. The seven or eight tiny out buildings, as well as two houses, all in addition to the large house in which the Horners lived, served as dwellings for clients hailing from faraway places like Kansas City or Louisville from Tulip Time in May until after Labor Day. In addition to her maintenance and laundry functions, Charlotte did the meal planning, cooking and serving with only the assistance of a hired neighbor, while Bob was pretty much a complacent observer of the activity around him.

Bob was the adopted son of "Skipper" Horner who had both inspired and encouraged me to build a twenty-three foot deep keeled sailboat that sat unfinished on its supporting blocks in a building on my parents' property for fifteen years until I finished it during my accumulated leave after World War II. Now he had little to do around Pine Lodge so he decided to run for and was elected to the office of justice of the peace, an archaic position that handled cases brought by the township constable.

There was a large house in disrepair on the forty acre parcel of heavily wooded land, also belonging to Charlotte, lying to the north of her Pine Lodge operation. The old house had not been occupied for years, and perhaps it was for this reason that Martje and Vickie decided they should occupy it. They had used the decrepit dwelling as a headquarters for several months, roasted hot dogs and marshmallows over the coals of fires in the ancient fireplace.

Inevitably Judge Horner, as he liked to be called, became aware of these illegal activities and when the girls next took up occupancy he arrived, accompanied by the constable who arrested them. The judge then proceeded with a trial back at the lodge, also illegal, and sentenced them to two months of probation with provision that the two girls were forbidden to see each other during that period. The separation of the girls required by this sentence was viewed by the girls as both a challenge and an opportunity.

The canoe that was a part of our assembly of watercraft lay upside down on the beach when not in use, so it was an obvious solution to the challenge. A rendezvous was arranged by telephone and with that mischievous girls were back in business. In an incident similar to that involving the Lyman, I strolled down to the dock one morning and noted that the canoe was missing. Casting my eyes over the bay I saw the canoe some distance away, and apparently unoccupied. I jumped in the Lyman without any thought as to how or why the canoe had removed itself from its normal place inverted and well up on shore. I motored out to tow it in and restore it to its normal position next to the dock. On arrival at the canoe, there were the two girls lying on its floor thinking, apparently, that they were somehow going to elude detection.

We were never able to control Martje and guide her into positive behavioral patterns. She started smoking cigarettes while still a child and soon discovered the relaxing effects of alcohol, becoming a severe alcoholic as an adult with disastrous results and all the while puffing away on her coffin nails, and convincing Buck at a tender age to start smoking, a habit which almost became fatal when he contracted tuberculosis some years later, an experience that taught him smoking was not a good idea.

The friends of the Bertsch siblings were always welcome at our house, but on occasion made themselves overly welcome, as in the time we arrived home and found two of Martje's boy friends fencing in the recreation room, one with a decorative lodge sword and the other with my navy dress sword neither of which was designed for actual combat, and either of which might have been ruined in the duel that was going on.

When Buck entered the eighth grade at the new junior-senior high school, he was an expert at skipping classes and somehow evading detection in the as yet fully organized West Ottawa Junior/Senior High School. During small game hunting season, that activity occupied his time. When finally detected at the end of the first semester, the punishment awarded was to attend study hall during the final period of the day, but the teacher/supervisor, through some oversight, was not notified of the new enrollee, and he left promptly at the end of the previous class and walked or hitch-hiked his way to freedom.

One of his additional adventures followed his reporting to the school nurse with what he thought was a bellyache hoping get out of school for the rest of the day. The school nurse took his temperature and found it elevated followed by a touch of his abdomen and rightly concluded he had appendicitis and his appendix should be removed in the immediate future. We picked him up after calling our doctor and arranging a hospital meeting at which the physician verified the diagnosis and quickly had Buck in the pre-operation process. As he was being wheeled to the operating room on a gurney we had an opportunity to wish him well. He peered out from above the sheet covering his body and plaintively cried out, *Mom, Dad, they're making a big mistake.*

By the time Buck had completed driver education and began to drive regularly, the Jeep was gone and replaced by a beautiful but small red Volkswagen station wagon. In light of all our son's shenanigans, we decided that the atmosphere at Holland High would be better for Buck, particularly in that I could monitor his activities to some degree from my position as principal and he could ride with me to school each day. We happily paid the tuition this required, as we were not residents of the Holland school district. An added reason important to me was that upon graduation he would become the third Fred S. Bertsch to graduate from Holland High School.

Toward the end of the school year a classmate, Cindy Marlink, invited him to attend the Cotton Cotillion with her, and he now says of that relationship, *The rest is history.* I would add that it not to be without untoward incidents. Having completed driver education, Buck received his driving license toward the end of the school year and he and Cindy had frequent dates. The time for the almost-traditional teen accidents had arrived.

Buck drove the new red Volkswagen to Zeeland to pick up Cindy and say hello to her parents, who in the nature of parents, had yet to be reassured that this young man was an appropriate date for their daughter. As Buck entered the city of Zeeland, he found the street on which she lived and then proceeded with some caution to read house numbers in the gloom of night. There was a sudden and continuing shriek marking the metal-to-metal contact on the passenger side of car. The sound alerted the residents of several houses who assembled quickly to see what had happened. Two of these residents in addition to Cindy's parents were her Uncle Lornie, who was the Zeeland Chief of Police and his wife. Wilma, who were visiting the Marlinks. This was a painful experience for the young suitor. He met some of Cindy's extended family before being arrested and carted off to the Zeeland jail by her uncle, who called and notified us of his action. After a bit of conferring we decided to allow him to remain in his cell until morning when we would pick up both Buck and the damaged vehicle.

Roughly a year later in midwinter and the roads lined with banks of snow piled higher than the roof of the car, Buck and Cindy were returning after a date and driving at a moderate speed well below the speed limit when a car ran a stop sign on a street joining that on which Buck was driving. The car hit them virtually head-on, propelling Cindy against the windshield and she was taken to the hospital for examination to determine what injuries she ha suffered. As in the previous case, the driver was uninsured and we were stuck with the loss, although this loss was to a degree offset when he reappeared as a customer in a dining room where Buck was his server. The offender emptied his wallet to leave a large tip.

There were other bruises, bumps, dents and scrapes over the years, but none serious until six years later, following many other adventures and encounters, including his year at the naval academy narrated elsewhere and he became a freshman at Hope College. He was offered a summer job as an assistant roofer by the Mooi Roofing Company whose slogan appeared to have a double meaning, "We Keep Holland Dry." This kept him busy until the beginning of the first semester, when he fell off a roof while carrying a bucket of hot tar and was burned from wrist to elbow leaving a king sized scab on his right arm.

That year marked the end of the red VW station wagon when Buck used it one night to visit friends living in the freshman dorm, where he parked the car on the street alongside the building. As Buck was getting out of the car a drunk driver with his wife and baby in the car with him, slammed into the rear of the VW, projecting it over the curb and crumpling it such that it was not repairable. Although his front tires were flattened in the crash, the driver of the offending car attempted a getaway. At the sound of the crash the dorm was vacated as its residents sought to view the scene, and they chased the car until the rims of the wheels on the car, digging into the pavement forced it to stop. The driver found himself surrounded. A student departed to call the police, and when they arrived, it was the wife who claimed to be driving knowing her husband would be jailed because he had been arrested numerous times before for the same offense.

Mary Jo received her license after her completion of driver education and promptly decided she should drive to Grand Rapids, a metropolitan area much larger than Holland. When she drove straight ahead from the clearly marked left turn lane it caught the eye of the policeman driving behind her and she was ticketed for the offense. The result was that I had to appear in juvenile court with her at which hearing the judge awarded her a small fine and a year of probation. I don't know, but I don't think she has had a traffic violation since.

HOMECOMING ROYALTY — Mary Jo Bertsch (left), 21, majoring in physics/chemistry, an Thomas Maas, 22, a business administration major, were announced as Hope College' homecoming queen and king at halftime of the Hope-Olivet football game this past weeken Miss Bertsch is the daughter of Mr. and Mrs. Fred Bertsch, 149 Crestwood Dr., Holland, and graduate of West Ottawa High School. Maas is the son of Mr. and Mrs. Leonard Maas Grandville. Hope defeated Olivet 42-14.

Photo: The Holland Sentinel

CHAPTER THIRTY-FIVE
DENOUEMENT 1977-1978
The Gratuitous Insult

As was becoming customary, in the spring of 1977, I, along with every professional of the staff of teaching professionals, received a "pink slip", a letter actually and appropriately duplicated on pink paper, informing us that we would not be hired for the ensuing school year, 1977-78.

My letter read,

Dear Mr. Bertsch:

In light of the recent defeat of the school millage election by the voters of the School District of the City of Holland, and after full and careful consideration of all the pertinent circumstances, the Board of Education has determined that due to economic conditions it will be necessary to implement a reduction-in-staff of the School District's administrative personnel, effective July 1, 1977...this letter is to inform you that the Board of Education will be unable to offer you a contract.....for the school year
1977-78. ....This notice is being provided to enable you to make plans for the coming year."

It struck me as ironic then, and even more so in retrospect, that in effect I was being fired before I had a chance to resign.

I had been having several physical indications that the stress of my professional position was injurious to my health. Although always a light sleeper, I began to have nights when I barely slept at all even though there were no unusual crises at the school. There were also the times when there actually *were* crises or perceived crises to disturb my sleep. The interactions among the teachers, the board of education, parents, townspeople and other groups seemed increasingly to place demands on both my time and my patience.

About this time I wrote a little note for the retirement file:

Working for the Board of Education is a bit like working for a committee composed of the seven blind men of India famous for their legendary descriptions of an elephant, each based on a different tactile examination of a different part of that animal. In my view, I was trying to satisfy a number of irreconcilable constituencies without the slightest hope I could satisfy them all.

A letter from the Assistant Superintendent for Personnel dated June 15, 1977, shortly after the end of the school year, with all of its harrowing details, rescinded the earlier action awarding all professional staff "pink slips." The letter read in part, *The "yes" vote on the millage issue assures the Board of adequate funds to continue the operation of the schools.*

There followed a paragraph thanking staff for their support during the campaign seeking a favorable vote in the millage election. The final paragraph was less reassuring: *Contracts for your employment will be issued later in the summer after consideration by the Board.* As noted before, this usually meant that Principals would get to share the leftovers following the negotiation of a settlement with the bargaining unit.

For the entire summer and during the fall semester in 1977, Don and I had intermittently discussed the fact that I was getting worn out in the job and wanted to leave it before I became a bitter and worn out old man. Finally, in a letter to him dated February 25, 1978 I wrote, *"This letter is written to confirm our previous conversations in which I indicated that this would be my last year as principal of Holland High School. Please consider this letter to be my resignation from the principalship effective June 30, 1978.....*

"The support which you have personally given my efforts during these nearly fourteen years has been sincerely appreciated, and I have been thankful of the supportive efforts of the Board of Education, the teaching and administrative staff, the students and the community."

Following the announcement of my resignation, a flood of letters and phone calls came to the principal's office. Most commended my performance; I assumed those with more negative views withheld their comments

One letter came almost immediately from Helen Brownson, the former Holland High special education teacher, now the "Special Needs Coordinator" on the vocational education staff of the county:

The news of your retirement came as a real surprise, and I wanted to write you a letter as soon as possible to tell you I am personally sorry to see you leave us as principal. We will miss your leadership!

I feel I owe a great deal to you – the opportunities for growth and service which I gained in working with you through the years. You never "clipped my wings"....and I always felt free to develop programs and try innovative and creative ideas.....You provided a wisdom and political awareness in relating to the community that weathered us through many a storm from the days of "proper dress code" to "break supervision." I know it hasn't been easy, but I trust you feel somewhat rewarded for your service in administration....thank you ...Helen.

A letter dated February 13, 1978 on the letterhead of Immanuel Baptist Church read, *Thank you for taking the time out from your busy schedule to write such a kind letter regarding our daughter Beth.* (I had sent a letter of congratulations to the parents of all seniors.) *As parents, we want you to know that we deeply appreciate all that you and your staff are doing to mold young people to be responsible and dependable. We moved to Holland five years ago and we are most happy for the excellent education our children are receiving from the Holland Public School system.*

We respect your decision to resign as Principal, but are sorry to see you leave this position. Congratulations on your many years of excellent service. May God's blessing be yours as you embark upon a new chapter of experience.

Sometime before my resignation was announced, my hands broke out in sores that resembled the blisters one gets from touching a hot stove, but these were all over my hands. I could hardly hold the pen or pencil that seemed indispensable in performing my functions. I consulted our family physician, my friend Walter Kuipers. He prescribed some innocuous salves that had no effect whatsoever on the problem.

After a few months of the ineffective treatment he attempted, Dr. Kuipers recommended a dermatologist in Grand Rapids, and I arranged to have appointments with him prior to my weekly Naval Reserve obligations, further disrupting my already life under pressure.

On office visits this worthy skin doctor would examine my sore and blistered hands, utter a few incantations and then have me hold my hands under an ultra violet lamp. He prescribed more and different medicines in the form of salves or powders to be applied in generous quantities at bedtime, and then held in place by plastic gloves secured at the wrists by rubber thongs, making it difficult to scratch my nose or perform any other activities involving a hand or hands. A couple of months of this were enough for me. Spring was passing and eventually my resignation would become effective.

After six or eight more of these ineffective visits, the dermatologist said, *They don't seem to be getting any better, do they?*

I agreed. *What do you think I should do?* I inquired.

Quit your job, was his terse but highly accurate response. He went on with a rather lengthy dissertation explaining why this phenomenon had occurred. By this time the effective date of my resignation was imminent, and a few weeks later, when the school year ended and the tensions of the principal's job disappeared, the sores on my hands, had also disappeared.

Bertsch Resigns As Principal

Holland High School Principal Fred S. Bertsch Jr. announced his resignation at a special meeting of the Holland Board of Education Monday night.

Bertsch, in his 14th year as principal, will remain in the position until June 30 of this year. He said he was resigning for personal reasons and has tentative plans of returning to teaching.

"I would like to keep the doors open," Bertsch said of his plans for the future.

If he returns to the classroom, he would prefer to teach mathematics at the high school level, as he did at Holland High from 1958 to 1964, when he was head of the mathematics department. He also is qualified to teach social studies and English. He indicated he may teach another two to three years.

Bertsch graduated with an A. B. degree in mathematics from Hope College in 1941. He received a masters degree and teaching credentials from Western Michigan University, and did further graduate work at the University of Michigan.

After a 33-year combined regular and reserve Navy career, including teaching navigation and marine engineering as the assistant professor of naval science at the University of Minnesota, Bertsch worked from 1955 to 1957 in Lear Inc. Aviation Instrument Division. He was hired to teach mathematics at Holland High School in 1958.

Bertsch was named principal of the high school in the summer of 1964 following the resignation of Jay W. Formsma who left to become principal of Stevenson High School in Livonia, Mich.

Bertsch has seen and had a hand in many of the physical and curriculum changes that have occurred since he became principal of the then 2½-year-old campus.

"The high school maintained its freedom and responsible philosophy during the rather turbulent period of the late 60s and early 70s. Curriculums were developed that have been intended to prepare students for life as well as for future academic work in an atmosphere of relative student freedom while insisting on student responsibility," Bertsch said.

Of Bertsch, Supt. Donald L. Ihrman said: "Fred Bertsch is a professional administrator. The high standards which he upheld as a high school principal have

Fred S. Bertsch Jr.

been sincerely appreciated. We wish Fred well as he returns to the classroom following a successful assignment as principal of Holland High School."

Board President Deanna De Pree expressed apprececiation for Bertsch's 14 years of dedicated service as principal, and Bertsch replied he always appreciated the support of the Board of Education as well as the superintendent and administration. "I will always support Holland schools," he said.

A Holland Sentinel editorial commented favorably on my principalship:

A Good Principal

The first official act Donald L. Ihrman did as Holland school superintendent was to select Fred S. Bertsch, Jr. as Holland High School principal.

It was Aug. 17, 1964 and the Bertsch selection met with approval throughout the community.

"Fred Bertsch was the No. 1 choice of Ihrman and the board endorsed his preference 100 per cent," school board president Harvey Buter said.

Bertsch was selected because "by training and experience he possesses administrative and organizational abilities," Ihrman said. Bertsch had been a teacher in the Holland system for six years prior to his appointment.

The former Naval captain accepted the challenge of leading Holland High School and since that time has run a "tight ship."

Bertsch was a Holland High School graduate, left the community for several years to serve in the Navy and then after obtaining his teacher's degree became a high school mathematics teacher.

When his predecessor and his boss (Jay Formsma) took a post in Livonia, Bertsch applied for the job and was selected over all of the applicants. He appeared to be and was the man for the job.

Bertsch and Don Ihrman had both graduated from Holland High under J. J. Riemersma, a principal who emphasized the importance of discipline and learning.

In the turmoil of the late 60's, Bertsch's selection proved to be an excellent one. He knew how to handle the students when they began challenging administration policies.

He has continued to emphasize what he thought was important in present day high school education. Like any person who makes decisions, Bertsch has had his backers and his foes. But he leaves no doubt that he is in control at Holland High School.

We know he did a good job. Holland High School is better because of what Bertsch did.

His early announcement gives Ihrman and the Holland board plenty of time to look for a successor. They will have to decide if they are to look outside for a replacement or to promote within the system.

Bertsch's selection was Ihrman's first decision. It was a good one.

We know his choice of a successor will be made after thorough study and will be another good decision.

The Holland Sentinel

As the school year melted away, there were many small acts of kindness that I greatly appreciated. One of these was an assembly given by the students during which Student Mayor David Trask presented me with a beautifully finished maple cribbage board equipped with brass pegs, made by a combination of students in the wood shop and machine shop classes. In his remarks, the mayor included some favorable comments about my cheerleading, as well as my Santa Claus and "pie-in-the-face" activities that had sparked our assemblies and pep rallies.

Another student read a paper, no doubt in collaboration with a member of the teaching staff that purported to be a commentary on the way in which I conducted teachers' meetings:

There has been a great deal of consternation and speculation about Captain Bertsch and a secret weapon of his aboard the U.S.S. Holland High that keeps staff meetings number one across the sea. Brother Piersma has elucidated that it is the Captain's memos. I have often thought it was in his use of the confuser, I mean computer, in scheduling. However, I am always reminded that these are tickets, not bodies, used by the Captain in the scheduling process. Sister Van Lente (a counselor) thinks that the secret weapon lies in the Captain's sea stories. On the other hand, others think it is how he massages the meetings. But now, as we continue down the pike, at this point in time, and with all hands on deck, we would like to present the Captain with some hardware which does contain the secret weapon forged this very day for all future recalcitrants to see. With that he pulled out from the back of the lectern a gigantic paddle of the type used in fraternity initiations, and presented it to me.

In the final week of school my Ghia was filled with balloons for one last time. The cheerleaders were the perpetrators, and the tennis team, practicing on the courts below the faculty parking lot and several other students, lingering about, gathered to watch my reaction to this harmless prank.

An annual event on the morning preceding the rehearsal for commencement was a seven o'clock outdoor breakfast held at Kollen Park, a beautiful area on Lake Macatawa, about a half mile from the high school campus. This affair was hosted by the athletic staff, and prepared by them on charcoal grills of several sorts. The standard menu was fried or scrambled eggs, bacon, beans assorted home-made breads and coffee, always enough of everything to satisfy the most ravenous appetite. When everyone had been served, it was customary to present retiring or departing staff members with a gift, a trinket for those with brief service, and more significant and costly gifts for retirees with many years of service.

Retirees from previous years were always invited to this event, and most joined in the festivities. All such attendees were recognized amid much laughter and applause. Usually, this had been the time to adjourn, and time for the hosts to put out the fires, stow away any remaining food and police up the area. This allowed plenty of time for all hands to retire to the civic center a few blocks away and practice for the commencement to be held that evening.

The routine was modified in 1978 to allow for one more event in recognition of my departure as the principal who had served longer than any predecessor, excepting, of course, the revered Jock Riemersma, whose long career set a record not likely ever to be broken. From the back of pickup trucks, the trunks of cars and various other hiding places came a variety of equipages to support a skit.

As I watched the scenario unravel, the thought passed through my mind *Was this to be a celebration of my departure at long last, or was it to be recognition of a job well done?* It was an interesting group that surrounded me: supporters and opponents; active staff and retirees; male and female, young and old. At least I didn't feel I was about to be assassinated. All the non-participants gathered around my ancient, decrepit, long retired canoe snatched for the occasion from the back of Dirk Bloemendaal's pickup truck.

I was encouraged to take a seat in the canoe as a place of honor and escorted to the canoe by Carol Van Lente, who placed my scrambled egg emblazoned uniform cap on my head, and helped me into my leather flight jacket, displaying the badges of several aviation units in which I had served. These were provided by Lory, cooperating with the perpetrators from behind the scenes. When seated in the canoe, Carol handed me a paddle, and it appeared that the show was ready to get on the road.

The program for the event survived in my collected notes, letters, anecdotes, etc., but, unfortunately little more. I wish it had all been recorded, as my memory has dropped the details and this report of the proceedings is thus totally inadequate. My principal memory is that "A good time was had by all." The program:

> *Subject: The Fred S. Bertsch, Jr. Hour*
>
> *When: Thursday, June __, 1978*
>
> *Time: Approximately 0830*
>
> *Where: Kollen Park*
>
> *Theme: "F.S.B. in Retrospect"*
>
> *MC: Don Piersma*
>
> *Order of Events:*
>
> *1. Setting the Scene: Tom Carey & Nat Bosman*
> Kind words from a couple of stalwart supporters.
>
> *2. F.S.B. in the Navy: Ed Damson*
> Ed wore his navy lieutenant's uniform and reflected on my naval service.
>
> *3. Pearl Harbor Revisited: Ted Boeve*
>
> This was a spoof in which Ted impersonates a Japanese pilot who participated in the attack on Pearl Harbor being interviewed by "Z" (Zeke Piersma) As corny as it is, it is the only piece of script remaining from that Thursday morning so long ago:

" Z: Our distinguished guest this morning, having traveled all the way from Japan to help celebrate this occasion is Yamamoto Hirohito Habachi." (Habachi enters, in his bathrobe, bowing and smiling and then completes his entrance with a shout of : "Bonzai!

"Z: Is it true Captain Hibachi that you piloted the lead plane in the attack on Pearl Harbor?

"B: Ah So; I pilot first plane in the attack – it was a Focke Wulfe. See here, this is the Focking medal they gave me for the attack.

"Z: You have to be kidding. The Focke Wulf is a German plane left over from World War I.

"B: Sukiyaki! No wonder we lose the war. Where is this 'Fried Rice,' that hero from Pearl Harbor we honor today?

"Z:" (Pointing) "You mean Fred Bertsch, not Fried Rice. He's over there in his ship.

"B: Kawasaki! How can that be? Are you sure you won the war? Ah so, now I remember him. He used to be a good swimmer, but he looks more like a floater now.

"Z: What gift do you bring to commemorate this solemn occasion?

"B: Nippon have special gift for Captain Bertsch: a bowl of fried rice and a life membership in Tokyo Massage Parlor. Now that he's no longer principal, we're gonna massage him good."

4. Headaches Through the Years: Carol Van Lente
I don't remember a word of what she said, but we had been confidantes for years, so it no doubt was good.

5. Shedding of Blood: Roger Plagenhoef
Roger, of course, had been my opposite and opponent on many periods of negotiations and conferences, but on this occasion was in a jovial mood, and made a kind and funny little speech about our many confrontations.

6. A-Fishing We Will Go: Dirk Bloemendaal
Dirk told of several of our adventures while fishing, emphasizing our misfortunes and sometimes dangerous adventures as in fishing from icebergs and fishing from a twelve foot boat used as an ice-breaker.

7. From Roast to Toast: Harold Tregloan
Kind words from a veteran of non-partisanship.

8. *Response – Words of Wisdom: Mr. Fred S. Bertsch, Jr.*
What could I say? It was great fun. The pressure was off and I felt
Honored. I hoped my few words of appreciation were adequate.

The senior class invited me to deliver the commencement address. I was pleased to accept the invitation, and felt it to be an honor. That year I was identified as a "Distinguished Graduate of Holland High School." I was determined to make my speech one of the shorter ones on record:

I have been invited to speak on this happy occasion. Congratulations to the outstanding class of nineteen seventy-eight.

Floods of thoughts have been going through my mind during these recent weeks as I prepared to sever my official ties to this institution with which I and my family have had such a long relationship. My father and I and my son all graduated from Holland High School. About seven thousand students have graduated from this school since I joined the faculty; about five thousand of them since I became the principal in a year when most of this year's graduates were four years old. It would be easy to launch into a nostalgic recital of the past, but I do not propose to do so. In fact, I will be mercifully brief.

There are limitless challenges in this world, and it would be appropriate enough to present many of them to the members of the class of 1978 for their consideration. I choose to present to you tonight only one challenge and that a very simple one: the challenge of work and service; the challenge to you to produce to the very best of your abilities and for the betterment of mankind. I challenge you to project yourselves into the work ethic, and to reject the idea that the world owes you a living. John Kennedy's admonition, "Ask not what your country can do for you, but rather what you can do for your country:, is closely akin to this idea.

So also is the notion that it is wise to use the physical spiritual strengths of youth to produce a better world - - not for loafing, but for producing more for everyone. The strength, the aggressiveness, the confidence and the brashness of youth is often wearing on older generations, but these are valuable qualities which can only be used by you while they are still available. I am reminded of the cut-line

under a cartoon saying to his college-aged son, "Why don't you quit school and apply for a job as president of General Motors or some other big corporation while you still know it all?"

I am also reminded of the hullabaloo that was caused some years ago by the comment made by Charles Wilson. President Eisenhower's Secretary of Defense, to the effect that all people can be likened to either hunting dogs or kennel dogs; that the hunting dogs go out and get the job done, while the kennel dogs sit on their tails and howl about it. This is an oversimplification, but the idea is clear.

In another version of this same general theme, the populace of the world is conceived as divided among builders, painters and wreckers. We always have too many wreckers in our society and never enough builders. We need good builders, generous builders, unselfish builders. If you can't be a builder, at least be a painter who supports the builders; one who maintains the good that surrounds us. Never be a wrecker.

So my challenge to you of the class of 1978 is simple indeed: Be workers. Be producers. Be of service. Be hunting dogs rather than kennel dogs. Be builders and painters rather than wreckers. Build a better world. Good luck!"

There was a reception after the ceremonies concluded, and many gracious words were spoken by the guests reinforcing my belief that I, as a retired sailor could say in grammar I wouldn't accept from either students or faculty, "I seen my duty an' I done it."

For fourteen years I had viewed the scene from my office window, including the unpaved parking lot and the oval around which student speeders raced, sometimes on motorcycles. I had tolerated the minimal salaries accorded me and the tiny annual raises offered. When my successor was about to be named, she negotiated with the board for a number of things including the paving and the speed bumps and was given a salary several thousands more than mine, even though she had only served as an administrator for a year before that time. She held the position for one year before retreating back into the classroom. I swallowed hard and enjoyed my retirement to the extent I could.

I was given the opportunity to reflect on my performance when a student correspondent for The Sentinel interviewed me.

A Visit With Fred Bertsch

By Kirk Emerson
Holland High Correspondent

After 14 years of being principal of Holland High School, Fred Bertsch will will retire this June. During those years there has been a great deal of social change in attitudes, styles and morals.

In keeping with the times, Bertsch and Holland High have been able to change while still remaining the unique educational institution it is.

In order to get to know the man and his job, I spent some times asking questions and letting him talk. His answers were frank and they were honest.

Here is the interview that took place.

Kirk Emerson: Have these last fourteen years been good years?

Bertsch: I think so. I have been headof an educational institution that is unique in many ways. It survived the tough and bitter days of the late 60s and early 70s with few of the scars other educational institutions shared. Also, we have produced quality graduates during these years as Holland High School has over more than 100 years of its history. I think it's quite an honor to be head of such an institution. It has served the community well and it's no means perfect, but we've tried to operate Holland High School as a pragmatic institution that molds itself with the times.

Emerson: The first years, what were they like?

Bertsch: Holland High School was very highly structured in which everyone was in study halls or class all the time. Movement was only on a bell system. The big change came when we moved to the new campus under my predecessor, Jay Formsma. It was at that time we started the freedom and responsibility program, the open campus system and so on.

We've changed many, many things over the years. When I was first principal, we had detention after school for people who missed classes; we instituted a form of in-school suspension that recalled instruction and personal-discipline (IPD).

I must say that it wouldn't surprise me at all if we re-institute those things at some point and time. Because, as you know, although we emphasize student responsibility, our student body isn't always responsible as it might be, particular on matters of promptness and attendance.

These are national-wide problems, they are not peculiar to Holland High School, but, never-the-less for performance in adult society, attendance and promptness at one's job are usually considered to be qualities that people should have.

There is some concern about this problem not only at the school level, but there's also concern out in the community. We are aware of that.

Emerson: When you first started, were the teachers and students different to work with as compared to today's teachers and students?

Bertsch: I think we all were more highly structured in those days. In many ways I think there was a greater distance between the teacher and the student.

The Vietnam war changed a lot of attitudes; it changed a lot of things. It charged many, many superficial stylistic kinds of things. Here at Holland High, we were better able to adapt to those changes (hairstyles, clothes, attitudes toward the "establishment") than the other schools.

Emerson: Any reasons why Holland High was able to adapt better?

Bertsch: I think so because of our fundamental philosophy of education here at Holland High School. We place great emphasis on student freedom and responsibility. That is the opposite pole from the school that takes the philosophy that students are no good and therefore should be locked up all the time in a highly structured atmosphere. These notions are 180 degrees apart.

If you take the philosophy that basically students are no good, then what follows from that is an atmosphere in which you have bells and signals and little passports that allow you to go from one area to another, while being watched by the hall monitor. And, since you don't trust students to be on their own, you have to have study halls to hold them in place when you don't have something else for them to do. Now if you take the opposite philosophy which is that our student-body is at least as good as its adult counterparts, then many things flow from that.

Emerson: Such as?

Bertsch: Well, first of which is freedom of action and freedom to choose. Basically we like to think that students being counseled by parents, teachers, counselors, administrators, etc., can make good life choices.

Now that isn't universally true, but, never-the-less we believe all people, including students, living in a free society should be allowed freedom of choice including freedom to error. If indeed a true society such as ours is to persist, we think people approaching adulthood should be educated in a free, not less freer atmosphere.

Emerson: After 14 years of being principal and a teacher before that, what are some of your observations of teenagers?

Bertsch: Well, number one I have a tremendous amount of faith in the United States and in our youth. There have been thousands of great graduates over the 109 years of Holland High's existence. but, that doesn't mean they were all graduated so many years ago. There will be great graduates in the class of '78, '79, and '80, just as there were in the 20s, 30s, 40s, 50s, and the 60s. We will continue to have outstanding alumni. I have no doubt about it at all. I have great faith in the youth. In fact, I haven't seen any great negative change in my 14 years.

Emerson: What are some of the major problems you face in this job?

Bertsch: Many of the problems we face are centered around the students growing up. As we all grow, we invariably face problems. Here at Holland High a very large proportion of our student body come from broken homes where there is just one parent at home. There are many parents not equipped to be parents. And there are many parents not equipped to be parents. And there are serious inter-faces between parents and students. Parents don't necessarily understand youth and youth don't necessarily understand parents.

Now that's nothing new to you and it's nothing new to me but those situations go on year after year after year. Now adults are not perfect by any matter or means; many of them create problems and consequently a very great deal of an administrator's time is spent in trying to minimize the effect of family and social problems upon the performance of the student. What is really comes down to is helping students survive.

Emerson: The job of being a principal must be a thankless job. You could have so many people angry at you all the while you're trying to help them. Ever thought about packing up and deciding it just isn't worth the trouble?

Bertsch: Yeah (hearty laughter). Yeah, I have. I think everything has its time and I feel very strongly that this is the time for me to leave the principalship with grace and dignity. And I hope that's what I'm doing.

Lory continued teaching for a year in order to qualify for full retirement at age sixty. One fall day after I had prepared her breakfast and sent her on her way for another day of teaching the fourth grade at Lincoln School, I retreated down the hallway to the bedroom area where my office had been relocated to Susan's former bedroom. I did not fully close the front door as it was a mild day and I knew the storm door, although glass above the knee level, was fully closed.

Before I got to the end of the hall, there was a tremendous crash of broken glass and the front door was slammed open. For a moment I thought perhaps it was the action of a former student who had decided to seek some pent up vengeance against his principal, but then I heard footsteps on the half flight of stairway that led to the level of the recreation room and utility room. By this time I was peering out from behind the wide open front door. There followed a once again a great crashing

UNEXPECTED VISITOR — An eight-to-ten-point buck was a morning caller at the Fred Bertsch home, 149 Crestwood Dr., at about 8:15 a.m. The buck entered the front storm door, breaking the pane, and bursting through the apparently not tightly- latched wood front door and then blundered its way to the lower level into Bertsch's workshop and furnace room where he jumped through a small (40 x 19 inch) window. Bertsch is shown at the exit window. The deer was injured badly in its encounters with the door and window and suffered further injury when it fell into the Bertsch's partially f swimming pool. A DNR officer was called and shot the ani while it was struggling without success to get out of the p Outside of quantities of blood, deer hair and the damage to door and window, which made a big cleanup job, very l other damage was done, according to Bertsch, who said noise was the most terrifying part of the whole experie especially until he and his wife were sure just what had vaded their home. (Sentinel photo by Mark Cop of broken glass as a half dozen cases of cheap soft drinks were tossed around the utility room. There ensued nothing but silence.

A short time later I became courageous enough to venture down to the utility room. There was broken glass and pop everywhere and also some blood and hair or fur. A small window above my workshop was broken, but there was no other sign of who or what had wreaked this havoc. However, when I peered out through the broken window I saw a deer treading water in the bottom of the deep end of the swimming pool. We had lowered he water level in the pool as one element in preparing it for the winter weather ahead. Perceiving there was nothing I could or should do myself about the deer, I called the office of the area conservation officer in Grand Haven. *He's on another mission and we expect him to be gone for the rest of the day. In his absence we have called for the deputy sheriff covering your area to take whatever action he can,* was the response I received.

Within minutes a *Sentinel* reporter with a photographer in tow arrived on the scene and my picture was taken as I peered once again out of the broken window while explaining what had happened. The deputy arrived with a coil of one-inch manila rope in his hand, planning, it appeared, to lead the deer to safety, but he quickly concluded that it might not be a good idea to get the young buck to solid ground only to have him charge the deputy, as he had the reflection of his own image in the glass storm door. The day was wearing on and I had to leave for a dental appointment. The story, somewhat amplified, was already on the local radio station, so I dropped by the school to reassure Lory I was all right. When I got back home, I found the deputy had shot the deer and hauled it off to a butcher who dressed fresh road kill game to be served as food for the county jail inmates.

A picture of me was published in the *Holland Evening Sentinel* in December following my resignation from the principalship as a part of a story about all Holland area residents who were in or near Pearl Harbor at the time of the Japanese attack.

The photograph was taken in the library/den of the house we built after returning to Holland following my active navy career. The picture I am holding was taken at the time of my commissioning in September, 1941. To the left behind me are my medals and a picture of the personnel and planes of the aviation patrol squadron in which I served in during the Korean War. To the right behind me are pictures of the ships in which I served and insignia representing the aviation squadrons in which I served. The final picture was taken at an "all hands party" in La Jolla, less that a week before I sailed as an officer in my first ship *U.S.S. CASE (DD370)*.

I was a newly commissioned officer and the only engineering officer aboard the ship at the time of the Japanese attack. CASE was in an overhaul condition alongside the destroyer tender, U.S.S. WHITNEY lying about five hundred yards from the battleship U.S.S. ARIZONA when she blew up in an explosion triggered by a Japanese bomb. A more detailed description of the events of December Seventh, 1941, and my subsequent naval service through fourteen years, including World War II and the Korean War can be found in my second autobiographical volume titled *Every Day Is Navy Day.*

CHAPTER THIRTY-SIX - ROTARY III
(1979-81)
"What about Me?"

My days of intensive involvement in manifold activities were over or at least so I thought.

Among my desires were yearnings to attend the meetings of the Holland Rotary Club, to do some traveling other than ACDUTRA, some wood working and some small game hunting in season, none of which fit into the schedule of a high school principal whose life was largely programmed by the demands of his occupation. In recognition of my situation and the fact that I now had been a Rotarian for a number of years, I was nominated and elected to serve as club president for the year immediately following my resignation as principal, with my term to begin on the first of July.

While I was entwined with my Rotary obligations in 1979 we received a call from Susan informing us that her always somewhat rocky marriage to Jim Shipley was coming to an end. She had filed for divorce. At that time Jim was reassigned to Vincenza, Italy, while Sue remained at Walter Reed Army Medical Center. To advance in her career, Sue planned to start the academic phase of a doctoral degree in nursing administration at Catholic University.

The logistics of all this were fairly complicated, involving the selling of the large house a hundred miles south of her duty station; moving to quarters at Walter Reed and providing care for her two children. As a result of her call we left the following day, a Saturday, to provide whatever assistance we could including caring for the children until such time as their mother became able to relieve us of those duties.

During our drive from Holland I began to have a feeling in the right side of my jaw that I recognized as one I had experienced several times before. I knew I had a molar that was about to become an abscessed tooth and root canal surgery would inevitably follow. I spoke to Sue on the phone to give her the details of our forthcoming visit and in the process mentioned my tooth. By the time we got to our destination about fifty miles south of Washington in late afternoon my tooth was ready to explode and I was in agony.

It was my good fortune that Sue had had several appointments with a dentist who had established a practice in his basement only a mile or two from her house. How he happened to choose this remote area for his practice remained a mystery to me, but it was fortunate for me he had done so. Sue had called the doctor and advised him of my potential need and he had responded he would see me anytime the need became great. It was late Saturday afternoon when Sue called to tell him I was on my way. By the time I got to his office I was in agony and restraining myself from screaming in anticipation of even greater pain to follow.

My new acquaintance put me in the chair, took a quick look at the tooth, took an X-ray of it to verify its identity, put a burr in his air driven drill and bored a hole through the filling in the tooth into the area where the pus had built up and caused the intense pain I was suffering. Relief was immediate. The professional handed me an envelope containing some penicillin capsules and a prescription for some more as needed. *Take three of these capsules every six hours or so on your way home and make an appointment as soon as possible after your arrival.* As I got up from the chair I started fishing for my wallet planning to pay the bill by credit card if he would accept it, and in the process began thanking the dentist profusely for having seen me outside of office hours late on a Saturday afternoon and for relieving me of the agonizing pain.

What do I owe you? I asked expecting a fairly hefty charge.

Nothing, he said, *You have enough problems on your hands and don't need even a trifle more. Drive carefully on your way back to Michigan and get a root canal started as soon as possible.* That was it. I had never seen the man before and never would again, but his empathic approach to my problem made a tremendous impression on me.

It was then time to return to Sue's and address the situation there. It had already been decided that Lory and I would take the children to Michigan for the time being and allow Susan to get her life back together, pursue her career and her academic goals. Under the circumstances it was decided that I should leave as soon as possible in the Ghia, taking with me the family dog and the limited quantity of the children's clothes and other belongings. Lory would follow a day later in one of the Shipley cars with Skipper and Gail and all the clothing and equipage that could be packed in it to provide for the undetermined visit ahead.

The result of all this was that Lory and I became foster parents for a time, participating in all the joys, laughs and attendant problems that come with children.

This turned out to be a temporary arrangement as planned, but for a time we had a sizable family living with us once again as Martje's two boys, Kasey and Spencer, were deposited with us while their parents went their several ways. We attended cub pack and Parent Teacher Association meetings, chased wandering kids around the neighborhood, attended Little League baseball games and all the other things that parents do.

Susan continued her graduate studies, wrote her thesis and was awarded a doctoral degree in nursing administration. The children rejoined her, and all went on to her next duty station, the Army Research and Development command at Fort Detrick, Maryland, where she was promoted to lieutenant colonel and awarded the Legion of Merit medal for her services. This tour was followed by a two year stint with the headquarters of the U.S. Army Recruiting Command at Fort Sheridan,

Illinois. Her final assignment was as Deputy Commander at Ireland Army Hospital. She retired in 1993.

The Rotary District to which the Holland club belongs is an international district with Canada, but at the time I became club president all of the clubs except for three in Canada lay in the United States. Holland's club was the oldest club in the district, having been chartered in 1921. The Rotary Club of Sault Saint Marie, Canada had been chartered the following year. Through some obscure agreement the Canadians claimed to have entered into at the time the Canadian Sault club was chartered provided for the Canadians to have a district governor every three years.

While this agreement must have seemed to be reasonable at the time with only two clubs involved, but by the time I was elected president of the Holland club it appeared to be quite unreasonable as the district had grown to about sixty clubs and included only three in Canada. In 1978 when I became club president the three Canadian clubs had provided about fifteen district governors, virtually all of them from the Sault club while the fifty five United States clubs shared the other forty-two. A couple of the American clubs claimed two governorships and the remaining thirty-eight were doled out among the other fifty-three clubs.

By failing to press for a governor from within its own ranks the Holland club had never had a district governor. Somewhat chafed by this situation a small group of Holland Rotarians determined on the occasion of his annual visit to press the present governor, who was a Canadian, for assurance that the next governor elected would be a member of the Holland club. On the surface this seems like skullduggery, but at the time and in the reality of things, when a club put forward a nominee, it was tantamount to his election, provided all this occurred within the provisions of the agreement originally made between Holland and the Sault.

All this preparation was then in place and it was incumbent on Holland Rotary to provide a nominee to succeed the present governor two years hence. The principal requirement was that this person be a past club president. It would seem providing a nominee would be an easy task as the club had a long list of past presidents who were active in the club, most of whom at one time or another had decried the fact
Holland had never had a district governor elected from its membership.

Several former presidents had perfect attendance records for years, and two had perfect records for the period of their entire Rotary membership. Others had attended Rotary International conventions in many parts of the world, and still others were serving as leaders of important club committees supporting Rotary's four avenues of service. Several past presidents had been leaders in the local versions of Rotary's famous fireside gatherings designed to instruct new Rotarians.
All had far more Rotary experience than I.

As club president, I requested that all living past presidents in the club gather following a regular club meeting to decide which of these many well qualified members should become governor. I proceeded down the list of the living past presidents present in the order in which they served to inquire if they would accept the nomination. Each in his turn, including those who had previously expressed a desire to become governor, declined the offer, giving excuses such as "too old," "too busy," "ill health," "wife's illness," "business pressures" and so forth through the entire list. I tried some cajoling with no success. After a few minutes I realized that at the end of my Rotary year I would fulfill the requirement that the nominee had served as club president. I ventured to state this fact and that I would be willing to

Holland Rotarian to serve as district governor

Holland will have its first Rotary district governor next year as a result of the recent election of Fred S. Bertsch to head Rotary District 629. Bertsch, a past president of Holland Rotary Club, is the first district governor to be named from the Holland club in its 58 years.

Bertsch assumes the post on July 1, 1979, succeeding present District Governor Edward H. Calkins of Gaylord. The district includes Rotary Clubs in the western section of Michigan, from Holland north to Sault Ste. Marie and into the Canadian province of Ontario. It includes 50 clubs with a membership of 2,778. Each club must be visited at least once during the governor's term.

Active in Holland Rotary Club for 16 years, Bertsch also has served as commodore and director of Macatawa Bay Yacht, is former president of the Century Club and is a member of Holland Country Club. Michigan Association of

Fred S. Bertsch

Secondary School Principals and National Association of Secondary School Principals, the Navy League, U.S. Naval Institute, Naval Reserve Association and Reserve Officers Association.

He enlisted in the Navy following graduation from Hope College in 1941 and was on active duty until 1955, advancing from ensign to commander. From 1955 to 1973 he was on inactive duty with the U.S. Naval Reserve, retiring as captain.

He was affiliated with Lear, Inc., as a sales engineer for several years, until joining the Holland High School faculty in 1958. He served as Holland High principal from 1964 to 1978.

Bertsch earned a master's degree from Western Michigan University and did graduate work at University of Michigan. For his Navy service, he was awarded the Distinguished Flying Cross and 15 other decorations and medals.

Bertsch and his wife, the former Lorraine Timmer, have four children, Mrs. James L. (Susan) Shipley, Mrs. Karl (Martie) Nadolsky, Lt. Fred S. Bertsch III, U.S. Navy, and Mary Jo Bertsch.

The Holland Sentinel

serve, subject to the approval of the club, which was readily given by a voice vote. Thus in effect I elected myself governor.

What followed was a series of experiences that took Lory and me to many parts of the world we would otherwise not have visited and to establish friendships with Rotarians, their spouses and in many cases their children. Our relationships extended beyond geographical, international and cultural boundaries and placed us in a world of common ideals, sharing not only thoughts, but through both financial and personal involvement to accomplish great things, such as the elimination of polio, just one of many goals achieved by Rotarian on both the local and international level.

What followed was a series of experiences that took Lory and me to many parts of the world we would otherwise not have visited and to establish friendships with Rotarians, their spouses and in many case their children. Our relationships extended beyond geographical, international and cultural boundaries and placed us in a world of common ideals, sharing not only thoughts, but through both financial and personal involvement to help accomplish great things, such as the elimination of polio, just one of many goals achieved on both the local and international level.

The Holland Sentinel

Below, L to R: Lory Bertsch, Governor Fritz. Mrs. Renouf, Clem Renouf, then Immediate Past President of Rotary International

In those years, the governor did not have a staff, an office or other support. The governor in our district served almost entirely as a "one man band" in the words of my predecessor. In addition to visiting all sixty of the clubs in the district distributed over a three hundred mile stretch of Western Michigan and Ontario, he was expected to plan a district conference, appoint committees to execute the plan and insure that all went well at the conference, the agenda for which included discussion groups aimed at improving club performance, ideas for the avenues of service and other serious topics as well as leisure activities, activities for the women, as the ladies were not yet included in the actual Rotary membership, and , finally, a banquet. We decided to shoot for the top and requested the Immediate Past President of Rotary International, Clem Renouf, of Australia, to serve at our conference as the Personal Rep-representative of the current president, and he graciously accepted the commission to attend the District 629 conference.

Among other activities we hosted a cocktail party at our house in the woods for all of the past district governors and their wives who were in attendance.

Although I had attended only one district conference in all my time in Rotary, my research told me that past conferences had been held at country clubs, hotels, private banquet facilities and yacht clubs and provisions were made for attendees to be placed in local hotels or motels. As I made my visits to the clubs of the district, I inquired about why the district conferences were not better attended by more of the membership. The average attendance over the years had been in the range of three hundred to three hundred fifty. During my visits I routinely asked the reason for the limited attendance, and found that most answers were *It is too expensive.*

I determined we would attempt to eliminate this reason for non-attendance and thereby radically increase the participation. After some consideration of the matter and a few inquiries, our conference committee decided to negotiate with the authorities at Hope College to provide all of the facilities needed for the conference; meeting rooms, sleeping accommodations (although not air conditioned), recreational facilities, including tennis, golf and gymnasium together with three meals per day including the district conference banquet on the final day.

Total cost? Three hundred dollars per couple as compared to the cost of previous district conferences of about five hundred dollars. Our conference offered more amenities than the more expensive conferences in the past. The total attendance at the Holland conference? Three hundred twenty-five. Non attendees would now have to come up with a new excuse rather than *It's too expensive.*

CHAPTER THIRTY-SEVEN
MACATAWA BAY YACHT CLUB–III
Retirement Yacht

I had been a past commodore of Macatawa Bay Yacht Club for a number of years by the time I retired as the principal of Holland High School but had never owned a sailing yacht larger than Susan's International 110 class boat, nor had Lory and I as adults competed in the club sponsored races other than the practice races described earlier. The races the club sponsored for adults were sailed in The Ensign, a one design keel boat almost exactly the size of the *Lorelei* I had built many years earlier had been selected as one of the classes for adult competition and we planned to participate. Recognizing we were novices sailing against crews that had been competing for years, we elected to name her after one of the famous clipper ships of the previous century, *Criterion.* The name was appropriate, but never understood by the many fellow sailors who questioned it or asked if the name had a special significance. We never revealed its true meaning to us, the novices who were entering competition for the first time. *Criterion* was to be the yacht against which all other yachts of the Ensign class and in particular those competing at Macatawa Bay could be compared. In our first year of competition we finished roughly in the middle of the fleet and our presence among the racing yachts made the upper half of the fleet possible. *Criterion* was thus the standard against which all others were measured.

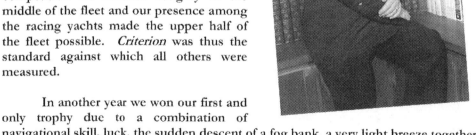

In another year we won our first and only trophy due to a combination of navigational skill, luck, the sudden descent of a fog bank, a very light breeze together with the fleet's self-imposed two hour time limit.

We had rounded the first mark of the triangular course when the wind dropped, but we had tacked up far enough that I estimated we were on the course for the buoy. At that point a dense fog bank enveloped the entire fleet.

The visibility quickly reduced and our vision lowered to little more than fifty feet. I sailed by our compass course, and prayed it would take us to the mark. The wind dropped until it was little more than a breeze. My watch told me we were into the second hour of the time limit as we peered ahead hoping to spot the mark. Suddenly it appeared out of the white cloud in which we were sailing. As we rounded the mark another Ensign with its outboard engine running appeared out of the fog and hailed us. We hoisted the spinnaker for the downwind leg, but there was hardly enough wind to fill it. Eventually we slipped out of the fog and the breeze picked up.

The committee boat was dead ahead. The question then was, *Would we beat the time limit?* The clock was running and as we approached the finish line the committee boat's crew was heaving up to short stay anticipating we would not make the deadline. The wind from astern suddenly quickened and *Criterion* slipped over the finish line with only minutes to spare.

Back at the club when the result was posted awarding *Criterion* the win, several other skippers wrote protests claiming we could not possibly have rounded the mark properly but none was upheld because of the testimony both of the race committee and the skipper of the yacht who observed our windward rounding. Trophies were awarded on a basis which allocated points in each race in descending order based on the number of entries in the series, plus an additional one point was granted to the winner of any race in the series. When the points were calculated by this method for this series *Criterion* was awarded a third place trophy, a little silver plated bowl which I have on display, filled with chocolates, on our coffee table. It is the first and only trophy we received for our efforts during my racing career.

The Sligh brothers, Charlie and Bob, pretty much dominated the Ensign races at Macatawa Bay and went to the Ensign National Championship Series each year, wherever they were held. They towed their boats behind relatively new and powerful cars. A requirement for entry was that a boat had won a series trophy within the past year and we thus qualified because of our win in the fog.

Our car was an under powered Buick and the trailer had come with the boat. Charlie Sligh persuaded me against my better judgment to compete in the national Ensign races to be held that year at the Yachting Club of Old Greenwich Connecticut. I had my doubts about towing the heavy deep keel boat with our aging and under powered Buick, but Charlie prevailed, assuring me that the only hard pull would be the "Lorain Grade" south of Lake Erie. *The rest will be easy going,* said Charlie, *the highway US80 from there on has gentle upward slopes until we coast down into the Hudson River Valley.*

I checked over everything I could think of on car and trailer, had the tires, oil and coolant changed on the car and on the trailer the supports for the boat, the lights, hitch, brakes. Unfortunately, I did not check the lugs holding the wheels to the trailer. It was planned that we start early in the morning and spend one night in a motel en route. By the time we huffed and puffed our way to the top of the Lorain Grade, our speed was down to fifteen miles per hour and the engine was overheating. We stopped and let the idling engine cool things off, and then proceeded, when we should have gone home.

Charlie was right about the grades we encountered until it was time for the descent into the Hudson River Valley where we encountered a steep downward grade designed to wear out our brakes as we strived to stay behind two trucks rather than try to pass them. At this point, the left wheel on the trailer came off, dropping the trailer on its left brake drum and the wheel sped past us on the down grade.. As I struggled for control of the weaving load and we ground to a stop, one of the truckers announced *George, that rollin' boat yard behind us is comin' apart!* Repairs took a full day, but we finally rolled into Old Greenwich and were greeted cordially.

The national competition turned out to be a fiasco through no fault of our hosts. There was little or no wind on Long Island Sound for the entire period of scheduled races and only one was completed within the time limit. We filled our usual role in this drifting contest and finished in the middle of the fleet. The return trip was essentially without incident, but the entire affair convinced me I did not want to enter any more national or international competitions.

Criterion was finally sold to a Cleveland man who owned fifteen Ensigns which he relocated to his summer home in the Les Cheneaux islands of Lake Superior to establish a fleet there. When we moved to Florida some time after the Ensign was gone, we found that the new owner of *Criterion* had shipped her to his winter home in Stuart where he was our neighbor. At his invitation, I sailed frequently around the bays and the inlets of the South Fork of the Saint Lucie River aboard our former yacht.

CHAPTER THIRTY-EIGHT
A LOOK BACK
How Did We Do?

This book is intended to be an informal anecdotal memoir, rather than history, but much of it discloses my educational insights, understandings and beliefs together with, I'm sure, some prejudices. I believe these to be accurately portrayed in the document below, written in response to a questionnaire I was asked to complete by a member of the Holland Professional Club for a presentation he was planning for a forthcoming meeting of the organization. My answers to his questions, written eleven years after my retirement as principal are printed below in their entirety. Unfortunately, the questions themselves did not survive but they can be surmised for the most part from my answers.

It is my desire to respond to your questionnaire to the best of my ability, since I have very strong feelings about what is right or wrong, not only about education, but society as a whole. I make the following observations before I attempt my responses:
  (1) I have been retired from education for over eleven years, and, while I try to keep an eye and ear on what is going on, I am not completely current;
  (2) Most of your twenty questions are so broad in nature that whole books have been written (and more will be in the future) on the subjects they encompass;
  (3) Many of your questions by their very nature require equivocal or conditional answers.

FIRST OF ALL – A brief course in problems of education in the classroom,(thus excluding problems of financing, etc)., can be summed up in two phrases:
  (1) The degree of student motivation, and
  (2) The treatment of individual differences.
Please keep these to in mind as you read my responses.

1. I do not necessarily agree that education in the United States, per se is at such a low point, but rather that student performance within the educational system is at a low point. The average U.S. student is not highly motivated, and for good reason. In many cases he already has everything his little heart desires, from (video games) in the elementary grades to automobiles, boats and protected and readily available sex at the high school level. I could easily write a book, or at least a large pamphlet on this subject alone, but you get the idea.

2. Schools are definitely a reflection of our society; the self-indulgence and hedonism of our recent generations is not lost either on our educational system or the students in it.

3. This is one of your highly conditional questions and both of the points under our "brief course" above apply.

a. We are all highly sensitive to the needs and problems of "special education" students. Here we wrestle with the treatment of individual differences. It would be ridiculous to require our mentally handicapped students to pursue a college prep curriculum; it would be similarly ridiculous to expect a paraplegic to meet the physical education requirements imposed on physically strong students.

b. In our moralistic society, our proclaimed goal is to "educate all of the children of all of the people", and, for the most part, we have been successful in doing this up to about the junior high level, or through the eighth grade in the old agrarian country school system. Keep in mind that as we have fifty percent of our people (including students) who are "above average", it follows that we have fifty percent who are "below average", and their educational needs must be met. These needs are not necessarily (or even generally) identical with the needs of those who will be designing our space modules, aircraft, medical procedures or developing new techniques in our highly complex society. However, this group of people (those categorized as "below average"), in my opinion, has been one that has not really received its share of emphasis in the educational system. The range of individual differences in this group is great enough that considerable curricular flexibility should be available to them, and hence all the attempts in the past to provide practical course in a broad range of subjects from math and English to vocational subjects. The (members of this) group form a part of the backbone of our society; they pay their share of the taxes, maybe more than their share; the truck driver and the carpenter, the retail clerk and the hamburger-flipper all have their places in our society, not to mention the gallant, underpaid souls who clean up our slops in nursing homes or pick the fruits and vegetables on our farms.

c. For the above average and the truly talented (not to mention the "geniuses", who can be a really expensive burden on society) who comprise the upper fifty percent of the spectrum, high standards should be established and great challenges offered. MOTIVATION is the key word here. Why does the Viet Namese immigrant outperform the indigenous pampered U.S. citizen? One word: MOTIVATION.

Incidentally, I have been monitoring the recent hullabaloo about education in the U.S. through the recent Presidential-Gubernatorial conference on the subject. Much was said about finances, teacher preparation, certification, evaluation, setting of standards, etc., but I didn't detect a single reference either to MOTIVATION or TREATMENT OF INDIVIDUAL DIFFERENCES!

d. (Ideally) Each individual student should be challenged to perform to the best of his abilities and goaded by his family and society to perform as nearly to that level as possible.

e. Discipline is a familial and societal problem. If there is rioting and gang warfare in the streets or in the family structure, similar problems will exist in the schools, and the schools are ill-equipped to control such uncivilized behavior. Both as a school administrator and observer of our society I have frequently made the observation that "We are not as far out of the jungle as we would like to think we are."

e-f. Unions are caused. When Boards of Education insisted on relegating teachers to the lowest-paid of all professions, the result was inevitable. If I may be permitted a personal observation, when I began teaching in the Holland Public Schools, my salary was less than one third of what it had been as a naval officer, the latter profession not being widely renowned as highly paid. Fortunately, this situation has been largely rectified, but since collective boards of education by their actions (in effect asked for them) unions are here to stay.

Likewise tenure. Unsatisfactory teachers can be removed under tenure by use of proper procedures. Some adjustments in the evaluating systems should be made to facilitate removal or demotions when unsatisfactory performance warrants such action. As I observe other professions where "birds of a feather flock together" e.g. law, medicine, dentistry, I don't think the system in education suffers too much by comparison. (To my horror, I observe that even commercial airline pilots are objecting to drug testing, but on the positive side, they must pass regular and rigorous flight and instrument checks to determine whether they have maintained the necessary proficiency to continue their profession, which is not true in most other professions.)

g. This is one of the most equivocal of all your questions. How could you possibly develop an instrument that would treat with the entire spectrum of individual differences? If you are referring to some test that might be applied to potentially college-bound students, such tests already exist in the form of the SAT, ACT and others, but even with these, the results are often criticized..

h. It is my impression that present teacher salaries are adequate and competitive, but, of course, as we continue to inflate the dollar, they will have to rise commensurately.

i. (Are teachers recognized appropriately in ways other than pay?) Generally, "Yes", but unfortunately, because our evaluation and elimination systems are not perfected, there is still the stigma attached to George Bernard Shaw's epigram, "Those who can do; those who can't teach." Obviously, this is an unfair simplification.

Thousands of books have been written on this subject.

k. The magnet school idea sounds attractive, but how do you handle the practical aspects of it when all the kids' parents want their children to go to a Jefferson School (on snob hill) and none want their kids go to a Lincoln School (In a poor section of town).

l. (Removing unmotivated students from the classroom scene) I've offered a few comments on this subject in c., above. Some of my ideas here probably would not be met with great approval in a society intent on educating "all of the children of all of the people." Students who are not MOTIVATED to do anything in school comprise a serious handicap to those who are MOTIVATED, at whatever level of learning. I could write a book on this subject but don't propose to do so today.

m. (Mandatory evaluation of both students and teachers) YES!!!! I was never very popular (with teachers) for my stand on this subject. Evaluation is important in the performance of an aircraft pilot, a surgeon, an astronaut or a farmer. Teachers should be evaluated and students should be evaluated. Development of a comprehensive set of instruments for this purpose would be challenging indeed, but much work has already been done in this area. Some reference to these matters had been made above. Your question implies to me that you are talking primarily about testing of college-bound high school seniors on the one hand and profession-bound college seniors on the other. Presumably much of this is already being done. Professional engineers, physicians, accountants, etc. are so tested. Weaknesses in these systems lie in the failure to provide "in or out" testing at various time intervals. This can and is done in the military, but I am not conscious of any other profession where it is practiced.

n. *(Extra pay for superior teachers)* Always, but how do you pay for them? Evaluation is a problem here, too.

o. *(Motivating students to learn)* This is primarily a family problem. Education cannot compete with the pleasure-seeking hedonism of the day unless the student is MOTIVATED to LEARN, rather then be spoon-fed entertainment from the tube, or whatever else might attract him.

p. *(?)* Such a law might provide a considerable additional "club" for unions to hold over the heads of boards of education. My personal preference would be that such differences be settled early on, but implementation could be a problem.

q. *(Treating all students alike)* WOW!!! WOW!!! And WOW!!!. Think of individual differences. If you had a mentally handicapped grandson, or even one slightly below average (not college bound) would you like him to be subjected to a continuing and arbitrary reinforcement of his already aroused sensitivity to the fact that he cannot compete on the same basis with those of his age group who completed calculus as a junior in high school, or even with those who are "whizzes" in handling the college-prep curriculum at the high school level?

r. Team teaching is simply a tool or mechanism among many in the educational inventory. This technique is effective under some circumstances and inappropriate in others.

THERE - You have the bases for at least ten books and a minimum of fifty theses or articles on education, and I haven't even touched on some of my stronger notions on the subject(s)! *GOOD LUCK.*

APPRECIATION

The author wishes to express his sincere thanks to all who have contributed to this saga, and, in particular to Mrs. Carol Van Lente, who served as a student counselor on the staff of Holland High School during my years as principal, and Mrs. Charles Howell, the former Janet Lightfoot, both of whom filled in many blanks in my memory and among my notes, and also corrected errors in my manuscript.

I also acknowledge the help of my children for their memories of their lively childhoods. Bill Jesiek and Shirley Wiersema reminded me of the times at the Macatawa Bay Yacht Club which entwine the rest of the story. Ken "Fuzz" Bauman and Dave Kempker, among others, stepped in and helped with details long since forgotten.

The help and cooperation of Mr. Peter Esser, publisher of *The Holland Sentinel* in allowing the republication of materials originally published in that newspaper are noted with appreciation.

Any errors remaining in this story are attributable to me alone, as are the opinions offered.

APPENDIX I
TWO VIEWS

1964-1979

The Holland High School campus as it appeared during the time I served as its principal. My office was behind the long windows to the left of the door into the library building (at right in the above picture). This building also contained the library, counselors' offices and the home economics suite. The west academic unit lies behind and beyond the Holland High School sign and flag pole. The east academic unit was to the right of this camera view. The Butler building housing the industrial arts and shop classes was to the north of the west unit and the faculty parking area.

2010

Dirk Bloemendaal Photos

The campus today (2010) from a similar perspective, although from a different camera position. Extensive additions and modifications have been made to the campus and its buildings. In both pictures the performing arts center is at the left out of camera view while the Herrick art center is at the right out of view in both photographs. The Herrick center is west and north of the east academic unit.

APPENDIX II
The Influence of B. Frank Brown

Doctor Brown was an educator and educationist who attempted to reform the educational process in the schools of the United States and who had a considerable influence on Walter Scott and my predecessor, Jay Formsma. The design of the campus and its buildings; the curriculum, the open school concept were all advocated by Dr. Brown, as were the projected concepts of a school system without either grades for achievement or grades for placement of students in classes. Students would advance at a rate compatible with their academic achievements; not grades or grade point averages. His ideas and conclusions, as supplemented by his committee were published in a document titled *Recommendations for Improving Secondary Education; The Report...by the National Committee on the Reform of Secondary Education; B. Frank Brown, Chairman.* This document contains thirty-two recommendations which, if implemented, would revolutionize the process of high school education.

The new Holland High School in 1963 was built to support an "open campus" curriculum, the inclusion of some of B. Frank Brown's ideas and an objective for the future of incorporating more of his proposed reforms. Implemented upon the completion of the new high school, a period when I was teaching mathematics, were a number of Dr. Brown's proposals, but by no means all. In preparation for the move to the campus, numerous staff meetings were held to expose the teachers to the changes they could expect, such as team teaching, flexible scheduling, with classes assigned by modules of time and complete student freedom to come and go when not scheduled for a class or other activity. I was one of the staff members who volunteered to visit other schools where some of the Brown proposals were introduced. As might be expected, opinion on the staff was divided roughly into three groups, those who looked forward to the change, those who opposed it and those who expressed indifference.

When the new school year began, I was assigned to teach two sections of "Senior Mathematics, each section composed of two "blocks" (periods of time composed of two modules each) combined with one module of "Senior Mathematics" to make a five module week for this subject employing programmed learning materials supported by a shelf of reference books on the various aspects of the mathematics involved. The remainder of my assignment was three classes of Advanced Algebra similarly scheduled and using programmed learning materials. As predicted by Dr. Brown and supported by long teacher observations and experience, students completed the courses at various rates and this left the problem of how profitably to challenge the faster learners. This problem was partially solved by the establishment of a cooperative program with Hope College under which the rapid learners were exposed to regular college classes.

The other mathematics classes bore the same old titles, "Algebra I," "Geometry," "Basic Math" and "Business Math" with their attendant problems of individual differences and student motivation. The thirty-two recommendations of Dr. Brown's Commission were in many ways in conflict the laws of the land, community expectations and the ideas of teaching staff.

Here are the titles of a few selected recommendations:

Recommendation No.5: <u>Bias in Textbooks</u>
This remains a controversial subject today, fifty years later; there is much bias in high school texts, pandering to particular ethnic groups as there was during my time as principal;

Recommendation No. 6: <u>Bias in Counseling</u>
My book offers a number of examples of bias and our efforts to combat it.

Recommendations Nos.8, 9 and 10 deal with practical and career educations.
Holland was a leader in these efforts.

Recommendations Nos. 16, 17 and 18 deal with the use of television in the school.
Holland was a leader in the use of television, but we found as a practical matter such use merited constant surveillance to prevent indolent teacher use.

Recommendations No. 20: <u>Rank in Class</u>
This recommendation is an ideal that easy to propose, but almost impossible to implement without the articulation with post secondary schools recommended by Dr. Brown.

Recommendation No. 24: <u>School Newspapers.</u>
We tangled with this problem successfully in Holland, controlling school sponsored publications, but allowing unofficial outlets.

Recommendation No. 28: <u>Compulsory Attendance.</u>
The Commission Report states, *If the high school is not to be a custodial institution, the state must not force adolescents to attend ....The formal school-leaving age should be dropped to age fourteen....Other programs should accommodate those who wish to leave school.* I would only add that those forced to remain in school as a custodial function greatly hamper the learning processes of others. Unfortunately union sponsorship of laws requiring youth to attend school until age sixteen complicates this problem, and no relief appears to be in sight.

For the proposed reforms to take place strong community participation and support would be required (Recommendations No. 1 and 2). In talking to present day educators, they almost universally report it is the school that is virtually the last support of the community rather than the community supporting the school, a phenomenon resulting from lack of family structure and the prevalence of family breakup through divorce or separation with the result that the school is forced into attempts to fill the role of the family in many cases.

In the case of Holland High School my sources tell me the reforms introduced by me and my predecessors and executed with great enthusiasm have largely gone by the wayside. The problems inherent under present circumstances remain unsolved and the challenges to educators greater than ever. For the most part, the running commentaries from influential individuals who are not personally involved in the educational process are not helpful. These well-meaning folks would learn a great deal by actually teaching, for at least a year, five classes per day of students who will become good citizens, in part through the efforts of these teachers, but who will never qualify to become rocket scientists or developers of new drugs or improved medical techniques. As one observer remarked, *If you don't play the game you should not be allowed to make the rules.*

APPENDIX III
Where Are They Now?

The ranks of those who taught at Holland High School during my time as teacher and principal are thinning rapidly, but after many hours of searching by telephone I have managed to produce the following list of survivors. It is by no means complete, but it is the best I can do with my limited resources. When I have not been able to speak to the individual, I have sought information from others when possible; thus non-vicious hearsay is included in a few instances. Among other observations, it is interesting to know what many have accomplished in retirement.

Alice Beukema, now living in Sun City, Florida, succeeded me as principal for two years, and then returned to the classroom.

Barbara Fleming a flight instructor at the local airport, and lives on West 20th Street.

Zeke Piersma, true to his athletic spirit, died while participating in a softball game, leaving a wife suffering from Alzheimer's disease.

Kit Leggett maintained a long correspondence with Dick Giordano, but never did marry him. I'm told she is now selling real estate in the Holland area, but in numerous tries both to her home and office number, I have failed to reach her.

Karla Spence is teaching in a neighboring school, and lives within a block or so of the apartments I built long ago on 20th Street.

Ted and Muncie Boeve continue to live in a Centennial Farm condo on the south side of Holland.

Roger Plagenhoef lives in Lake Town Township in Allegan County, south of Virginia Park and is active in church and community affairs.

Don Ihrman became seriously ill and died while I was writing this book.

Dirk Bloemendaal is still writing and photographing while tending to the needs of a disabled wife.

Fuzz Bauman spends much time at the Dow Center on the Hope College campus keeping himself fit for the next hundred years.

Ray Backus lives in the Zeeland area and broadcasts Hope College basketball games and other events on the local radio station.

Judy Mastenbrook, the librarian, lives quietly in the southern section of Holland.

Dave and Mary Kempker came into some money, spend summers on Beaver Island and take long cruises and European canal boat vacations during the rest of the year. In a recent conversation Dave tells me that this year, after a European adventure, they are going to fly to Korea for a tour of the Korean War battle areas at the expense of the Korean government, a reward offered to all veterans who served in Korea. I'm envious, but I really can no longer travel.

Walt Kooyers coaches Hope College track and encourages all to join him in his physical fitness efforts.

Dick Darby has made his fortune in medical buildings and would like to retire, but is said to find it difficult to disentangle himself from his financial responsibilities.

Olin Van Lare and Bob Chard were the only two active staff members who died during the time I was the principal.

Evelyn Vukin, well into her nineties, continues to live in the Central Park area of Holland.

Fred Winter is retired as a chief yeoman in the naval reserve as well as from the Holland School District. He lives with his wife, Darlene north of Holland.

Don and Pat Gebraad live in Brook Village, Holland.

Myles Runk and his wife are deceased, but their daughter, Pamela, continues to live in the family home on Beech Street in Holland Township.

Dan and Janet Goodwin live in Park Township, north of Holland. As the director of vocational education the physical location of his office was moved four times during his tenure in the position. Dan is active in Red Cross and other volunteer work in the community.

Jeanne and Bob Visscher live in Bonita Springs, Florida.

Dan Poretta, now a widower, lives in the Virginia Park area of Holland and spends much time helping his children and grandchildren.

Helen Brownson and her husband Bill live at Freedom Village, a Holland retirement community,

Rein Wolfert lives near the college in Holland

Marilyn Tremml, Joe's widow, lives in the Central Park area of Holland.

Richard Beyer and his wife operate an antique store in the Zeeland area.

Gardner Wieringa died shortly after I resigned as principal. His widow, Lorraine, has continued to live in their house.

Carol Van Lente is widowed but continues to live in the former Dunn house that she and Jim inherited many years ago.

Don Johnson left Holland suddenly not long after my retirement and is said to live in either Georgia or Florida.

The former Janet Lightfoot, the home economics teacher, now Mrs. Charles Howell, lives on Spring Lane Drive, just off Graafschaap Road.

David Lightfoot lives in Ada, Michigan, having survived his years as superintendent of the Ravenna school district. He married a Kent City elementary teacher; they later moved to Winter Park, Florida where Dave taught fifth grade for several years. It was then back to Michigan to be near family and friends.

Ruth Vrieling, now widowed, lives in an assisted living apartment in Edmond, Oklahoma, a suburb of Oklahoma City near her daughter, Vicki, who teaches at the university. Ruth, a long-time bridge addict, is a Silver Life Master in duplicate bridge.

Don and Pat Gebraad live in Brook Village across the street from Graafschaap cemetery.

Clyde Line lives on State Street in Holland

Richard Rust, former assistant superintendent for instruction, lives in Holland as does Jack Lowe, assistant superintendent for administration.

Paul Payne, master of the machine shop and his second wife live in Hamilton, a few miles south of Holland. I am reminded that students under his instruction who (1) made the splendid cribbage board with which we play a game virtually every night, and (2) re-bored my boyhood .410 shotgun to accommodate three-inch shells.

Joyce Bertrand lives in Holland but I have been unable to contact her probably because her phone number is unlisted.

APPENDIX IV
Humor

Educators are not without humor. Expressions of humor vary widely, some bitter, some wry and some gently examine the educational process, the students, the teachers and others involved in education at all levels.

Here are some examples:

Choosing Titles for Educational Writings, Speeches, Innovations or Projects

From the following list choose a word from each column. The three words will indicate a title that may be appropriate for your work. If you don't like the first one as a subject or title for your EdD thesis, try again with a different set of selections. Don't be discouraged; there are thousands of potential titles here:

Column One	Column Two	Column Three
Computer	Oriented	Instruction
Input	Articulated	Simulation
Concept	Structured	Teaching
Field	Correlated	Program
Behavior	Modulated	Guidance
Output	Directed	School
Resource	Based	Process
Reality	Integrated	System
Value	Compensated	Curriculum
Discovery	Centered	Learning

There could be more; for example, consider adding "Personal" to Column One, "Generated" to Column Two and "Activity" to Column Three. The options go up astronomically as words are added to each column. One authority suggests one or more of these combinations can be used arbitrarily within a speech to a group of people interested in education, giving your remarks a ring of authority that can make a great impression. His conclusion is that no one in the audience will have the vaguest idea of what you are talking about, but no one is likely to admit it either.

The following is a widely distributed all-purpose performance appraisal similar to the one developed for use in evaluating Holland's educational staff, although that form contained much different wording in the individual blocks.

DATE OF EVALUATION:_____

EMPLOYEE EVALUATED: _____

INSTRUCTIONS; Place a distinct check mark (_/) in the box that best describes the performance of this employee during the past six months.

AREA OF PERFORMANCE	FAR IN EXCESS OF JOB REQUIREMENTS	EXCEEDS JOB REQUIREMENTS	MEETS JOB REQUIREMENTS	NEEDS IMPROVEMENT	DOES NOT MEET MINIMUM REQUIREMENTS
Quality of Work	Leaps tall buildings in a single bound	Leaps tall buildings with a running start	Can leap short buildings if prodded	Bumps into buildings	Cannot recognize buildings
Promptness	Is faster than a speeding bullet	Is as fast as a speeding bullet	Would you believe a slow bullet	Misfires frequently	Wounds self when handling guns
Initiative	Is stronger than a locomotive	Is strong as a bull elephant	Almost as strong as a bull	Shoots the bull	Smells like a bull
Adaptability	Walks on water	Keeps head above water	Washes with water	Drinks water	Passes water in emergencies
Communication	Talks with God	Talks with the angels	Talks to himself	Argues with himself	Loses argument with himself

The following suggestions are from a sardonic list titled *How to Become an Instant Evaluator without Changing Anything.* Some of them strike close to home with our efforts in Holland, while others are wildly off the target as is the implied ridicule of computers in a document that was prepared on an old fashioned typewriter and duplicated by use of carbon paper.

1. Make a survey of innovations in your school by having a teacher who needs a subject for a master's thesis go around and make a list of things that look new. Call a meeting of the Parent-Teachers Association or other gathering of those interested in education and present the list and refer to each as an innovation.

2. Build flexible facilities. Be sure they include carpeting, no windows, hexagonal rather then rectangular classrooms and commons areas where students can idle away their time.

3. Initiate something called flexible scheduling by extending some instructional periods and shortening others. Use a computer to assign students to classes.

4. Create an instructional resource center by renaming the library and equipping it with carrels which are primarily used to store sample books left by the salesmen hawking them.

5. Use instructional technology, especially the overhead projector and numerous movies whether or not related to the subject matter. This relieves the overburdened teacher who can relax and rest during such presentations.

Use team teaching; it reorganizes mediocrity.

Offer a course titled "Independent Study" which allows the student to lounge in the commons, the library or any other niche he can find.

The following comprise a teacher's fantasy of the characteristics of those holding leadership positions in his school district. Note particularly his high regard for the principal.

INDIVIDUAL MEMBER OF THE BOARD OF EDUCATION

Leaps tall buildings in a single bound;
Is more powerful than a locomotive;
Is faster than a speeding bullet;
Walks on water;
Advises God on educational policy.

SUPERINTENDENT

Leaps small buildings in a single bound;
Is more powerful than a switch engine;
Is just as fast as a speeding bullet;
Walks on water when the sea is calm;
Talks to God.

ASSISTANT SUPERINTENDENT

Leaps small buildings when winds are favorable after a running start;
Is almost as powerful as a switch engine;
Is faster than a pellet fired from a paint gun;
Occasionally walks on water at an indoor swimming pool;
Talks to God provided his special request is approved.

CURRICULUM DIRECTOR

Can barely clear an outhouse;
Is often towed by a switch engine;
Can fire a paint gun;
Can swim;
Is occasionally addressed by God.

TRANSPORTATION DIRECTOR

Runs around buildings;
Is frequently run over by locomotives;
Can sometimes fire a BB gun without injuring himself;
Can dog paddle;
Talks to dogs.

PERSONNEL DIRECTOR

Runs into buildings;
Can identify a locomotive two out of three times;
Owns a BB gun, but is required to keep it in a locked cabinet without BBs;
Can stay afloat with a life jacket;
Talks to the walls.

PRINCIPAL

Trips over the doorstep when trying to enter the building;
To anyone who will listen, he says "Look at the Choo-Choo;
Wets himself with his own water pistol;
Plays in mud puddles;
Talks to himself.